Palgrave Critical Studies in Human Rights and Criminology

There is growing interest in the connection between criminal justice concerns and human rights, including in topics from global migration and youth justice to mass imprisonment. This series combines the latest theory and research in criminology, criminal justice, and related fields with a critical perspective on the theory and practice of human rights. It explores in depth what human rights can bring to criminology and what criminology and related disciplines can bring to our understanding of the real-world practice of human rights. Books in the series link specific human rights instruments and institutions with core criminological settings such as policing, youth justice, prisons and courts to critically explore how they have influenced criminal justice policy, practice and theory. Alongside contributions that see human rights applied in these criminal justice contexts, the series welcomes contributions that critique human rights in the context of what justice is, and who defines it, and how this may matter to cutting-edge debates such as gender equality, Black Lives Matter, decolonising criminology and others. The intention is for these books to be accessible to a wide audience via e-books, short Palgrave Pivot books as well as full-length books. Authors from the Global South are particularly encouraged to submit proposals and translations of suitable works already published in languages other than English. The series invites both monographs and edited collections on well-defined groups of rights including youth rights, disability rights and Indigenous rights, as well as on topics that stretch the boundaries of the discipline such as border control, environmental regulation, global crime and international development, when viewed through a criminological lens.

Book proposals are invited to the Editor: Josephine.Taylor@palgrave.com. Palgrave Macmillan will work actively with authors to explore opportunities for open access funding.

Leanne Weber · Marinella Marmo
Editors

A Research Agenda for a Human Rights Centred Criminology

palgrave
macmillan

Editors
Leanne Weber
Canberra Law School
University of Canberra
Canberra, ACT, Australia

Marinella Marmo
College of Business, Government & Law
Flinders University
Adelaide, SA, Australia

ISSN 2731-412X ISSN 2731-4138 (electronic)
Palgrave Critical Studies in Human Rights and Criminology
ISBN 978-3-031-46288-7 ISBN 978-3-031-46289-4 (eBook)
https://doi.org/10.1007/978-3-031-46289-4

Cover illustration: A.Martin UW Photography/gettyimages

This Palgrave Macmillan imprint is published by the registered company Springer Nature Switzerland AG
The registered company address is: Gewerbestrasse 11, 6330 Cham, Switzerland

Paper in this product is recyclable.

Injustice anywhere is a threat to justice everywhere.

Martin Luther King, African–American civil rights activist

Acknowledgements

The editors would like to express their appreciation to Josie Taylor, Palgrave Senior Commissioning Editor, Criminology and Socio-Legal Studies for her belief in this book and in the Critical Studies in Human Rights and Criminology series.

We also thank our authors for their thoughtful and ground-breaking contributions to this volume.

Contents

Notes on Contributors

Rebecca Annorbah is a doctoral candidate in the Interdisciplinary Health Program at Northern Arizona University. Her primary research focuses on the evaluation of health equity projects aimed at promoting equitable health outcomes for children, women and individuals incarcerated.

Julie Berg is a senior lecturer in Criminology at the School of Social and Political Sciences, and the director of the Scottish Centre for Crime and Justice Research (SCCJR), at the University of Glasgow. Her research interests include a focus on the impacts of new and emerging global harmscapes on security institutions, collaborative arrangements and democratic safety governance. Further to this, she is interested in the impacts of these new harmscapes and associated responses, on the evolution of criminology as a field of inquiry and, related to this, the nature and implications of a decolonised criminology, given the impact and governance of new harms in the Global South and the need for innovative responses and an adaptive criminology.

Stella Black Ko Ngāi Tūhoe, Whakatōhea, Te Whānau-a-Apanui me Ngāti Whakaue ahau. Stella is a proud "He Ture Kia Tika/Let the Law Be Right" Māori social justice researcher and advocate. She is inspired by the words of Moana Jackson a staunch Māori activist for Māori rights in a discriminatory judicial system, who encouraged Māori "to dream." Stella brings kaupapa Māori research methodologies and methods to each project she works on because these work for everyone. She is particularly passionate about working with whānau, hapū, iwi and hapori organisations who courageously share their pūrākau for others to dream too. Ngā mihi e ngā māreikua me ngā whatukura mō tō rātou pūrākau, kei te mihi, kei te mihi, kei te mihi.

Mary Bosworth is a professor of Criminology at the University of Oxford and at Monash University. She has published widely on issues to do with immigration detention in the UK, but also in France and Greece. She is currently working on the first academic study of deportation and immigration detention transportation staff in the UK. Mary is co-Director of Border Criminologies, an international research network and website based in Oxford.

David Burnside has a lived experience of mental health challenges, problematic substance use, homelessness and incarceration. He has worked for Odyssey, a service supporting people experiencing addiction, for over 10 years, mostly in peer and consumer roles and now sits in the Odyssey Executive team as the Lived Experience Lead. Dave has a Postgraduate Diploma in Health Science, Mental Health and Addiction (PGDipHSc), a Master of Law (LLM, Hons), and is involved in supporting the Post Graduate programmes at AUT and Auckland University focusing on recovery concepts and principles and social justice. He identifies as Pākehā/tangata tiriti and is a proud father of one son.

Steven Caruana is a coordinator of the Australia OPCAT Network, a coalition of over 200 non-government organisations, academics and statutory officer holders interested in the effective implementation of oversight to Australian places of detention. Steven is also the specialist advisor on Immigration and OPCAT to the Australian Human Rights

Commission and is involved in monitoring mental health units in New South Wales as an Official Visitor.

Steven's past roles include working on restrictive practices reform with the Royal Commission into Violence, Abuse, Neglect and Exploitation of People with Disability. Steven was also a detention inspector for the Office of the Inspector of Custodial Services Western Australia and the Office of the Commonwealth Ombudsman as well as a senior policy officer and senior quality assessor with the Aged Care Quality and Safety Commission. Prior to this Steven worked for the Department of Immigration and Border Protection within its immigration detention network both onshore and offshore.

Steven is an expert member and newsletter co-editor for the External Prison Oversight and Human Rights Network with the International Corrections and Prisons Association; an advisory board member for Deadly Connections Community and Justice Services and an editorial board member for *Current Issues in Criminal Justice.*

Pablo Ciocchini is a researcher at the National Scientific and Technological Research Council (Argentina), research fellow of the Institute of Legal Culture at the National University of La Plata (Argentina) and honorary fellow in the Department of Sociology, Social Policy and Criminology at the University of Liverpool (United Kingdom). His research explores the relationship between law and legal professionals and state violence in the Global South.

Andriani Fili is a Wellcome Trust postdoctoral research fellow at the Centre for Criminology, University of Oxford and an associate director of Border Criminologies. Her Ph.D. research was the first national study of immigration detention centres in Greece, mapping the immigration detention system and recording resistance mobilised against it. Her current research project will explore the role and impact of health provision on people inside immigration detention centres and after release in Greece. Drawing on a range of sources of evidence, it will further examine the continuity of experiences of medical care across and beyond these spaces and through time, tracing connections between zones of quarantine and confinement for those deemed undesirable in the country. In Greece she is also involved in counter mapping activities of migrant containment spaces in collaboration with local civil society actors.

Katja Franko is a professor of Criminology at the University of Oslo, Norway. She has published extensively on globalisation, migration and border control, international police co-operation and the use of advanced information and communication technologies in crime control strategies. Her recent publications include globalisation and crime (3rd edition, 2020, Sage), The crimmigrant other: Migration and penal power (2020, Routledge) and Profiting from Pablo: Victimhood, Memory and Consumerism (with D.R. Goyes, OUP, forthcoming).

Joe Greener is a lecturer in the Department of Sociology, Social Policy and Criminology at the University of Liverpool. His research interests lie in critically orientated and theoretically informed analyses of state power and political economy across a range of issues including welfare, social care, crime control, neo-imperialism and racism.

Claire Hamilton is a professor of Criminology and head of Criminology in the School of Law and Criminology in Maynooth University, Ireland. She has published widely on the comparative politics of crime and security, spanning criminal procedure reforms, counter-terrorism and penology. Recent publications include the *Research Handbook of Comparative Criminal Justice* (with D. Nelken, Edward Elgar, 2022) and *Contagion, Counter-terrorism and Criminology: Justice in the Shadow of Terror* (Palgrave, 2019).

Jessica Hastings was born and raised in Pōneke (Wellington). She is Pākehā with Polish ancestry. Since completing her degree, she has been able to pursue her dream of creating better outcomes for people within the criminal justice system. Jessica brings insight and empathy to all of her roles. Her passion to work in this area stems from my own personal experiences with mental health, drug addiction and incarceration. Jessica served one year in prison for the supply of methamphetamine before turning her life around in 2011. She has been active in the alcohol and other drug recovery network since. Jessica believes in equitable outcomes for whānau in the justice system.

Will Jackson is a senior lecturer in Criminology and a member of the Centre for the Study of Crime, Criminalisation and Social Exclusion (CCSE) at Liverpool John Moores University, UK. His research is focused on the nature and regulation of political activism and, since 2013, he has been researching developments in public order policing in the UK. His recent work has been published in *Policing and Society*, *Critical Social Policy*, *Social Justice*, *Feminist Review* and *Probation Journal*.

Lamese Laponi is a police inspector in the Tuvalu Police Service and has served various sections in the police including the Criminal Investigation Department, prosecution and general policing. He holds a bachelor's degree from the University of the South Pacific, majoring in Pacific policing, management and public administration.

Claire Loughnan is a lecturer in Criminology in the School of Social and Political Sciences at the University of Melbourne. Her research focuses on the modes, practices and experiences of confinement in places of 'care' and control, ranging from detention and prisons, to aged care, for example. Her first monograph is under contract with Routledge on the institutional effects of mandatory immigration detention. Claire is a committee member of the Carceral Geography Working Group, a co-convenor of the University of Melbourne branch of Academics for Refugees, and a research partner with the Comparative Network on the Externalization of Refugee Policies. She is an editorial board member of *Decolonization of Criminology and Justice*, and *Criminological Encounters*.

Marinella Marmo Professor Marinella Marmo is the director of Teaching Program of Flinders Criminology. She holds a Ph.D. in Applied Social Science (University of Lancaster, UK) and an LLB Hons (Università di Salerno, Italy). She is a multiple award-winning tertiary education academic, and she has published extensively in the area of critical criminology and human rights. Her research has been cited by academics and senior policymakers worldwide, profiled by several prominent international media outlets, formed the base for a British Parliamentary Q&A session and used to inform documentaries in Britain and Australia. She is an active contributor to national and state inquiries in the field of crime and public policy matters. She has attracted external funding from a number of sources, including the joint initiative EU-Australian Government, the Australian Research Council (ARC), the Academy of the Social Sciences in Australia (ASSA), the Ian Potter Foundation and the South Australian Law Foundation.

Raymond Michalowski is a sociologist and regents professor emeritus of Criminology at Northern Arizona University. His books include *Order, Law, and Crime, Crime, Power and Identity, State-Corporate Crime, State Crime in the Global Age,* and *Run for the Wall: Remembering Vietnam on a Motorcycle Pilgrimage.*

George B. Radics is a senior lecturer in the Department of Sociology and Anthropology at the National University of Singapore (NUS). He teaches Law and Society, Selected Topics on Law and Justice, Sociology of Emotions and Classical Sociological Theory. After receiving his Ph.D. in sociology from NUS, he earned a Juris Doctor with a concentration in Asian law from the University of Washington and worked for the Supreme Court of Guam for two years. He is a member of the New York Bar. His articles have been published in the *Journal of Human Rights, Columbia Human Rights Law Review, Asian Journal of Social Science* and the *Philippine Sociological Review.* He is also co-editor of *Criminal Legalities in the Global South: Cultural Dynamics, Political Tensions and Institutional Practices* (Routledge, 2019) and *Criminal Legalities and Minorities in the Global South: Rights and Resistance in a Decolonial World* (Palgrave, 2023).

Elizabeth Stanley works in the areas of state crime, human rights, incarceration and social justice. She co-edited '*The Aotearoa Handbook of Criminology*' (Auckland University Press, 2021) and '*State Crime and Resistance*' (Routledge, 2013). In 2009, she wrote '*Torture, Truth and Justice: The Case of Timor-Leste*' (Routledge, 2009) and her monograph '*The Road to Hell*' (Auckland University Press, 2016) contributed to the 2018 establishment of a Royal Commission into Abuse in Care in New Zealand. She is a Professor of Criminology at Te Herenga Waka-Victoria University of Wellington, Aotearoa-New Zealand.

Sydney Shevat is completing the doctoral program in sociology at the University of Tennessee, Knoxville. Her research focuses on climate change and environmental justice, feminism and gender inequalities, criminology and social inequality, as well as social movements, activism and strategies for social change.

Silvana Tapia Tapia is a doctor of Philosophy in Socio-legal Studies (University of Kent, UK). Her interdisciplinary research addresses the paradoxes and limitations of the penal apparatus as a mechanism to counter violence against women. She is currently Leverhulme Early Career Fellow at Birmingham Law School, University of Birmingham, where she conducts a research project on anti-carceral feminist responses to human rights penality.

Katey Thom is a pākehā interdisciplinary social justice researcher exploring the spaces where law and health interface. Her overall aim in research is to inform policy, practice and legal reform that improves outcomes for some of the most marginalised people in society. Katey's current research has a strong focus on social justice issues in mental health and addiction, covering various aspects of mental health law, human rights, and therapeutic initiatives within the criminal justice system. Katey has a strong interest in considering the implications of the United Nation Convention for the Rights of Persons with Disability in Aotearoa and realising supported decision-making across mental health services. Katey is proud to be part of He Ture Kia Tika, working with diverse communities to re-envisage the criminal justice system to better respond to people with intersecting mental health, addictions and criminal justice histories.

Sandra Walklate is Eleanor Rathbone Chair of Sociology at the University of Liverpool and was conjoint Chair of Criminology attached to the Monash Gender and Family Violence Prevention Centre from 2016-2023. She is internationally recognised for her work in victimology particularly criminal victimisation as it pertains to violence(s) against women. Her most recent publications include, *An Advanced Introduction to Victimology* (2023, Edwin Elgar), and *Victims' access to justice: what* *would a 'just' criminal justice system look like?* (an edited collection with Pam Cox) (2022, Routledge)

Danielle Watson is an associate professor and Academic Lead Research Training in the School of Justice, Queensland University of Technology. She conducts research on (in)security in Pacific Island countries, capacity building for security service providers, recruitment and training as well as many other areas specific to improving security in developing country contexts. Her research also focuses on policing, police/community relations, policing culturally and linguistically diverse communities, and plural regulatory systems in the Caribbean and the Pacific.

Leanne Weber is a research professor of Criminology in the Canberra Law School at the University of Canberra, Australia and a research associate at the Centre for Criminology, Oxford University. She researches policing and border control and is interested in the nexus of critical criminology and human rights. She has held six major research grants from the Australian Research Council as either Chief Investigator, CI or sole CI and has produced or co-produced 10 academic books, including *Globalization and Borders: Death at the Global Frontier*, 2011 (Palgrave, with Sharon Pickering), which was awarded the inaugural Christine M Alder Book Prize by the ANZ Society of Criminology.

Nancy Wonders is a professor emeritus of Criminology and Criminal Justice at Northern Arizona University and a past chair of the American Society of Criminology's Division on Feminist Criminology. She has published extensively on the relationship between social inequality, difference and justice; gender and justice; globalisation and the increasingly transnational character of crime and justice; the criminology of borders and mobility; and the development of effective strategies to create sustainable and just communities.

1

Towards a Human Rights Centred Criminology

Leanne Weber and Marinella Marmo

Criminology and Human Rights

Human rights undertakings by governments seldom translate seamlessly into human rights compliance. In the worst-case scenario, governments may have little or no intention of upholding human rights standards to which they have publicly committed and can use their ratification of international instruments and domestic implementation as a veneer to obscure or even legitimise continuing abuses. Even in the best-case scenario, local implementation of international human rights agreements may be patchy, overlook the needs of diverse population groups or give rise to unforeseen consequences. The criminal justice system and related

L. Weber (✉)
Canberra Law School, University of Canberra, Canberra, ACT, Australia
e-mail: leanne.weber@canberra.edu.au

M. Marmo
College of Business, Government & Law, Flinders University, Adelaide, SA, Australia
e-mail: marinella.marmo@flinders.edu.au

L. Weber and M. Marmo (eds.), *A Research Agenda for a Human Rights Centred Criminology*, Palgrave Critical Studies in Human Rights and Criminology,
https://doi.org/10.1007/978-3-031-46289-4_1

areas of crime, harm and law enforcement are key sites for the exercise and contestation of state-corporate and personal power. Critical criminological research, therefore, has a significant role to play in identifying whether state and state-corporate power is exercised in ways that align with human rights law and principles, and, more fundamentally, whether human rights undertakings reflect the best interests of the populations they purport to protect. And yet, the discipline as a whole has been slow to advance this critical agenda.[1]

The aim of this edited collection is to articulate a future direction for research at the nexus of criminology and human rights by bringing together experts from different subject areas who, while they may be sceptical about certain aspects of human rights theory, law or practice, share an interest in realising many of the objectives set out in human rights instruments. As we have argued elsewhere (Weber et al. 2014, p. 83), '[c]riminologists who engage actively with human rights, while they may vary in many other respects, all see the pursuit of human well-being rather than the smooth functioning of state institutions as the key objective of criminological enquiry'.

It is now more than half a century since US scholars Schwendinger and Schwendinger (1970, p. 77) urged criminologists to 'redefine themselves, no longer to be the defenders of order, but rather the defenders of human rights'. This began what Stanley (2011, p. 168) calls a 'criminological shift' in some parts of the discipline that directed attention towards the international, and purportedly universal, norms of human rights. This shift has included sustained questioning of how crime is defined and constructed by state actors, and critiquing of the role of governments as both protectors and violators of human rights. Criminological scholarship in this vein has sometimes applied the language and concepts of human rights (Cohen 1993), but has also developed through the lens of social harms and social justice (Canning and Tombs 2021) and the emergence of the cognate study of state and state-corporate crime (Michalowski and Kramer 2006; Chambliss and Michalowski 2010; Stanley and McCulloch 2012). Whatever the focus, the primary contribution for human rights conscious criminologists has been overwhelmingly empirical, intended to 'unpack the involvement of various powerful actors in violations' (Stanley 2011, p. 175).

These steps towards a criminology with a critical perspective on the state have coincided with a growing preoccupation with transnational crime and the operation of power on a global scale. As Stanley (2011, p. 176) has noted, this requires moving away from 'a strict individualist model of criminal responsibility to consider the collaborative power arrangements that exist at local, national and global levels'. This, in turn, opens the way for new normative frameworks, as we have argued previously: 'A perspective that stretches beyond the narrow confines of state-based law and criminal justice institutions is needed to address this extra-territorial research agenda, and criminologists are turning increasingly to human rights to provide a supra-national normative framework' (Weber et al. 2014, p. 82). A critical, human rights-centred criminology will not take the normative claims of governments at face value, but will seek to uncover where the language, and sometimes the practice, of human rights is deployed to sustain global inequalities. For example, Katja Franko (2019) has argued that European governments have sought to maintain an illusory commitment to human rights, while exercising harsh exclusionary controls over those they define as 'crimmigrant others', thereby sustaining global inequalities.

Empirical criminological research holds the promise of grounding otherwise abstract notions of human rights in practice; extending our understanding of the operation of human rights in particular contexts, taking into consideration broader relations of power; and supporting calls for the accountable exercise of power (Marmo and Fishwick 2022). Overall, much of what has been published at the nexus of criminology and human rights could be said to reflect a concern with developing a criminology that works *for* human rights, but not necessarily *through* them. In other words, while legal scholars may focus on the international human rights framework itself as a *process* for achieving change, the focus for critical criminologists is generally on achieving human rights goals as an *outcome*, by revealing the failure of governments and other actors to meet these standards in practice and drawing on a wider range of political, legal and social interventions to ameliorate and prevent them. The knowledge produced by a human rights-centred criminology therefore supplements the focus on legal process often adopted by scholars of international law.

In a previous publication (Weber et al. 2014, p. 3), we invited criminologists to engage more closely and critically with the actual content and practice of human rights and avoid using the term merely as a slogan. This is because, in order to undertake applied research that defends human rights, it is important to have a sound understanding of the substance of international human rights law: 'To defend human rights, criminologists must be able to sufficiently identify the violations of these rights – by whom and against whom; how and why' (Schwendinger and Schwendinger 1970, p. 146). Yet, many criminology undergraduate and postgraduate studies worldwide do not offer an adequate education in human rights. And, on the increasing occasions when human rights are invoked in academic writings, this is mostly cursory. This is inadequate to implement—or even critique—human rights concepts and practices in an adaptable and effective way, since they provide key advocacy tools, shared across cognate disciplines and political institutions and processes (Marmo and Fishwick 2022).

Just as there are many approaches to criminological scholarship, there are contrasting perspectives that can be taken to the study of human rights. Dembour (2012) has identified four schools of human rights thinking which she sets out as 'ideal types'. What she calls the *natural* school takes universal human rights as a 'given', embodied in law without the need for further justification, and by definition universal. In contrast, the *deliberative* school of thought is more mindful of the contingent and socially constructed nature of human rights, while recognising the potential to achieve universality in human rights law through consensus building. The *protest* school depicts the contest over human rights in more combative terms, recognising that extant human rights law often falls short of alleviating human suffering and must therefore be a site of perpetual political struggle. Most sceptical of all is the *discursive* school which sees the supposed universality of human rights as a pretence that enables governments and other authorities to couch their actions in human rights language, irrespective of their compliance with human rights law. Dembour describes this position as being 'nihilistic' with respect to human rights.

We have previously attempted to map these contrasting perspectives onto the discipline of criminology, noting that individual criminologists or schools of criminological thought might combine elements of more than one (Weber et al. 2014). Broadly speaking, we speculated that more legalistic approaches and perhaps positivist empirical approaches such as crime science, might approximate a *natural* position that applied human rights norms without seeking to problematise them. We proposed that branches of applied criminology that aspire to consensus building such as peacekeeping criminology, transitional and restorative justice might share at least some methodological similarities with the *deliberative* human rights school, drawing on human rights norms and concepts as a *lingua franca* in community deliberations over standard setting. Critical criminologists who are preoccupied with the critique of power in relation to crimes of the powerful, state crimes, colonialism and other systemic forms of discrimination and oppression might feel most at home in the *protest* school, deploying human rights claims as demands for accountability. While Foucauldian, radical feminist, and possibly Marxist scholars might be the most inclined to dismiss human rights norms as merely *discursive* tools, albeit for quite different reasons. Despite these disparities, we concluded that '[h]uman rights frameworks can potentially be accommodated within any criminological approach that eschews empiricism and the purely technical approaches to criminal justice and crime control associated with much of mainstream criminology' (Weber et al. 2014, p. 75).

One fundamental tension that must be acknowledged when seeking to integrate human rights and criminology is the difficulty of squaring human rights concepts with critical structural analysis. As early as 1970, Schwendinger and Schwendinger called for both individuals *and systems* that deny the basic human rights essential for human flourishing to be identified as criminal (cited in Weber et al. 2014, p. 77). However, human rights frameworks on their own are often viewed as too individualistic and too focused on civil and political rights to address the full range of structural harms and inequalities that threaten human flourishing:

> Human rights discourse is useful in terms of couching claims as agreed 'social wrongs' (Smart 1989: 143); however, if we want to challenge the wider harms that cause death and suffering, we sometimes need to look beyond the current hierarchy of human rights that elevates individualism and legal responses. Research has to understand local and personal 'troubles' in terms of histories, ideologies, relations and structures at a global level. (Stanley 2011, p. 177)

This is a call for an active engagement with social, economic and cultural rights, alongside the incorporation of structural frameworks, such as counter-colonialism, feminism, critical race theory or anti-capitalism. This follows from our earlier writing on criminology and human rights where we noted that:

> Scholars working from radical perspectives often advocate fundamental structural change that goes beyond the enforcement of minimum standards set out in human rights instruments, reject the abstraction and assertions of universalism of orthodox conceptions of human rights, and consider that existing human rights institutions are incapable of delivering on social justice goals in the face of state imperialism and growing corporate power. (Weber et al. 2014, p. 78)

Despite legitimate misgivings about the ability of human rights instruments to address structurally entrenched harms, Murphy and Whitty (2013, p. 574), in an assessment of criminological engagement with human rights conducted a decade ago, noted that at least some strands of critical criminology have recognised rights pragmatically as 'potential tools' for working towards broader social justice goals. Even criminologists who are mindful of the *discursive* potential of human rights to obfuscate state responsibility and legitimate harmful state or corporate practices, may choose not to abandon reference to human rights entirely, but rather to use human rights frameworks as a reference point within broader analyses that integrate multiple critical perspectives to hold governments to account. As Stanley (2011, p. 189) concludes: 'Criminology, therefore, needs to be attentive to the ways in which civil and political human rights approaches, by powerful nations and bodies, can be used as a cover to pursue individual geographic, political, social or economic interests'.

Rationale for Collection: New Thinking and Future Research Agenda for a Human Rights Centred Criminology

New Thinking About Criminology and Human Rights

Contributors to this volume display varying dispositions towards human rights that reflect the diverse 'schools' of human rights thinking outlined above. Not surprisingly, given their positioning as critical criminologists, a predilection for the more politicised (*protest*) and sceptical (*discursive*) approaches, and often a combination of the two, is readily apparent. As Dembour herself noted, individuals may align themselves strategically—whether consciously or otherwise—with elements of more than one of the ideal types, depending on the purpose of their analysis. We contend that there is no inherent contradiction, for example, in deploying extant human rights norms as an analytical tool to compare with actual criminal justice practice (adopting elements of a *deliberative* or *protest* position viz-a-viz human rights), while also pointing out the state capture of human rights *discourse* to legitimate abusive practices and identifying shortcomings in the construction of the human rights framework itself.

The contributions vary in the extent to which they engage with the specific content of human rights instruments and concepts, but together they span a range of civil, political, social and economic rights from the right to life and personal integrity, to protest, to health and an adequate standard of living, to freedom of identity and expression and the right to be free from arbitrary detention and cruel, inhuman or degrading treatment. This breadth, and the focus on human rights violations arising from structural harms, acknowledges that human beings may experience a 'continuum of violations', as was argued by Stanley (2011) more than a decade ago. Because of this breadth of vision, all contributors integrate critical analytical frameworks into their human rights discussions. For some authors, their contribution represents a relatively new engagement with human rights law and concepts, while for others it is the culmination of many years of scholarship at the nexus of criminology and human rights. In each case, their chapters present new and critical thinking that enriches our understanding of both the value and limits of human rights in real-world contexts, while extending the boundaries of the criminology discipline.

The volume opens with a thought-provoking contribution by Elizabeth Stanley who reflects on the challenges of developing a criminology for human rights, building on her earlier work (Stanley 2011). She opens provocatively with the observation that '[i]t can sometimes be hard to get behind human rights', noting that political, economic and technological structures globally, including institutions charged with managing crime and criminal justice, are organised in ways that actively promote mass human rights abuses. This is facilitated by processes of normalisation and distancing that disguise underlying systems of inequality and sustained by ineffectual accountability mechanisms in systems that affirm the power and primacy of the state. But rather than abandon any engagement with human rights, Stanley sees a crucial role for criminologists—discussed further in the next section—as human rights champions.

In her chapter on 'governing through rights', socio-legal scholar Claire Hamilton notes the ease with which human rights regimes have accommodated authoritarian securitisation measures following the 9/11 terror attacks, while at the same time claiming to 'emancipate and protect often vulnerable lives'. Adopting a Foucauldian lens, she presents two security case studies operating at the international and national level, respectively, in which human rights became a legitimising force to pursue draconian policies in the name of national and global security. Despite this excoriating critique of human rights practice, Hamilton maintains that human rights law cannot be dismissed as entirely ineffectual or as merely a legitimation device but has also been successfully applied to force some constraints on sweeping security laws in the United Kingdom.

Will Jackson's chapter is a call to radically overhaul policing research, much of which continues to be conducted *with* and *for* police. Jackson charts major milestones in the public exposure of abuses of power by UK police, while noting that relationships between police organisations and mainstream policing researchers have become closer over the same period, often diminishing the critical edge of the research. Jackson argues that human rights focused criminologists should conduct research *on*, rather than *for* police. He recounts an empirical case study on the policing of protest, where a decision was taken to adopt a 'one-sided approach' in order to gain the trust of heavily policed protest groups. This uncovered many violations of the Human Rights Act 1998 [UK] that had gone unreported in previous, police-orientated research.

Next, Katja Franko examines the right to life as it applies, or more often does not, to the deaths of border crossers at the external borders of Europe. She notes that scant scholarly attention has been paid to this fundamental right with most work in criminology being centred on the use of the death penalty. She depicts borderlands as places where migrants' rights come into direct conflict with the border control objectives and sovereign violence of states while offering ideal conditions for the avoidance of responsibility. For one thing, migrant status decreases the capacity for border crossers to be seen as the bearers of rights. As a consequence, the protection of 'precarious life' in Europe has typically been framed as a humanitarian issue, whereby offering assistance is considered to be an act of grace.

Andriani Fili and Mary Bosworth maintain a focus on the particular difficulty of securing the rights of migrants. Despite a damning record of cruel, inhuman and degrading treatment in immigration detention facilities, they argue that Greek authorities have used the often 'timid' and 'reformist' reports of human rights agencies, including government funded monitoring bodies, as 'discursive legitimation' of their abusive practices. Drawing on interviews with human rights defenders, lawyers and activists, and with reference to specific human rights instruments such as OPCAT, the authors show how human rights protections have proved ineffective in moderating the state's prerogative to control its borders, reflecting a lesser degree of human rights protection for non-citizens and the incapacity of human rights mechanisms to effect systemic change.

Silvana Tapia Tapia shines a light on carceral violence in Ecuador, using an abolitionist and post-colonial lens to expose what she calls 'human rights penality' in government responses to violence against women. Whereas many authors direct their critique to governments who use human rights discourse as a camouflage for abusive practices, her critique of human rights is more fundamental. She sees the international human rights system, derived from Western liberal thought, as playing a facilitating role within an ongoing colonial paradigm that directly supports carceral violence. This generates false assumptions that prisons can be made human rights compliant, often displacing non-carceral, pre-colonial systems and consistently failing to deter or reform perpetrators or meet the needs of survivors.

Continuing with a critique of human rights as legitimising Western ideology, Pablo Ciocchini and Joe Greener reflect on the power dichotomy of human rights in the Global South. While human rights could be used to address state and state-corporate harm, they are in fact implemented to maintain the status quo. Therefore, these authors argue, human rights are used to maintain the current structures of power. They claim that the principle of human rights universality is undermined at local-operational level, because the higher-level infrastructure of human rights is brought to the local level via a dispersed system of accountability. This implements a selective inclusion of what is and what is not human rights abuse and confines human rights interventions to ad-hoc mitigation or prevention of crisis, rather than long-term sustainable societal transformation.

Along similar lines, the chapter by Danielle Watson, Julie Berg and Lamese Laponi analyses the issues linked to a Western-centric interpretation of 'access to justice'. Despite this principle being recognised as a fundamental human right almost 85 years ago with the UN Universal Declaration of Human Rights, its definition and frameworks are limited, since the current interpretation of 'access to justice' is not sufficiently inclusive of justice mechanisms beyond Western-centric systems or other broadly accepted, and in many cases colonised, systems. In turn, this excludes a comprehensive approach to access to justice, forcing other systems to either conform or to be not accepted or even to be negated to the point of being pathologised for being non-state and plural systems.

As part of this reflection, Stella Black, David Burnside, Jessica Hastings and Katey Thom point out that Indigenous people are those who are 'apprehended, arrested, incarcerated, institutionalised or in rehabilitation or recovery', in highest proportion. They reaffirm Māori rights are fundamental human rights, as recognised in te Titiri o Waitangi [Treaty of Waitangi], and by the United Nations Declaration on the

Rights of Indigenous Peoples. They argue that criminal justice processes become truly inclusive when they embrace a Māori-led approach, from research to their genuine operationalisation within the justice system. They point out that often a Western-centric theoretical and methodological approach to criminology does not allow such inclusion, distorting representations. A different commitment to research ethics in the co-production of knowledge is central to a true human rights discourse of criminology. They reflect how this is important for those with an intersectional lived experience (of incarceration, of minority identity, of intergenerational trauma).

George Radics moves the focus onto queer criminology, highlighting how colonialism in the Global South does not permit the fulfilment of a human rights-centric project. Radics traces the UN's positioning against discriminatory laws and acts of violence based on sexual orientation and gender identity expression. Yet, despite this top-down movement, it is pointed out that the rights of LGBTQ people are formulated and entrenched in, and for, systems of the Global North, leaving behind the Global South. Using some key examples of police and courts, Radics points out how culturally embedded the issues are in the Global South, because systems of colonial oppression are maintained and reproduced via the criminal justice tools.

Sandra Walklate focuses on a victimology of human rights. In this chapter, we are invited to reflect on how victims' narratives, and mechanisms for addressing injustice, had been left behind when the human rights discourse came to the fore, especially after the second world war and onwards. This may explain their structural absence as human rights mechanisms of justice that still reverberate into the present day. Indeed, Walklate closes the chapter with the consideration that, in her educated opinion, there is no one 'single jurisdiction that has successfully negotiated the challenges of rendering victim rights as human rights'.

While they agree that the impact has been limited, Nancy Wonders and Sydney Shevat conclude that the international human rights system *has* been effective to some degree in raising worldwide awareness of gendered violence and mobilising political action. They see gendered violence as one of the most prevalent and yet least recognised human rights violations, noting that the international human rights architecture has been developed to prioritise violence experienced by men in the public sphere. Their chapter provides a comprehensive, critical review of the major human rights initiatives in this field to date, identifying punitive approaches, reliance on states and failure to address root causes of violence against women as key shortcomings, underpinned by state complicity in the perpetuation of wider gender hierarchies.

Raymond Michalowski and Rebecca Annorbah take up the challenge posed by several of the authors of bringing social and economic rights to the forefront of criminological enquiry. They contrast the concentration on individual acts of violence in criminology and domestic criminal law, with the much greater harm done by government failures to address systemic, avoidable, and often racialized, health inequalities. Presenting a mass of public health research, originating largely from the United States and with a particular focus on the policies of former President Donald Trump, they argue that disparities in health outcomes both *within* and *between* nations should be considered violations of human rights and become the subject matter for a 'human rights criminology for public health'.

As with the previous chapter, the contribution by Claire Loughnan and Steven Caruana stretches the boundaries of mainstream criminology as they bring an engagement with the aged care sector to the discipline of criminology and human rights. Aged care facilities are a growing sector, in Australia and worldwide, with many reported episodes of violence, neglect, abuse. Often these spaces are run by poorly trained and paid staff. Sadly, these places are also becoming known for being places of confinement and control, where human rights are breached, with similar emerging patterns comparable to prisons and detention centres. Loughnan and Caruana's chapter brings to the fore the role criminologists have to monitor and critique human rights applications, and the role of the state, when vulnerable people are harmed.

Articulating a Criminological Research Agenda for Human Rights

In relation to a future research agenda for a human rights centred criminology, our authors identified both crucial *topics* for further study and critical *methods* they consider to be best suited to this task. Some contributors also offered observations on using criminological scholarship to challenge the architecture of the international human rights regime itself. We summarise some of their key suggestions here.

Stanley proposes a *relational* research agenda that is capable of exposing the discursive hijacking of human rights by governments, and identifying the role of criminal justice institutions and wider structural factors in perpetuating human rights abuses. At the core of this agenda is the need to adopt empathetic approaches towards the victims of human rights violations that cut through the distancing processes that often prevent abuses from being identified as serious state harms, and to engage as allies with harmed individuals and communities.

In setting out her future agenda, Claire Hamilton alerts legal scholars and practitioners to the dangers of a narrow and overly technical focus on law. She argues that 'doing rights criminologically' may help 'make rights matter' in the security field. This entails, *inter alia*, the borrowing of critical criminological concepts such as 'popular punitivism' to bring into focus the contested and political dimension of human rights practice. She advocates using Foucauldian methodologies to examine how human rights emerge and work as governing devices under certain conditions and uncover the mentalities, knowledges and technologies deployed by various parties.

In line with Stanley's call for criminologists to work as allies with the victims of human rights abuses, Will Jackson advocates adopting the 'view from below' to expose human rights abuses perpetrated by police, ideally through ethnographic work with heavily policed populations. The objective of human rights centred police research should be to identify the impact of policing on these populations and interrogate the official account of human rights compliance with a view to increasing police accountability, not merely bolstering their operational efficiency. Key here is the need for researchers to retain total independence from police organisations in order to avoid capture in the organisational perspective of this powerful arm of the state.

In a world marked by enormous global inequalities, Franko argues that we need a better conceptual, methodological and theoretical apparatus to understand the unequal protection of human life at the global level. This includes adopting different conceptions of state sovereignty, by privileging perspectives from the Global South. Adopting these perspectives may reveal that human rights do not stand up to scrutiny as protectors of life where there is no one to enforce them, and that new thinking may be needed through the building of 'more democratic knowledge structures'.

Fili and Bosworth suggest that research into human rights abuses in immigration detention needs to refocus on how institutions charged with monitoring human rights observance perform their duties. Greater awareness is needed of how monitoring systems can become compromised, deflect attention from larger questions about the use of detention and provide 'normative cover' for harmful practices. It is vital, in their view, to document human rights abuses and other state failures. And while translating evidence into the dismantling or reform of abusive systems 'is not an easy task', there is benefit in joining in solidarity with colleagues dealing with similarly 'bleak landscapes'.

For Tapia Tapia, the human rights system itself is the rightful object of criminological research, necessitating the adoption of anticolonial, abolitionist and feminist perspectives to ensure that human rights do not 'perpetuate a hegemonic order'. With respect to violence against women, this agenda includes mapping the relationship between 'human rights penality' and the decline of non-penal (including socio-economic) approaches to gender justice; engaging with the activism of abolitionist feminists and counter-carceral movements; and assessing the damaging effects of punitive approaches advocated by the international human rights regime in tackling violence against women.

Ciocchini and Greener acknowledge the potential human rights can offer if they are interpreted more inclusively, through a southern criminology lens. They claim that the principle of self-determination can bring real societal changes. Human rights should be able to reshape global economy and give a more equal access to wealth and resources. A human rights-centric project should address corporate crime. Only through such a structural-cultural shift, can experiences of crime and violence change too.

To render human rights principles effective, and appreciate all justice mechanisms that are operational within local contexts, Watson, Berg and Laponi argue that 'access to justice' would benefit from a process of decolonisation. As it stands, informal and hybrid systems may be inaccurately dismissed as ineffective in advancing access to justice, because they are mapped out against a Western theorising. Such local and informal systems could in fact actualise access to justice more in line with human rights principles, and therefore engaging with these players and systems may be the step necessary towards an inclusive and fairer approach.

Black, Burnside, Hastings and Thom point out the violent outcome for Indigenous people in the current Western-centric legal system. Indigenous rights have not been properly protected in the current regime. They argue that a human rights criminological lens can accelerate the re-envisioning of an inclusive system and can promote the voices of lived experience. They see the co-production of knowledge at the centre of such a vision, for a significant and much needed human rights shift away from the current approach. This may require 'resisting westernised ideas' on methodological approaches, to minimise and avoid further marginalisation.

Radics argues that queer criminology has a role in highlighting the systemic and cultural differences between Global North and Global South to make progress. This should include questioning how to progress inclusive human rights instruments and mechanisms, if colonialism is still acutely operative. Radics points out that a more nuanced understanding of the societal issues triggering negative responses towards LGBTQ rights should be a high priority in the human rights agenda of key stakeholders, such as the United Nations.

Walklate urges for a global political commitment to systemic change, where human rights can find the conditions to be central and meaningful to and for victims. Walklate adopts a framework of good practice to engage with victim story-telling and suggests expanding it through the lens of human rights. This may be more reflective of time, place and voice and therefore act on inclusivity at a societal and individual level.

Wonders and Shevat argue that future research should draw on the rich body of existing criminological research to enable the international human rights architecture to target the structural drivers of gendered violence. These include the role of states in maintaining gender inequalities, the gendered impacts of conflicts and climate change, gendered barriers to mobility and the rise of nationalist and right-wing politics. They argue that empirical research makes otherwise invisible power dynamics visible and can be used to empower populations in ways that challenge the dominant order, including the masculinist, neoliberal and colonial frames that have shaped the international human rights order itself.

Michalowski and Annorbah urge criminologists, especially those already versed in the study of state and corporate crime, to direct their scholarship and activism towards the proximate and distal drivers of 'public health crimes', carving out some new terrain for a human rights criminology for public health. They contend that critical criminologists are well placed to 'pull the lens back' from the immediate infliction of harm to identify the 'upstream drivers' or wider context of these systemic harms. They present an expansive analytical framework for this purpose that integrates the individual, organisational and macro-social levels of social action.

In the 'quasi-carceral' space of aged care facilities, Loughnan and Caruana use the lens of international agreements aimed at preventing torture and cruel, inhuman or degrading treatment or punishment. They are concerned that, without a real application of international human rights frameworks, there is little possibility to detect and address harmful practices. A human rights centred criminology would focus on the harm and on tools to prevent it. Their work is inspirational, because they continue the expansive analytical framework of the chapters before and point out how a human rights lens permits pushing the boundaries of criminology further.

Conclusion

A human rights-centred criminology brings benefits both to the study of human rights practice and to criminology as a discipline. On the one hand, the place-based, empirical approach of criminology complements the juridical perspective of human rights lawyers. At the same time, the injection of human rights thinking into criminology provides a recognised normative framework to complement the analytical frameworks already adopted by criminologists to uncover entrenched, structural harms. Moreover, the focus in *critical* criminology, on critique of the state and of patriarchy, colonialism and other hegemonic systems of thought, provides the tools to unmask the manipulation of existing human rights systems by governments and the conceptual inadequacies arising from the imposition of dominant modes of Western liberal thought at a global level.

The critical, human rights centred criminology our contributors imagine works *for* human rights, but not necessarily *through* them. It is not intended to be a discreet sub-discipline, but a way to do both criminology and human rights better by bringing together a range of intellectual tools to analyse and respond to a continuum of harms that extends beyond both state-defined crimes (the focus of mainstream criminology) and individual violations of civil liberties (the primary substance of legal scholarship in human rights). Our collection here covers many of the core and emerging areas of critical criminological concern but is far from comprehensive. We hope to deal in more depth with many of the issues identified here, and many others not addressed in these pages, in further publications in the *Critical Studies in Human Rights and Criminology* series.

Note

1. But see Weber et al. (2017) for a selection of critical writing on criminology and human rights.

References

Canning, Victoria, and Steve Tombs. 2021. *From Social Harm to Zemiology: A Critical Introduction*. Abingdon: Routledge.

Chambliss, William, and Raymond Michalowski. 2010. *State Crime in the Global Age*. Uffculme, Devon: Willan Publishing.

Cohen, Stanley. 1993. Human Rights and Crimes of the State: The Culture of Denial. *Australian and New Zealand Journal of Criminology* 26 (2): 97–115.

Dembour, Marie-Benedict. 2012. What Are Human Rights? Four Schools of Thought. In *Handbook of Human Rights*, ed. Thomas Cushman. Abingdon: Routledge.

Franko, Katja. 2019. *The Crimmigrant Other: Migration and Penal Power*. Abingdon: Routledge.

Marmo, Marinella, and Elaine Fishwick. 2022. Criminology and Human Rights. In *Research Handbook of Comparative Criminal Justice*, ed. Nelken David and Hamilton Claire, 274–288. Cheltenham: Edward Elgar.

Michalowski, Raymond, and Ronald Kramer. 2006. *State-Corporate Crime: Wrongdoing at the Intersection of Business and Government*. New Brunswick, NJ: Rutgers University Press.

Murphy, Therese, and Noel Whitty. 2013. Making History: Academic Criminology and Human Rights. *British Journal of Criminology* 53 (4): 568–587.

Schwendinger, Herman, and Julia Schwendinger. 1970. Defenders of Order or Guardians of Human Rights? *Issues in Criminology* 5 (2): 123–157.

Stanley, Elizabeth. 2011. Towards a Criminology for Human Rights. In *Expanding the Criminological Imagination*, ed. Alana Barton, Karen Corteen, David Scott and David Whyte, 2nd ed. Uffculme, Devon: Willan Publishing.

Stanley, Elizabeth, and Jude McCulloch, eds. 2012. *State Crime and Resistance*. Abingdon: Routledge.

Weber, Leanne, Elaine Fishwick, and Marinella Marmo. 2014. *Crime Justice and Human Rights*. Basingstoke: Palgrave Macmillan.

Weber, Leanne, Elaine Fishwick, and Marinella Marmo, eds. 2017. *The Routledge Handbook of Criminology and Human Rights*. Abingdon: Routledge.

2

Criminological Research for Human Rights

Elizabeth Stanley

Introduction

It can sometimes be hard to get behind human rights. Global economic, political and technological structures are organized to facilitate and normalize mass violations. Our state and corporate institutions routinely act in criminal ways and frequently make capital out of doing so. They employ self-serving talk and processes around rights, sustaining global violence, inequities and impunity as they go. Nowhere is this more apparent than in the systems created to manage crime and justice.

There are many different contexts in which human rights violations occur. However, one aspect is clear: violations often happen when distancing is present. There are many ways that distancing is built including in our politics, use of language, the production of data, the development of algorithms, the culture of bureaucracies or the

E. Stanley (✉)
Te Herenga Waka-Victoria University of Wellington, Wellington, New Zealand
e-mail: elizabeth.stanley@vuw.ac.nz

L. Weber and M. Marmo (eds.), *A Research Agenda for a Human Rights Centred Criminology*, Palgrave Critical Studies in Human Rights and Criminology,
https://doi.org/10.1007/978-3-031-46289-4_2

construction of our academic disciplines. At their worst, our structures, institutions and frameworks normalize violence, fear, inequities and a lack of care. At the same time, violations can also be supported through progressive means. Committed and thoughtful justice-conscious actors—including those who work in human rights organizations or academia—can also prop up violatory systems, as systems for monitoring, compliance or knowledge-making become part of the ritualistic 'dance' in which states or corporates (re)claim legitimacy. Complaint processes can just work to make violations manageable, and to redeem and re-power violators (Ahmed 2021).

How might criminological researchers be responsive to any of this? And, how might we act to bolster solidarity with those at the sharp end? A crucial element, as outlined in this chapter, could be that we become more attentive to the distancing that regularly props up human rights violations, and to the relationality of our research.

Rights and the Problem of Distance

Rights can only be fully developed within a relational sphere—where there are close, empathetic relationships between humans, or between human animals and other beings (including non-human animals, invertebrates, other species, environments, eco-systems or planetary systems) (Jackson 2020; Monod de Froideville 2021). These relationalities, and the rights that may flow from them, depend upon the reduction of distance. Yet, states and corporations engage in diverse forms of distancing to place *others* or their problems out of *our* relational orbit. Our connections are often diminished through spatial, socio-cultural, political, economic, algorithmic and structural forms of distancing. Indeed, our current era is defined by ideologies, bureaucratic rationalities and technological shifts that actively sustain distance. The result is that rights are regularly eroded.

Sometimes this can occur in overt ways, such as when political parties calculate voter support for rights withdrawals and actively prioritize ideological exclusions and violations. Consider the persistent retraction of asylum rights for people who arrive via specific modes of transport, especially boats, in places like the UK or Australia. This targeted rights removal has been forged on mythical identities about those seeking asylum as 'illegal' or 'threats' to the nation's social cohesion and well-being (Grewcock 2010; Malloch and Stanley 2005). It has also relied upon steady ignorance-making about the role of Global North states in creating the conditions (such as of conflict, poverty or climate crisis) from which people so often move (Stanley 2021). In turn, many Western states have dismissed hospitality in favour of highly racialized criminalization. The *right to* asylum is now rarely mentioned by Western politicians—any *right to* is recast as a claimant's *lack of*—such that those who make asylum claims are seen in deficit terms, as the problem. Travel without required visas is now almost impossible, and asylum seekers are deemed to lack the skills, qualifications and language capacities that might allow them to migrate through other restricted channels—these patriarchal and racially targeted barriers maintain male whiteness without recourse to sexist or racist discourse (Franko 2020; Marmo 2023). Authorities classify *them*, instead, as a danger to rights—*they* will erode rights by 'taking' *our* jobs, houses, school places and welfare, or t*hey* are found to be 'immoral' in making rightful claims against ever-tightening bureaucracies (Aliverti 2021). The fundamental purpose of an asylum right—for individuals to arrive at the border, often without documents, and be provided with protection—has been repurposed as an offensive and offending act. This distancing shift is such that governments can even demand incarceration for those who arrive at the border—in New Zealand, detention without a warrant has recently been politically marketed as offering "an orderly and rights-compliant framework" (Graham-McLay 2023).

In other circumstances, politicians or government agencies appear to engage in progressive rights talk. Yet, distancing is maintained through bureaucratic rationalities. Here, the official enthusiasm for rights is rarely matched by a surge in resources or actions to ensure that rights-based cultures or standards might be achieved. Emerging political talk on dealing with the climate crisis, for example, has not been dove-tailed with substantive actions to stop the greenhouse gas emissions that continue to rise alongside the growth of new green economies (Lakhani 2023). Those who protest the lack of action on climate crisis are also heavily policed and punished, as seen in the UK's *Public Order Act 2023*. The problems here, that threaten every right we might imagine, need fundamental shifts to our global political and economic systems, yet dominant bureaucracies remain ambivalent (and sometimes hostile) despite the ever-increasing warnings from those engaged with the science (IPCC 2022). This situation is not helped by the ever-close relationships between law or policymakers and polluting corporations.

A core issue, then, is the limited bureaucratic commitment to rights, with state institutions frequently centring their own administrative needs, economic benefit or political popularity above all else. In this, the ability of state institutions to continually reinvent and re-empower themselves in relation to rights cannot be overstated. While ostensibly posing a challenge to states, rights standards and frameworks consistently re-establish the state as *the* legitimate power for solving problems of state or corporate violence, harm and exclusion (Spade 2015). This creates multiple tensions. To illustrate one: in settler-state contexts, the state must be unsettled, and other governance models developed to propel Indigenous self-determination—a move that is also at the core of the UN Declaration on the Rights of Indigenous Peoples 2007 (Matike Mai Aotearoa 2016). Yet, mainstream human rights logics and practices often deepen the role of the state as rights protectors. Part of the problem here is that state-led legal controls, policing and criminal justice measures are re-articulated as vital tools to prevent or control violations. More laws, more police and more prisons are frequently touted as solutions, despite their known failings in deterring or preventing violations, or in (re)habilitating violators (Gilmore 2022; McLeod 2015).

Over time, mainstream rights processes have also become increasingly professionalized—requiring administrative capacities that often go beyond the settings of small-nation states. States subsequently benefit from a heavy ritualism in how rights are bureaucratically managed (Stanley and Mihaere 2018). Monitoring or oversight bodies (including commissions for human rights, health, or children, or ombudsman's offices) often do not have adequate resources, staffing or actual independence from government. Under diminished settings, these bodies tend to focus on individual and ad hoc rights problems, rather than asserting power to propel necessary institutional or systemic changes. Related restrictions on change appear at the global level—for example, even in United Nations reporting, criticisms are espoused, acknowledgements are refined and new policies and procedures are promised across multiple reporting cycles (Stanley and Mihaere 2019). Any violations are forever 'in the past' and are always being addressed through recommendations or new programmes, strategic plans, policies, recruitment strategies or training agendas (ibid.). It is surmised that we just need a new form of bureaucracy, and everything will look different. Yet, at the next cycle, the same issues—whether that is the disproportionate targeting of Indigenous or minority people as offenders by police or prisons, or the lack of protection of women from male violence, or the criminalization and incarceration of those in mental health distress—will remain as central problems, not least because the structures (of colonialism, 'race', capitalism, patriarchy, cis-genderism or able-ism) that underpin these violations remain unchanged.

These difficulties in reaching beyond the surface—to unearth the structures and systems that facilitate violations—is increasingly made more complicated by the risk technologies and algorithmic frameworks that classify, observe and govern targeted populations. These technologies and rationalities are frequently presented under a neutral, scientific glow and with effusive claims of effectiveness by corporate owners and state users (Cunneen 2020). Newer systems (from AI tech to facial recognition) have been inserted into policing, immigration, corrections and other agencies with little transparency or regulation of their algorithm constructions, data inputs and corporate agendas or consideration of their implications (Ugwudike 2022). They operate to reinforce long-established forms of inequality, discrimination, power and violence. And they do so in a way that creates distance from state or corporate actors and the perpetuation of racist systems of violence and marginalization (ibid.), including through policing, punishment and border practices (Ugwudike 2021).

In summary, distancing is central to the perpetuation of rights violations. It creates conditions to limit the full recognition of state or corporate actors as violators, and to stymie chances for accountability. Distancing creates disconnections between those who suffer and those who benefit from violations, and it provides a ritual for dominant relations of inequities in doing so. In short, it creates the conditions for violence, harms and injustice—the critique of which must be at the core of any criminological endeavour.

Setting a Relational Agenda

What should be the role, then, of criminologists? There are many ways that researchers can take further positive action for rights. Here, I raise two broad approaches on how criminological researchers might positively impact on the relationships that produce violations and harms. The first is that we can further expose how rights are subject to distancing, and what might be done about it. And, the second is that we can be more attentive to the distancing within our own knowledge-production and research relationalities.

Researching Rights and the Production of Distance

Rights-focused criminologists have been adept in drawing attention to the ways in which rights are undermined, trodden over, dismissed, ignored, used as political cover, rolled back and removed (as just some examples, see: Barton and Davis [2018], Cohen [2001], and Scraton [2007]). In many areas, as in this volume, scholars track the insidious removal of rights and demonstrate how distancing operates to fuel marginalization, discrimination and violence in our formal policing and justice systems, and through our societies more generally. We cannot lose sight of the power of such work, not least as violators spend considerable energy and power in distancing themselves from violations. Blaming victims, casting them as a threat, ignoring harms, relying on bureaucratic measures to quell complaints, re-naming harms as positive acts, claiming there is no other option, among other practices: all serve to mis-direct responsibility and to airbrush out possibilities for change.

A significant part of our contribution, and one to which we must remain attentive, is to question the use of language or data to assert difference and create distance. There are many areas where this has resonance. Consider, for example, the language of *prison musters* (as if there are cattle), *over-representation* (as if some categorized groups just need to represent themselves in 'crime' a little less) or *illegals* (as if any person can be, in themselves, against the law). This language often serves to hide the humanity of those targeted. It can legitimize and normalize violations (*intensive questioning* or *behaviour management regimes*, anyone?), and it regularly assumes a homogenous nature to people caught in similar circumstances (*the* Muslim community as a case in point). Relatedly, we might further investigate the reliance on quantitative data or computational assessments to count and designate the risks of certain groups, dismissing their full humanity. Such data frequently hides nuanced personal experiences while presenting indicators of marginalization, structural inequality or discriminatory official interventions as individual failings or 'risks' (Stanley and Monod de Froideville 2020). All these representational approaches diminish human relationships and provide fodder for increased state or corporate controls.

Criminologists can also be useful in directing attention to the many and varied ways in which formal responses—including operations of law, policing and punishment—create distance between dominant actors and violence or harms, thereby bolstering mass inequities of power. One element, here, relates to our continuing need to engage with fuller versions of 'crime' or 'violation'. In this, our critical analyses must reflect the violence, social harms and risks that so often sit outside established legal categories or that are frequently downplayed in contemporary policing or justice measures (Canning and Tombs 2021; Pemberton 2016). There are many harms that should form central elements to our criminology, including climate crimes, environmental crimes, border crimes, crimes of globalization, state-corporate crimes, digital crimes, social harms and so on. Each of these, on their own, constitutes more violence and harm than the 'crimes' that currently make up our 'crime problem'. Including them as central tenets enables a more accurate picture. Moreover, this recognition can disentangle the political management of events (i.e. that defines what is criminal) and identities (who is criminal or victim) and what or who is made absent from these categories, and why.

Relatedly, we can be attentive to the ways in which old crimes are being given new leases of life through contemporary systems and practices. For example, to address the new violations that emerge out of online technologies that reassert powered identities, difference and conflict as a means of generating profit—seen in the corporate expansion of online porn sites that has led to women being increasingly confronted with different forms of violence, such as strangulation, by men (Keene 2023) or the social media companies that have facilitated new spaces for far-right groups to cohere, and for gross violence against Indigenous or minority groups to find celebratory audiences (Lindsay 2023). On these issues, among others, policing and regulatory agencies have historically failed to provide protection for those victimized, or to even count forms of sexual assault or hate crimes as violence (Botha and Poynting 2021). Criminologists are well positioned to track these historical violatory continuities.

In doing this work, there are multiple threads we might follow to explore how humans, other life forms and eco-systems are impacted by rights violations, how our systems facilitate and create impunity for mass harms and violence, and how we might resist. As just some examples, criminologists can make clear contributions around:

- Victimization—to continue our investigations into how victimization practices are structured into our systems, such that practices of victimization are normalized and sustained through everyday practices, and how dominant institutional systems fail to provide protections, redress, punishments or recovery.
- The Circular Perpetuation of Harms—to reflect on the continuities between the organization of our laws, institutions, policies and practices and how our 'crime problems' are built. For example, our inequitable systems of health, education, housing, economy and welfare all perpetuate mass violations and are frequently underpinned by processes of criminalization.
- State-Corporate Power—to expose the nature and operations of states and corporations, alongside other dominant global economic and political institutions that create harm, not least to show how violence and harms are not aberrational but intrinsic elements and a frequent source of their legitimacy to power.
- Borders—to call into question the nature of state boundaries by revealing their temporal and political nature, including how they are contradictorily impermeable (e.g. around asylum seeking) while also porous (e.g. around modern slavery).
- Global Structural Relations—to analyse the interconnected ways in which violations are embedded and secured as common and accepted

practice through multiple structures, including of advanced global capitalism, white supremacism, colonialism, patriarchy, cis-genderism or able-ism.

- Transformations—to create visions for alternative systems that allow rights—in all their many forms—to flourish.

Criminologists have a vital role, then, in connecting the role of institutions, laws, policies, structures and socio-cultural conditions to the perpetuation of violations, in removing the distance. Sometimes, this might mean that we need to direct our attention to the settings that appear benign or progressive in intent, including in the academic responses that we might hold most dear.

Closing the Research Distance

In April 2023, survivors and bereaved family members of the preventable Grenfell Tower fire called for a stop to two productions: a *BBC* television series and a *National Theatre* play that would each dramatize the many layers of this 'disaster'. Despite evolving from survivors' accounts, and being drawn from long-term research, survivors and those bereaved questioned the motives of non-local makers, their limited consultation processes and the potentially non-transformative nature of their contributions (Townsend and Thorpe 2023). They reflected on identity and ownership as well as the purpose of storytelling to expose new truths, provide repair or accountability, prevent future harms or improve lived realities. In doing so, they cut to the core of the purpose and practice of any knowledge-gathering and telling endeavour: "Who asked for this?" (Nabil Choucair) and "Who are they talking to?" (Maryam Adam) (Townsend and Thorpe 2023).

These questions are pertinent to any researcher, and especially for those of us working around crime, justice and rights. After all, the history of criminology has been continuously tied to concerns about the academic gaze with research undertaken: to uphold narrow versions of 'crime', to reassert targeted populations as 'criminals' or 'victims', to re-invigorate violent (and often ineffective) controls or to pump up the legitimacy of harm-producing state agencies and corporations, among others. Against all of this, the fundamental reasons for the emergence and purpose of research, and its longer-term impacts, require continual engagement by researchers.

We cannot underestimate the difficulties of doing this work. There has been a perennial tension around the 'real-life' impact of academic work—between theory and praxis, or between scholarly writings and activism. However, this is made ever more difficult in the current context of academia. Many criminologists now face a 'dark academia' (Fleming 2021) that feeds on precarious employment, increasing demands to manage larger classes with fewer resources, and new administrative and technological burdens. This is set alongside pressure for high-ranked publications, a surging quantum of outputs, metrics and citations. These institutional imperatives do not always sit easily with the work required for impactful or community-engaged research that might meet the concerns and aspirations of those most affected by rights violations. Trying to navigate these different routes is difficult and the potential for burnout can be high.

In this, we also need to recognize that a crucial part of the relational experience is concerned with how scholars relate to their own research meanings and practices. There are personal, emotional and political tensions in 'doing' rights work. University systems are still not adept in supporting scholars with mental health impacts or vicarious trauma from research experiences. Nor do they propel a clear understanding of or commitment to the prolonged time required to do research built on deep and trusting community involvements, or that necessitate different forms of 'output', such as bypassing journal articles in a focus on social education, alternative public reporting or community organizing. Moreover, universities may be indifferent or even opposed to the 'bad news' stories that create a challenge to state or corporate funders (ibid.).

The relational experience is also about how our research impacts on the world. The motivation for social change or renewed capacities for justice often guides rights work in Criminology and beyond. In this, scholars might also question whether they are the right person for a project. In my University (Te Herenga Waka—Victoria University of Wellington), all academics who request funding are now asked to consider their engagement with Mātauranga Māori—a broad term for Māori knowledge that encompasses Māori worldviews, values, creativity, cultural practices, life forces and of knowing and being in the world (Ruru and Nikora 2021; Tuhiwai Smith 1999). All researchers—from criminologists to engineers—must explain how their project will benefit or involve Māori. There is no research that cannot be unsettled. For many, this involves consideration of how Māori, as Indigenous peoples, will be involved in the research from its preliminary conception through to its methodologies, analysis, writing and means of distribution. For some, it will lead to a conclusion that they are not the right person to lead a project however benign they might be in intent. The days of settler academics writing *about* or *for* Māori, or writing with little or no consideration of or engagement with Māori, are beginning to recede. In short, criminologists also have to attend to our own discipline and research-making—to question the grounds on which our work is based, to reflect on where we are heading, and who we serve in taking on particular narratives, logics or approaches.

Conclusion

All of these developments point us to broader questions for criminology scholars, such as: How might criminologists work as allies to those who are repeatedly targeted for violations? And, how can our work prevent violations, change harmful systems or contribute to justice? In short, what purpose does our research, and our discipline, serve? Part of the process involves disentanglement from the 'gratifications' (Myers 2022) of White, patriarchal, cis-gendered, able-bodied and capitalist power and violence that benefit many scholars, institutions and state agencies. It also requires us to give increased consideration to the emotional and political considerations of doing rights research, and to know when to step aside, and take different (non-scholarly) actions that support others. This implicates us to work as allies to those who are commonly marginalized or subject to state-corporate harms.

This solidarity takes life-long diligence, self-reflection and humility. It can require political commitment for material social change, engagement in difficult and tiring public-facing work and even challenge to colleagues whose work might sustain oppressive, discriminatory or violent systems

(Land 2015). These political struggles generally run counter to university imperatives (despite the growing institutional narratives for scholars to be 'impactful'), not least as they often require researchers and institutions to cede space and power (McLachlan 2019). In all of this, it helps to recognize that these settings are always in a process of continual realignment and re-establishment—the crises or ruptures that emerge from violations will almost always be followed by a new capture of power. Our research and our related acts of challenge and solidarity will forever be unfinished.

References

Ahmed, Sara. 2021. *Complaint!* Durham: Duke University Press.

Aliverti, Ana. 2021. *Policing the Borders Within.* Oxford: Oxford University Press.

Barton, Alana, and Howard Davis, eds. 2018. *Ignorance, Power and Harm.* Cham: Palgrave.

Botha, Daniel, and Scott Poynting. 2021. Hate Crime, Racism and Islamophobia. In *The Aotearoa Handbook of Criminology*, ed. Elizabeth Stanley, Trevor Bradley, and Sarah Monod de Froideville, 107–118. Auckland: Auckland University Press.

Canning, Victoria, and Steve Tombs. 2021. *From Social Harm to Zemiology: A Critical Introduction.* London: Routledge.

Cohen, Stanley. 2001. *States of Denial*. Cambridge: Polity Press.

Cunneen, Chris. 2020. Youth Justice and Racialization: Comparative Reflections. *Theoretical Criminology* 24 (3): 521–539.

Fleming, Peter. 2021. *Dark Academia: How Universities Die*. London: Pluto Press.

Franko, Katja. 2020. *The Crimmigrant Other: Migration and Penal Power*. London: Routledge.

Gilmore, Ruth Wilson. 2022. *Abolition Geography: Essays Towards Liberation.* London: Verso.

Graham-McLay, Charlotte. 2023. NZ Mulls Harsher Law Against Refugee Boat Arrivals. *The Guardian*, March 23. https://www.theguardian.com/world/2023/mar/29/nz-mulls-harsher-law-against-refugee-boat-arrivals-despite-no-refugee-boats-ever-having-arrived. Accessed 18 May 2023.

Grewcock, Michael. 2010. *Border Crimes: Australia's War on Illicit Migrants.* Sydney: Sydney Institute of Criminology.

IPCC, Inter-governmental Panel on Climate Change. 2022. *Climate Change 2022: Impacts, Adaptation and Vulnerability*. Cambridge: Cambridge University Press.

Jackson, Moana. 2020. Where to Next? Decolonisation and the Stories in the Land. In *Imagining Decolonisation*, ed. Bianca Elkington, Moana Jackson, Rebecca Kiddle, Ocean Mercier, Mike Ross, Jennie Smeaton and Amanda Thomas, 133–155. Wellington: BWB Texts.

Keene, Sam. 2023. Defining Rough Sex Via Mainstream Pornography. In *Rough Sex and the Criminal Law*, ed. Hannah Bows and Jonathan Herring, 53–68. Emerald: Bingley.

Lakhani, Nina. 2023. Greenhouse Gas Emissions Rose At 'Alarming' Rate Last Year, US data Shows. *The Guardian*, April 6. https://www.theguardian.com/environment/2023/apr/06/greenhouse-gas-emissions-noaa-report-us-data. Accessed 18 May 2023.

Land, Clare. 2015. *Decolonizing Solidarity: Dilemmas and Directions for Supporters of Indigenous Struggles*. London: Zed Books.

Lindsay, Angus. 2023. *The Extremism Machine: Exploring the Effects of Digital Capitalism on Aotearoa New Zealand's Far Right*. PhD diss. Victoria University of Wellington.

Malloch, Margaret, and Elizabeth Stanley. 2005. The Detention of Asylum Seekers in the UK: Representing Risk, Managing the Dangerous. *Punishment and Society* 7 (1): 53–71.

Marmo, Marinella. 2023. Unmasking State Harm: The Border as a Theatrical Space of Gendered Violence. *Violence against Women* 29 (8): 1541–1561.

Matike Mai Aotearoa. 2016. *He Whakaaro Here Whakaumu Mō Aotearoa. The Report of Matike Mai Aotearoa—The Independent Working Group on Constitutional Transformation*. https://nwo.org.nz/wp-content/uploads/2018/06/MatikeMaiAotearoa25Jan16.pdf. Accessed 18 May 2023.

McLachlan, Leigh-Marama. 2019. Government Urged to Cede Power to Māori—Justice Advocates. *RNZ*, December 13. https://www.rnz.co.nz/news/te-manu-korihi/405435/government-urged-to-cede-power-to-maori-justice-advocates. Accessed 18 May 2023.

McLeod, Allegra. 2015. Prison Abolition and Grounded Justice. *UCLA Law Review* 62: 1156–1239.

Monod de Froideville, Sarah. 2021. Environmental Harm: Clean and Green, or Brutal and Contaminated? In *The Aotearoa Handbook of Criminology*, ed. Elizabeth Stanley, Trevor Bradley, and Sarah Monod de Froideville, 107–118. Auckland: Auckland University Press.

Myers, Ella. 2022. *The Gratifications of Whiteness*. Oxford: Oxford University Press.

Pemberton, Simon. 2016. *Harmful Societies: Understanding Social Harm.* Bristol: Policy Press.
Ruru, Jacinta, and Linda Waimarie Nikora. 2021. *Ngā Kete Mātauranga: Māori Scholars at the Research Interface.* Dunedin: Otago University Press.
Scraton, Phil. 2007. *Power, Conflict and Criminalisation.* London: Routledge.
Spade, Dean. 2015. *Normal Life: Administrative Violence, Critical Trans Politics, and the Limits of Law.* Durham: Duke University Press.
Stanley, Elizabeth. 2021. Climate Crises and the Creation of 'Undeserving' Victims. *Social Sciences* 10 (4): 1–14.
Stanley, Elizabeth, and Riki Mihaere. 2019. The Problems and Promise of International Rights in the Challenge to Māori Imprisonment. *International Journal for Crime, Justice and Social Democracy* 8 (1): 1–17.
Stanley, Elizabeth, and Riki Mihaere. 2018. Challenging Māori Imprisonment and Human Rights Ritualism. In *Human Rights and Incarceration*, ed. Elizabeth Stanley, 79–102. London: Palgrave.
Stanley, Elizabeth, and Sarah Monod de Froideville. 2020. From Vulnerability to Risk: Consolidating State Interventions Towards Māori Children and Young People in New Zealand. *Critical Social Policy* 40 (4): 526–545.
Townsend, Mark, and Vanessa Thorpe. 2023. Our Identity Is Being Stolen: Survivors Plead for Halt to Dramas About Grenfell. *The Observer*, April 16.
Tuhiwai Smith, Linda. 1999. *Decolonizing Methodologies.* London: Zed Books.
Ugwudike, Pamela. 2022. Predictive Algorithms in Justice Systems and the Limits of Tech-Reformism. *International Journal for Crime, Justice and Social Democracy* 11 (1): 85–99.
Ugwudike, Pamela. 2021. Data-Driven Algorithms in Criminal Justice: Prediction as Self-Fulfilling Prophecy. In *Data-Driven Personalisation in Markets, Politics and Law*, ed. Uta Kohl and Jacob Eisler, 190–204. Cambridge: Cambridge University Press.

3

Speaking Rights to Power or Governing Through Rights? Making Rights Matter in the Security Field

Claire Hamilton

Introduction

Human rights are commonly regarded as the antidote to excessive criminalization and securitization (Lazarus and Goold 2019). Yet, since 9/11, at both the national and international levels, human rights law has largely accommodated the security-oriented changes deemed necessary to combat terrorism (Hamilton 2018b, 2019). Indeed, Gearty (2017) identifies 9/11 as a serious 'hammer blow' to the fate of human rights in the contemporary era, one which tipped the scales away from human rights and towards security, and, further, one which, together with the economic crisis of 2008, exposed systemic faults in the architecture of

Parts of this chapter were first published as: Hamilton, Claire and Randy K. Lippert. (2020). Governing Through Human Rights in Counter-terrorism: Proofing, Problematization and Securitization. *Critical Criminology* 28 (1): 127–145. Springer Nature.

C. Hamilton (✉)
School of Law and Criminology, Maynooth University, Maynooth, Ireland
e-mail: claire.hamilton@mu.ie

L. Weber and M. Marmo (eds.), *A Research Agenda for a Human Rights Centred Criminology*, Palgrave Critical Studies in Human Rights and Criminology,
https://doi.org/10.1007/978-3-031-46289-4_3

the post-war global order. In exploring this further, this chapter deploys the notion of 'governing through rights' which views rights as potentially extending governance and securitization, even as they are claimed to emancipate and protect often vulnerable lives. Criminologists have used 'governing through' in work ranging from 'governing through crime' (Simon 2007) to 'governing through privacy' (Lippert and Walby 2016) and 'governing through security' (Valverde 2001). Governing here, following Foucault, is understood broadly as 'action upon action' (Rose 1999)—of 'conducting conduct'—and in each instance of governance, something is typically accomplished beyond what is claimed to be governed. Yet, it is not that these programmes reveal no effort to achieve, for example, violent crime reduction, enhanced personal privacy, enhanced physical security and so on. Rather, these aims are intimately constituted, preserved and 'worked through' as they are governed, and they yield other outcomes along the way.

Taking this as our conceptual lens, the following sections present two case studies of governing through rights in the counter-terrorism domain and provide the chapter's empirical focus. These cases—comprising some of the more egregious departures from human rights at an international and national level since 9/11—demonstrate, it is argued, how rights may act to simultaneously contain governmental interference and entrench securitization. The first examines the role of human rights within the United Nations (UN) given that the impact of the UN Security Council resolutions on the laws of member states has been nothing short of 'momentous' (Roach 2015, p. 3). The second case study, which examines coercive non-trial-based measures in the United Kingdom (UK), has met similar controversy, particularly given the violence such measures enact on basic assumptions of the criminal justice system (Zedner 2014). Both illustrate, it is argued, the emergence of human rights as a response to a given crisis or 'problem of government' (Foucault 1998) and their subsequent deployment as a means of governance. The analysis suggests the need for closer attention to the many ways by which human rights in the security field, via various legal and political 'proofing' mechanisms, may be transformed into an apolitical technical issue. Drawing on this, and recognising the continued ability of rights to 'speak to power' (Brysk

2018, 2021) in a troubled world, the chapter discusses some ways in which how 'doing rights criminologically' may help 'make rights matter' in the security field.

Case Study I: The UN, Counter-terrorism and Human Rights

The first case study concerns 'human rights proofing' mechanisms in the UN counter-terrorism 'assemblage' (a loose collection of elements that emerge together to govern). While counter-terrorism efforts were concentrated predominantly at the national level during the twentieth century, 9/11 marked a major shift in the capacity of international organizations, such as the UN Security Council ('UNSC'), to make and enforce the laws for the international community. In the immediate aftermath of 9/11, the Security Council used its mandatory powers under Chapter VII of the UN Charter to enact Security Council Resolution 1373 requiring all states to ensure that terrorism and terrorism financing were treated as serious crimes, but without guidance on defining 'terrorism' (Roach 2015). This represented an 'unprecedented ... legislative sweep' (Flynn 2007, p. 376), resulting in an explosion of counter-terrorism laws globally. Controversial measures included travel bans and freezing individual assets without any intervening judicial process. A second resolution (Security Council Resolution 2178), adopted in the face of advances by the Islamic State of Iraq and the Levant (ISIL) in Syria and Iraq in 2014, triggered another wave of legislation among member states, this time requiring the criminalization of so-called 'foreign terrorist fighters' (FTFs) (Roach 2015). These actions have been accompanied by the creation of a UN bureaucracy called the Counter-Terrorism Committee (CTC), which, in addition to monitoring and evaluating compliance with obligations set out in counter-terrorism resolutions, provides a list of best practices for domestic counter-terrorism legislation (Powell 2007). The consequences for human rights have been significant with virtually all member states of the UN changing their laws since 9/11 to comply with UNSC Resolution 1373 and subsequent Security Council edicts (Sheppele 2011).

Similarly, the requirement to comply with the most recent UNSC Resolution on FTFs (2178) has led to at least forty-seven nations passing 'foreign terrorist fighter' laws since 2013 (HRW 2018).

The decidedly authoritarian direction in which the UNSC has been pushing states with respect to counter-terrorism raises questions about the relationship between human rights and these types of security regimes. Evidently, the human rights deficit in the initial legislation created problems for the UN. UNSC Resolution 1373, which established the CTC, made no reference to respecting human rights in the design and implementation of counter-terrorism measures (except regarding refugee status), leading to almost immediate calls to integrate a human rights dimension into its work programme (Flynn 2007). Moreover, as 9/11 receded from view, some states complained that the UNSC was acting as a global legislator and that its sanctions were infringing on fundamental human rights (Blanco 2014). The UNSC also received pushback from UN special rapporteurs and independent experts, who adopted a joint statement (E/CN.4/2004/4, annex I) in Geneva in June 2003, expressing profound concern at the multiplication of counter-terrorist laws, policies and practices which, in their view, were affecting human rights negatively. In short, the new arrangements had become problematized.

The UNSC responded by passing UNSC Resolutions 1456 (in 2003) and 1624 (in 2005), requiring member states to 'ensure that any measure taken to combat terrorism comply with... international human rights, refugee and humanitarian law'. Recognition of human rights violations by states related to national and international counter-terrorism initiatives also led to two notable developments. First, the UN Human Rights Commission moved to appoint an independent expert to recommend how to strengthen UN protection of human rights and fundamental freedoms while countering terrorism (Goldman 2004). This in turn led to the appointment of the first UN Special Rapporteur on the Promotion and Protection of Human Rights and Fundamental Freedoms while Countering Terrorism (PPHRFFCT) in 2005. The second development concerned the appointment, also in 2005, of a senior human rights officer to a new Counter-Terrorism Committee Executive Directorate (CTED), who was charged with supporting the work of the CTC, as well as a mandate to this body to liaise with the Office of the High Commissioner for Human Rights (OHCHR) (Flynn 2007). Currently, CTED employs two senior human rights officers and claims a more proactive approach to human rights through liaising with OHCHR and the creation of a working group on the human rights aspects of counter-terrorism in 2008 (CTED, n.d.).

These initiatives represent the UN as 'right-eous' (Sokhi-Bulley 2016)—a virtuous human rights actor in an internationally controversial domain—thereby providing it with important symbolic legitimacy (Molnar and Warren 2020). Indeed, since 2006, 'ensuring human rights and the rule of law' has formed one of the four core pillars of the UN's Global Counter-Terrorism Strategy. The fact that rights ultimately were incorporated into the counter-terrorism assemblage of the UN, however, should not blind us to their potential to become instruments of governance. The complexity of the rights assemblage described by the International Federation for Human Rights (FIDH) (2017, p. 16) as a 'hydra-headed architecture of bodies' and 'an enigma' not only dilutes human rights effectiveness within the UN, but also renders rights technical and therefore governmental (Emmerson 2017; Sokhi-Bulley 2016). Moreover, beyond merely marginalizing human rights in practice, the inclusion of human rights has produced conditions for authoritarian practices to occur and expand. Human rights, for example, form a central plank of the UN Plan of Action to Prevent Violent Extremism (A/70/674 2015), with the phrase, 'human rights', mentioned almost fifty times. The plan emerged from a Preventing Violent Extremism (PVE) agenda—itself stemming from the UN Human Rights Council in 2015—and ultimately resulting in a resolution titled: 'Human rights and preventing and countering violent extremism'. This 'softer' approach recognized that law enforcement and security measures were insufficient to address terrorism, grounding counter-terrorism efforts in rights-based approaches developed in partnership with communities. Organizations, such as FIDH, however, have criticized how human rights have become securitized in this domain. For them, there is a danger of human rights being used 'as a legitimizing force for states to criminalize undefined violent extremism and pursue draconian policies that securitize social (PVE) programming in the name of national security' (FIDH 2017,

p. 121). The prosecution of human rights defenders and political opponents in nations such as China and Russia on charges of 'extremism' (as evidenced in FIDH's report) thus illustrates how an ostensibly rights-based approach to counter-terrorism can comfortably articulate with authoritarian regimes/practices.

Case Study II: The UK, Terrorist Prevention and Investigation Measures (TPIMs) and Human Rights

Our second case study moves to the national level where, similarly, counter-terrorism measures have been accommodated within, rather than in conflict with, the human rights infrastructure. The example considered here is legislation relating to Terrorist Prevention and Investigation Measures (TPIMs) in the UK—a form of hybrid civil-criminal order imposing onerous restrictions short of house arrest and much maligned for its role in the erection of a parallel or 'shadow' system of justice outside the ordinary criminal justice system (Zedner 2007, pp. 186–187). The story of TPIMs stems directly from the problematization of its forerunner—the control order—a similar non-trial-based measure designed to respond to a government defeat on December 16, 2004, in the House of Lords decision of *A. and others v. Secretary of State for the Home Department* ([2005] 2 AC 68). In *A.*, the House of Lords held that the indefinite detention of foreign prisoners without trial under section 23 of the Anti-terrorism, Crime and Security Act 2001 (ATCSA) was incompatible with the Human Rights Act 1998 (HRA)—the act incorporating into British law the European Convention on Human Rights (ECHR). It is difficult to overstate the ground-breaking nature of this decision and the challenges it presented for the UK government at the time. The decision in *A.* remains the only national security case in which (by a majority of 8:1) the House of Lords has issued a declaration of incompatibility with ECHR law. With the relevant sections of the ATCSA due to expire in a few months, a sense of crisis pervaded debates over the new legislation, hardly aided by the resignation of Home Secretary, David Blunkett, on unrelated grounds (Horne and Walker 2014). The new Home Secretary, Charles Clark, was faced with the unenviable task of, as Dyer and colleagues (2004, n.p.) put it, 'devis[ing] a solution' or risking 'more embarrassing court defeats in the run-up to the general election'.

The solution to this new 'problem' in governmentality terms came in the form of the Prevention of Terrorism Act (PTA)—the legislation authorizing control orders. The PTA achieved the difficult balancing act of allowing the government to appear 'tough on terrorism' in the public eye, with a nod towards human rights. The Act, which clearly mandated significant interferences with liberty, met with initial fierce opposition in the House of Lords and was criticized by the Joint Committee of Human Rights (2005–2006, p. 38), who foresaw problems with Article 5 of the ECHR. Despite this, the legislation was presented by the government as compliant with the HRA/ECHR, arguably derogating from the HRA/ECHR 'by stealth' (Fenwick 2013, p. 892). This, rather paradoxical, situation was aided by court decisions scrutinizing the new regime in 2007—decisions that were largely progressive, but which, as Ewing (2005, p. 47) observes, also contained 'the seeds of further restriction'. Thus, when decisions of the House of Lords sought to impose limits on the orders, these judicial modifications were welcomed by the government as 'giving the impression that the judges had, in human rights terms, supported the control orders scheme' (Fenwick 2010, p. 163). Central to this process were 'technical' rights-proofing mechanisms such as 'declarations of compatibility' mandated under the HRA. These declarations of compatibility were deployed by government ministers during the renewal debates on the PTA to advance claims that the control order litigation had, in effect, licensed the regime (Ewing and Tham 2008; see further Fenwick 2013 on 'ECHR memos'). Efforts to portray the government as 'right-eous' (Sokhi-Bulley 2016) in this area were further intensified with the replacement of control orders by TPIMs—part of a much-trumpeted 'correction in favour of liberty' announced by the government in 2010 (Syrett 2015). While TPIMs are deemed a form of 'light' control order (Zedner 2014), omitting some of their predecessor's most egregious features, the government again relied on the early House of Lords' decisions on control orders to resist calls for the abolition of non-trial-based measures in parliament and thus to entrench liberty-invading practices. This is arguably what transpired in the years following this 'correction', with the introduction in 2012 of Enhanced Terrorism Prevention and Investigation Measures (ETPIMs) and the enactment, in 2015, of legislation reinstating a controversial feature (forced relocation) of the old control order regime (Fenwick 2013, 2015, 2016). Indeed, for some commentators, the fact that the 2011 TPIM legislation, unlike its predecessor, is not required to be renewed annually represents a worrying normalization of emergency measures (Galli 2015; Roach 2011). Viewed through a governmentality lens—namely, as a methodology for understanding how government constantly reforms itself (Miller and Rose 1990)—we see a pattern of problematization–failure–and–solution, culminating in the consolidation and extension of 'governing through' freedom and rights since 2010 (Rose 1999). The result is that the control order/TPIM regime, despite a number of 'successful' challenges, survives largely unscathed with TPIM notices remaining, as per the October 2016 review of the legislation, 'a crucial component of the Government's national security response' (Home Office 2016).

Discussion: Making Rights Matter in the Field of Security

In these two cases of 'governing through rights', rights have served simultaneously to contain and entrench securitization and, indeed, extend it. Yet, while invoking rights can sometimes be ineffectual, this is not inevitable in all instances, nor can rights be dismissed as merely camouflage or legitimation. In the UN human rights assemblage, rights represent a powerful language for claims-makers, such as the UN Special Rapporteur, while also lying comfortably alongside coercive state practices. Similarly, in the UK, while the courts largely accommodated the control order/TPIMs scheme, the TPIM regime nonetheless became, in various respects, less repressive as a result of the litigation. Recognising this, while acknowledging the susceptibility of rights to redeployment and co-option to post-9/11 securitization, the intention here has been to act as a 'critical friend' and render rights more 'amenable to progressive intervention and reform' (Lippert 2016, p. 88). So how can 'doing rights criminologically' (Murphy and Whitty 2013, p. 580) help make rights matter in the security field?

First, if rights are not to be rendered 'technical' in both the political and judicial fora devoted to their enforcement—or worse still, if rights are to be 'governed through' in the security sphere—we must reject any suggestion that there is a 'right way to do rights' (Sokhi-Bulley 2016, p. 16) and return to the political content of human rights—the goal of justice for the individual against the power of the state. This involves a shift away from a 'legal model' of the human rights project—described by Shklar (1986, p. 10) as 'the belief that the rules are "there"'—towards a perspective informed by critical criminology. Too often, as we have seen above, the rights-protective architecture presumes 'what has yet to arise, namely a common concern about governmental encroachment in the name of security and a willingness of all parties to join in that discourse' (Krasmann 2012, p. 381). The advantage of critical criminology lies in its ability to locate rights within broader relations of power, governance and resistance (Marmo and Fishwick 2022), a reading which, as we have seen, is essential for unpicking the complex, labyrinthine workings of the transnational 'counter-terrorism order' (de Londras 2019). It may be argued, for example, that criminology, with its long expertise in penal populism, including 'populist leniency' (Jones 2010), is perfectly positioned to explore the instrumentalization of rights towards punitive ends such as the, increasingly pervasive, idea of a 'human right to security' (Lazarus 2013). Similar to the use of rights rhetoric above to justify the persecution of political opponents, the idea of the right to security has been used in the Philippines to justify former President Rodrigo Duterte's bloodthirsty 'war on drugs' (David 2016). Similarly, it has been deployed in Chinese official discourse as a vehicle to justify the treatment of Muslims in Xingjian and by Egypt to reaffirm the human rights prerogatives of states to impose harsh counter-terrorism measures (Mégret 2022). Writing to date in criminology has tended to view human rights in their traditional guise of 'speaking rights to power' (Brysk 2018), or, to borrow a metaphor from Christine Van den Wyngaert, a current judge of the International Criminal Court, as a 'shield' against punitive trends rather than a 'sword' (Snacken 2010; Daems et al. 2013; Weber et al. 2014). A more nuanced approach may also wish to consider the instrumentalization of human rights to justify authoritarian agendas, including their deployment by populist movements, what Mégret (2022) has termed 'human rights populism' (see further, Hamilton 2018a, 2018b).

A second important role for critical criminology plays to its strengths as an empirical discipline that allows for inquiry into 'the operational dimensions at specific sites' and thus the 'possibility to assess and concretise human rights concepts' (Marmo and Fishwick 2022, p. 284). As the above analysis has shown, Foucauldian themes (such as problematization) and focus on governing practices offer important tools for engaging with rights in critical criminology. Building on the work of criminologists already working from a Foucauldian perspective (see, e.g., Michael Welch 2012), these concepts provide a vital lens to examine how rights emerge and work as governing devices under certain conditions. To address the problem of securitization, for example, Krasmann (2012) has proposed a Foucauldian reconception of law 'as a practice', discernible only in the manner of its realization, and one that is highly contingent, political and relational. This places the focus firmly on modes of thinking (of all decision-makers, not only the judiciary); forms of knowledge informing such decision-making; and the mechanisms by which these are translated into reality. More concretely, this would involve the application of a Foucault-inspired governmentality analytic to identify: the process and context in which departures from human rights standards are made; the 'rationalities' (ways of thinking about) and the different types of 'knowledges' which facilitate them; the practices and devices ('technologies') that translate political reasoning into programmes of government (Hunt 2013; Rose et al. 2006); and the policy lessons we can learn from these observations (Lippert 2016). Foucault's conception of law and rights has historically been associated with the postmodern school of thought suggesting he would have no truck with the universalist concept of human rights at all (Weber et al. 2014). Foucault was an elusive thinker, however, whose thought was constantly evolving and, more recently, scholars such as Golder (2011) have detected in his later work a 'critical affirmation' of rights discourse, according to which he neither rejects nor embraces rights but rather engages 'critically within and against existing rights discourse' (Golder 2011, p. 286). On this view, rights are neither apolitical ideals nor 'an anti-politics — a pure defense of the innocent and powerless against power' (Brown 2004, p. 453), but rather political tools which may be implicated in relations of power as much as a means of criticising them (Ivison 2008). Foucault, then, forces us to pay attention to the power-knowledge networks inherent in the bureaucratic, political and juridical apparatus through which rights are negotiated. In so doing, his work offers critical criminology important possibilities for a politically richer, more self-reflexive and ultimately less disingenuous rights discourse.

References

Blanco, S. 2014. An Assessment of the Global Counter-Terrorism System Through the CTC, CTED and CTITF.

Brown, W. 2004. 'The Most We Can Hope For...': Human Rights and the Politics of Fatalism. *South Atlantic Quarterly* 103 (2–3): 451–463.

Brysk, A. 2018. *The Future of Human Rights*. Cambridge: Polity Press.

Brysk, A. 2021. Making Rights Rhetoric Work: Constructing Care in a Post-Liberal World. In *The Changing Ethos of Human Rights*, eds H. Mahmoudi, A. Brysk, and K. Seaman. Cheltenham, UK: Edward Elgar Publishing.

Daems, T., Van Zyl, D. Smit, and S. Snacken, eds. 2013. *European Penology?* Oxford: Hart Publishing.

David, R. 2016. Human Rights and the Poor, in Public Lives. *The Philippine Daily Inquirer*, August 7.

De Londras, F. 2019. The Transnational Counter-Terrorism Order: A Problématique. *Current Legal Problems* 72 (1): 203–251.

Dyer, C., M. White, and A. Travis. 2004. Judges' Verdict on Terror Laws Provokes Constitutional Crisis. *The Guardian*.

Emmerson, B. 2017. Report of the Special Rapporteur on the Promotion and Protection of Human Rights and Fundamental Freedoms While Countering Terrorism. A/HRC/34/61.

Ewing, K.D. 2005. The Futility of the Human Rights Act—A Long Footnote. *Bracton Law Journal* 37: 41–47.

Ewing, K., and J.-C. Tham. 2008. The Continuing Futility of the Human Rights Act. *Public Law* (Winter) 2008: 668–693.
Fenwick, H. 2010. Recalibrating ECHR Rights, and the Role of the Human Rights Act Post 9/11: Reasserting International Human Rights Norms in the "War on Terror"? *Current Legal Problems* 63 (1): 153–234.
Fenwick, H. 2013. Designing ETPIMs around ECHR Review or Normalisation of 'Preventive' Non-trial Based Executive Measures? *Modern Law Review* 76 (5): 876–908.
Fenwick, H. 2015. Redefining the Role of TPIMs in Combatting 'Home-Grown' Terrorism within the Widening Counter-Terror Framework. *European Human Rights Law Review* 1: 41–56.
Fenwick, H. 2016. Responding to the ISIS Threat: Extending Coercive Non-trial-Based Measures in the Counter-Terrorism and Security Act 2015. *International Review of Law, Computers and Technology* 30 (3): 174–190.
FIDH. 2017. The United Nations Counter-Terrorism Complex: Bureaucracy, Political Influence and Civil Liberties. FIDH. Retrieved January 25, 2020, from https://www.fdh.org/IMG/pdf/9.25_fdh_fnal_compressed.pdf.
Flynn, E. 2007. The Security Council's Counter-Terrorism Committee and Human Rights. *Human Rights Law Review* 7 (2): 371–384.
Foucault, M. 1998. Polemics, Politics and Problematizations. Interview by P. Rabinow, May 1984, In *Essential Works of Foucault*, vol. 1. New York: The New Press.
Galli, F. 2015. *The Law on Terrorism: The UK, France and Italy Compared*. Bruxelles: Bruyant.
Gearty, C. 2017. Is the Human Rights Era Drawing to a Close? *European Human Rights Law Review* 5: 425–431.
Golder, B. 2011. Foucault's Critical (Yet Ambivalent) Affirmation: Three Figures of Rights. *Social & Legal Studies* 20 (3): 283–312.
Goldman, R. 2004. Report of the Independent Expert on the Protection of Human Rights and Fundamental Freedoms While Countering Terrorism. E/CN.4/2005/103.
Hamilton, C. 2018a. The European Union: Sword or Shield? Comparing Counter-Terrorism Law in the EU and USA after 9/11. *Theoretical Criminology* 22 (2): 206–225.
Hamilton, C. 2018b. Sword or Shield? The Influence of International Organisations in Criminal Law Policymaking. *Revista Brasileira de Ciências Criminais* 147 (26): 67–88.
Hamilton, C. 2019. *Contagion, Counter-terrorism and Criminology: Justice in the Shadow of Terror*. London: Palgrave.

Home Office. 2016. Memorandum to the Home Affairs Committee: Post-legislative Scrutiny of the Terrorism Prevention and Investigation Measures Act 2011.

Horne, A., & W. Walker. 2014. Lessons Learned from Political Constitutionalism? Comparing the Enactment of Control Orders and Terrorism Prevention and Investigation Measures by the UK Parliament. *Public Law* (April): 267–288.

Human Rights Watch. 2018. Overreach: How New Global Counterterrorism Measures Jeopardize Rights. World Report 2017.

Hunt, A. 2013. Encounters with Juridical Assemblages: Reflections on Foucault, Law and the Juridical. In *Re-reading Foucault: On Law, Power and Rights*, ed. B. Golder. New York: Routledge.

Ivison, D. 2008. *Rights.* Stocksfield: Acumen.

Jones, R. 2010. Populist Leniency, Crime Control and Due Process. *Theoretical Criminology* 14 (3): 331–347.

Krasmann, S. 2012. Law's Knowledge: On the Susceptibility and Resistance of Legal Practices to Security Matters. *Theoretical Criminology* 16 (4): 379–394.

Lazarus, L. 2013. The Right to Security—Securing Rights or Securitising Rights. In *Examining Critical Perspectives on Human Rights*, ed. R Dickinson. Cambridge: Cambridge University Press.

Lazarus, L., and B. Goold, eds. 2019. *Security and Human Rights*, 2nd ed., 1–26. Portland, OR: Hart Publishing.

Lippert, R. 2016. Governmentality Analytics and Human Rights in Criminology. In *The Routledge International Handbook of Criminology and Human Rights*, ed. L. Weber, E. Fishwick, and M. Marmo, 80–90. London: Routledge.

Lippert, R., and K. Walby. 2016. Governing Through Privacy: Authoritarian Liberalism, Privacy Law, and Privacy Knowledge. *Law, Culture, and the Humanities* 12 (2): 329–352.

Marmo, M., and E. Fishwick. 2022. Criminology and Human Rights. In *Research Handbook of Comparative Criminal Justice*, ed. D. Nelken and C. Hamilton. Northampton: Edward Elgar.

Mégret, F. 2022. Human Rights Populism. *Humanity: An International Journal of Human Rights, Humanitarianism, and Development* 13 (2): 240–259.

Miller, P., and N. Rose. 1990. Governing Economic Life. *Economy and Society* 19 (1): 1–31.

Molnar, A., & Warren, I. 2020. Governing Liberty Through Accountability: Surveillance Reporting as Technologies of Governmentality. Critical Criminology: An International Journal, 28: 13-26.

Murphy, T., and N. Whitty. 2013. Making History: Academic Criminology and Human Rights. *British Journal of Criminology* 53 (4): 568–587.

Powell, C. 2007. The Legal Authority of the United Nations Security Council. In *Security and Human Rights*, ed. B. Goold and L. Lazarus, 154–184. Portland: Hart Publishing.

Roach, K., ed. 2011. *The United Kingdom Responds a Legislative War on Terrorism. In The 9/11 Effect: Comparative Counter-Terrorism.* Cambridge: Cambridge University Press.

Roach, K. 2015. *Comparative Counter-Terrorism Law*. Cambridge: Cambridge University Press.

Rose, N. 1999. *Powers of Freedom: Reframing Political Thought*. Cambridge: Cambridge University Press.

Rose, N., P. O'Malley, and M. Valverde. 2006. Governmentality. *Annual Review of Law and Social Science* 2: 83–104.

Shklar, J. 1986. *Legalism: Law, Morals and Political Trials*. Cambridge, MA: Harvard University Press.

Sheppele, K. 2011. The Migration of Anti-constitutional Ideas: The Post-9/11 Globalization of Public Law and the International State of Emergency. In *The Migration of Constitutional Ideas*, ed. S. Choudhry, 343–373. Cambridge: Cambridge University Press.

Simon, J. 2007. *Governing Through Crime: How the War on Crime Transformed American Democracy and Created a Culture of Fear*. New York: Oxford University Press.

Snacken, S. 2010. Resisting Punitiveness in Europe. *Theoretical Criminology* 14 (3): 273–292.

Sokhi-Bulley, B. 2016. *Governing (Through) Rights*. Oxford: Hart.

Syrett, K. 2015. The United Kingdom. In *Comparative Counter-Terrorism Law*, ed. K. Roach, 167–202. Cambridge: Cambridge University Press.

Valverde, M. 2001. Governing Security, Governing Through Security. In *The Security of Freedom: Essays on Canada's Anti-terrorism Bill*, ed. J. Ronald, P. Daniels, P. Macklem, and K. Roach, 83–92. Toronto, ON: University of Toronto Press.

Weber, L., E. Fishwick, and M. Marmo. 2014. *Crime, Justice and Human Rights*. London: Palgrave.

Welch, M. 2012. War on Terror, Human Rights and Critical Criminology. In *Routledge Handbook of Critical Criminology*, ed. W. DeKeseredy and M. Dragiewicz, 360–371. Abingdon: Routledge.

Zedner, L. 2007. Preventive Justice or Pre-punishment? The Case of Control Orders. *Current Legal Problems* 60 (1): 174–203.

Zedner, L. 2014. Terrorizing Criminal Law. *Criminal Law and Philosophy* 8 (1): 99–121.

4

Researching Policing from the Perspective of the *Policed*: Studying Human Rights from Below

Will Jackson

Introduction

This chapter sets out a critical approach to research on policing that has the potential to enhance a human rights-centred criminology. The approach advocated below draws upon the principles of critical social research, centralising a 'view from below' and highlighting the experiences of marginalised groups as a means of exposing injustice. Following in the anthropological tradition of 'studying up' (Nader 1972), such an approach reorientates our study of powerful actors and institutions, challenging dominant ideas about which perspectives and experiences are important. I argue that in the context of research on policing,

W. Jackson (✉)
Centre for the Study of Crime, Criminalisation and Social Exclusion, Liverpool John Moores University, Liverpool, UK
e-mail: w.h.jackson@ljmu.ac.uk

L. Weber and M. Marmo (eds.), *A Research Agenda for a Human Rights Centred Criminology*, Palgrave Critical Studies in Human Rights and Criminology,
https://doi.org/10.1007/978-3-031-46289-4_4

this requires a departure from the dominant approach to criminological research in this field, seeking instead to understand policing, and its impact on human rights, from the perspective of the *policed*.

The police are inextricably bound up in debates about human rights and a critical examination of policing is an integral part of a human rights-centred criminology. This is because the police have an unmatched capacity to act as both protectors of human rights and prime actors in their violation (McCulloch 2016; Weber et al. 2014). The debates about the impact of human rights on policing (Bayley, 2015; Mclanahan and Brisman 2016; de Lint 2016) suggest that there are limits to what human rights principles can do as the reference point for the reform, transformation or even abolition of the police. However, if our concerns are limited to developing a better understanding of the historical and contemporary relationship between policing and human rights, then critical research has a pivotal role to play. Taking the UK as a case study example, I argue in this chapter that criminology needs a human rights-centred research agenda informed by the type of critical research that can both examine the impact of policing on human rights and interrogate the official account of human rights compliance in this field.

The State of Policing in the UK

In March 2023, Baroness Casey published her report (Casey 2023) into the standards of behaviour and internal culture of the Metropolitan Police Service (the police force for the Greater London area, colloquially known as 'the Met'). This landmark review, commissioned in the wake of the 2021 murder of Sarah Everard by a serving Metropolitan Police officer, found 'institutional racism, sexism and homophobia' (2023, p. 7) in the largest police force in the UK. Casey recognised that she was not the first to highlight these problems. The existence of institutional racism in the Metropolitan Police was confirmed 24 years earlier in the landmark Macpherson Inquiry into the murder of Stephen Lawrence (1999) and, more generally, the headline findings of Casey's report have been highlighted by campaigners for decades. The report of more than 350 pages makes difficult reading for the police. The Chief Constable of the

Met, Mark Rowley, accepted the findings as a reflection of 'systemic' and 'cultural' problems in the force but rejected the label 'institutional' (in Dodd 2023). Despite the official refusal to accept the full diagnosis, the scale of the problem is set out in such a way to validate the claims that have been made by those communities who have long felt over-policed and under-protected.

The Casey review follows other official markers of fundamental problems in British policing. In 2021, the Metropolitan Police was described as 'institutionally corrupt' by an independent panel set up to inquire into the police handling of the murder of private detective Daniel Morgan in 1987 (Dodd and Sabbagh 2021). Data on issues such as racial discrimination, particularly in the use of stop and search powers (Home Affairs Committee 2021), the use of force (Grierson 2020) and deaths in police custody (INQUEST 2022) expose the nature and scale of the over-policing and under-protection of minoritised communities today. In the days following the Casey review, the Children's Commissioner for England released a report that detailed that there were at least 2,847 recorded strip-searches of children pre-arrest across England and Wales between 2018 and 2022 under stop and search powers (Children's Commissioner 2023, p. 29) and that black children were 11 times more likely to be strip-searched than their white peers. In addition to the rights abuses perpetrated by officers, the police's failure to prevent the abuse of rights by others is perhaps most starkly revealed in current data on police responses to men's violence against women; police in the UK have been accused of a 'systemic failure' to protect women as a 'highly vulnerable section' of the population from multiple forms of men's violence (Oppenheim 2019).

This evidence base suggests that British policing is in crisis and exposes the fact that while human rights discourse is central to the official presentation of policing, what the institution does, and fails to do, *as an institution* has a detrimental impact on the human rights of a substantial section of the population. In conjunction with the reviews, inquiries and reports, long-standing campaigns such as Black Lives Matter, Campaign Opposing Police Surveillance, Police Spies Out of Lives, United Friends and Families and organisations like The Network for Police Monitoring and INQUEST have opened the police institution in Britain to public criticism in a way not seen before. If criminology seeks to respond to this crisis and to better understand the impact of policing on human rights, we must think about the ways in which we approach the object of our research. This chapter suggests that the predominant approach to researching policing in criminology is ill-equipped to expose the true impact of policing on human rights. In response, the chapter advocates a critical (re)orientation of policing research to focus on the policed as a central strand of a research agenda for a human rights-centred criminology.

The chapter proceeds by providing a review of contemporary police research considering the potential of partnership research to inform a critical understanding of policing. From here it provides a short case study of research into 'human rights compliant protest policing' in England to demonstrate the requirement for critical research that focusses on the experiences of the policed. This case study highlights the under-appreciated role for research on policing conducted not just from the outside but from 'the other side'. The chapter makes a case for the study of policing from this position demonstrating the importance of research *on* rather than *with* police to enable us to accurately understand the impact of policing on human rights. The chapter concludes by arguing that we require a development of this type of critical research before we are able to make recommendations for the reform, transformation or even abolition of policing.

The State of Police Research

The expansion of police studies in the last thirty years has led to the development of new relationships between police and academic researchers (Reiner and Newburn 2008). Links between police institutions and universities in countries such US, UK, Australia and New Zealand have advanced a model of partnership working between police and researchers (Goode and Lumsden 2016). In this context, central issues of access and trust have been more easily addressed and the co-production of research has developed the study of police significantly. However, the advancement of co-production in this context has arguably effected a general shift to research *with* rather than *on* police, and the status of many researchers as 'outside outsiders' has been altered. For veteran police researcher Peter Manning, this general change in police research has intensified the development of a sociology *for* rather than *of* the police (Manning 2005).

The effect of these changes on the discipline of police studies has been considered at length (Loader 2011; Manning 2005) and there are serious implications for the study of policing. Eugene McLaughlin (2007, p. 58) has explained that the first wave of ethnographic studies of policing were 'unwelcome to police administrators because they demystified a number of problematic issues concerning police work'. Contemporary police studies is not without a critical edge (Cosgrove and Francis 2011), but the relationship between the institution and the academy raises questions about what is gained, and what is lost, when police research becomes a more welcome intervention. This does not infer that police research should be in conflict with police to be productive, or that partnership work is inevitably blind to problems in policing, but the issue here lies with the status of police research within a sociology *for* police.

A human rights approach to police research needs to challenge the predominant view that the study of policing should be done, or at least is done best, from the perspective of the police. There is a need to make a renewed case for the study of policing from the outside and to demonstrate the continued importance of research conducted independently from police. To understand fully the impact policing has on human rights, requires us to advocate for the study of the *policed*, centralising experiences of the exercise of police power. A critical human rights approach to police research arguably involves challenging dominant ideas about both the police and the individuals and communities who are the focus of policing. To understand the impact of police on human rights requires us to prioritise the experiences of those who are often disregarded as having little of value to add to our understanding of how policing is, and should be, done.

Critical Social Research

This critical approach to research on policing is underpinned by an understanding of the value of critical social research within criminology. Critical social research 'seeks out and champions the "view from below", ensuring that the voices and experiences of those marginalised by institutionalised state practices are heard and represented' (Scraton 2007, p. 10). This approach to research has been central to a critical criminology that has sought, at its core, to explore the experiences of marginalised groups and expose injustice (Hudson 2011). Critical criminology seeks to expose and respond to the 'persistent silences' (Hillyard et al. 2004) in mainstream criminology that result from a failure to consider alternative perspectives on crime and crime control. From this perspective, 'too much work in criminology is done by scholars who lack a critical distance from the subjects of their study' (Vitale 2017, no page) so the aim of critical research in this context is to reorient the discipline by changing who and what we study.

Critical criminologists 'take seriously Howard Becker's question of "whose side are we on?" and the answer is, usually, the side of the powerless, the marginalised and the excluded' (Hudson 2011, p. 333). In taking Becker's 1967 proposition seriously, critical criminologists assume that 'subordinates have as much right to be heard as superordinates' (Becker 1967, p. 241) and argue that the views and experiences of those ranked low on a 'hierarchy of credibility' should be investigated and taken seriously. This orientation of the critical researcher has pronounced implications for human rights-centred research into key institutions such as the police. We need to consider how this approach to engaging with subordinates can inform police research, and how this can, and does, affect the way that such research is received.

A critical approach to research suggests that we should consider what we might learn about policing and human rights if we considered this relationship from the perspective of the policed. In his classic study of the East End of London, Dick Hobbs referred to this approach as 'policing from below' (1988, p. 2), and this starts from a recognition that those who are the target of police have something to offer our attempts to understand policing. When confronted by the accumulated evidence of police misconduct, discrimination and violence, there is an obligation on critical researchers to reflect on how criminological research aids us in our quest to understand how policing is done and how it impacts on human rights.

Critical Research on Policing and Human Rights

Between 2013 and 2020, I was part of a team of researchers who conducted a longitudinal study of the policing of protests against hydraulic fracturing—better known as 'fracking'—in England (Gilmore et al. 2016, 2019). This work took the form of a critical ethnography of protest policing, examining public order policing from the perspective of protesters. We conducted site visits, observing protests and police responses, and conducted interviews with protesters at multiple sites around England. We took a decision to focus exclusively on the experiences of protesters following our initial engagements with protesters who told us that many people involved would be unwilling to engage with us if we were also 'working with the police'. What could be described as a 'one-sided' approach was in part a trade-off to enable access to marginalised groups, but also accorded with our understanding as critical ethnographers that this perspective could offer an important counter-position to most of the studies of public order policing in the UK.

By examining protest policing from this alternative viewpoint and including those voices that had been excluded (or had excluded themselves) from other research, we sought to provide a critical examination of a new model of protest policing introduced in 2009 that was based on compliance with the Human Rights Act 1998 (HMIC 2009). This new model sought to protect the right to peaceful protest through a commitment to principles of dialogue, communication and 'facilitation'. Examining protest policing from 'the other side' we were able to include very different experiences of policing from those documented in the bulk of protest policing research. A series of academic studies conducted since 2009 had been able to confirm that human rights awareness had infused a new model of public order policing (for a review, see Jackson et al. 2018). Studies conducted predominantly in partnership with police evidenced a wholesale transformation in police practice in line with human rights requirements. In contrast, our research demonstrated that for those protest groups who seek to be disruptive (while remaining peaceful and non-violent) very little had changed in the police approach.

In contrast to the partnership research done in this field, we were able to engage those protesters who had traditionally been unwilling to engage with both police, and their academic partners. Often (dis)regarded as 'transgressive', 'militant' or 'anti-systemic' due to their commitment to direct action tactics, these groups are largely ignored in police research. Without including these groups, it had been possible for multiple studies to highlight best practice and to confirm the police line that repression of protest is reserved only for those who break the law (see Jackson et al. 2018). In contrast, our research (Gilmore et al. 2016, 2019; Jackson et al. 2018; Jackson 2019) suggested that human rights principles have provided police with a new discourse through which to justify the repression of certain political protests that are considered to be a threat to order. Indeed, rather than seeing the recourse to human rights discourse as constraining what police can do, the mobilisation of, and the ability to control, this discourse is itself an aspect of police power. We concluded that public order policing had undergone a makeover in its presentation—to which human rights principles were central—but this had not had a substantive impact on the police response on the ground where protests sought to move beyond a symbolic register of opposition. We concluded that the boundaries between acceptable and unacceptable protest set by police—and used to determine whether the right to protest is protected—are not based on protesters' use of violence but rest on what a protest is focussed on, what it demands, and the form it takes.

This work, therefore, provided a different means of empirically testing reforms to police policy and practice. Our critical approach meant that we produced a radically different view of the relationship between policing and human rights and brought into question the nature of democratic policing in the UK. Our findings did not invalidate the findings of other researchers, but instead complicated the picture of policing they had provided. Research done in partnership with police is not inevitably blind to problems in policing or to human rights abuses. However, in this context, previous studies had identified a substantive transformation in police approaches to protest and highlighted a discernible commitment to human rights principles that had a marked impact on police policy and practice. Our research did not suggest that police do not respond to some, or even the majority of, protests in the manner documented by other researchers. Instead, our work made clear that the dangers of overgeneralisation are relevant in police research conducted from both sides. We did directly challenge the generalisation of findings in other studies to suggest that the process of empirically testing reforms to police policy and practice was complete. By examining the experiences of marginalised groups and considering police responses from the perspective of protesters—including those protesters delegitimised by police—we developed a very different view of human rights compliant policing in a limited but significant set of circumstances. We did not subsequently seek to argue that police respond in the manner we observed and documented in *all* cases, but just that they do in *some* cases, and that this is significant. We argued that our findings need to be factored into both scholarly and public debates about public order policing and the right to protest before we draw any general conclusions about human rights policing in this context.

The Case for Critical Research from 'the Other Side'

Critical criminological research aims to respond to criminology's silences by opening a space for alternative perspectives to be considered. Following in a tradition of sociological research initiated by C. Wright Mills (1959), such work seeks to counter 'academia's servile and servicing association with the state institutions and giant corporations' (Scraton 2007, p. 6). It is this relationship to state and corporate power that is understood to be responsible for the failure of much research to adequately address questions of power. Critical research on policing must begin from the recognition of policing as a key site for the exercise of power and should seek to monitor how police power impacts on those who encounter the institution. To do this we have to examine policing from alternative perspectives, even if we recognise that such work may struggle to be heard among the 'noise' (Hillyard et al. 2004, p. 372) of mainstream criminological research.

Critical research of this type is not wedded to any particular research method (Stubbs 2008), but the selection and application of method is usually underpinned by the drive to explore marginalised voices. This has led some to advocate methods that involve 'being there' (Sim in Scraton 2007, p. 5) to bear witness to the human rights abuses experienced by those whose voices are normally unheard. The goal, therefore, of human rights focussed research is to highlight the partial and skewed understanding that informs much of criminological theory and in turn often underpins official policy. In Phil Scraton's terms, critical research exposes the 'yawning gap between official discourse, inquiries or [inquest] verdicts and alternative accounts provided by bereaved families, [prison] regime survivors, rights lawyers, community workers and critical researchers' (Scraton in Scraton 2007, p. 12). This disjuncture is laid bare when researchers engage with those whose viewpoints or experiences are generally disregarded and this is significant in the study of policing.

The orientation of the critical researcher has pronounced implications for research on policing and human rights. Those who are marked as 'police property' (Lee 1981; see also McCulloch 2016) are simultaneously the ones who are most at risk of having their rights violated and the ones placed lowest on the hierarchy of credibility sustained by the institution. A research agenda for a human rights-centred criminology must challenge this hierarchy and consider marginalised voices. This is necessary to enable us to identify and expose any gap between the rhetoric and reality of policing. The central place of human rights discourse in the official presentation of policing in the UK and elsewhere means that critical research that examines policing from below is vital. A human rights-centred criminology must be able to critically assess the extent to which commitments to rights in police policy do more than simply legitimate business as usual.

References

Bayley, David. 2015. Human Rights in Policing: A Global Assessment. *Policing and Society* 25 (5): 540–547. https://doi.org/10.1080/10439463.2014.895352.

Becker, Howard. 1967. Whose Side Are We on? *Social Problems* 14 (3): 239–247.

Casey, Louise. 2023. Baroness Casey Review: Final Report—An Independent Review into the Standards of Behaviour and Internal Culture of the Metropolitan Police Service. https://www.met.police.uk/SysSiteAssets/media/downloads/met/about-us/baroness-casey-review/update-march-2023/baroness-casey-review-march-2023a.pdf. Accessed 24 April 2023.

Children's Commissioner. 2023. Strip Search of Children in England and Wales—Analysis by the Children's Commissioner for England. https://assets.childrenscommissioner.gov.uk/wpuploads/2023/03/cc-strip-search-of-children-in-england-and-wales.pdf. Accessed 24 April 2023.

Cosgrove, Faye, and Peter Francis. 2011. Ethnographic Research in the Context of Policing. In *Doing Criminological Research*, ed. Pamela Davies, Peter Francis, and Victor Jupp, 199–222. London: Sage.

de Lint, Willem. 2016. Bent to Good Authorities? Human Rights, Authoritarian Neoliberalism and Consent Policing. In *The Routledge International Handbook of Criminology and Human Rights*, ed. Leanne Weber, Elaine Fishwick, and Marinella Marmo, 342–353. London: Routledge.

Dodd, Vikram. 2023. Met Police Found to Be Institutionally Racist, Misogynistic and Homophobic, *The Guardian*, 21 March.

Dodd, Vikram and Dan Sabbagh. 2021. Daniel Morgan Murder: Inquiry Brands Met Police 'Institutionally Corrupt'. *The Guardian*, 15 June.

Gilmore, Joanna, Will Jackson, and Helen Monk. 2016. *Keep Moving!: Report on the Policing of the Barton Moss Community Protection Camp, November 2013-April 2014*. Liverpool: CCSE, Liverpool John Moores University.

Gilmore, Joanna, Will Jackson, Helen Monk, and Damien Short. 2019. *Protesters' Experiences of Policing at Anti-fracking Protests in England, 2016–2019: A National Study*. Liverpool: CCSE, Liverpool John Moores University.

Goode, Jackie, and Karen Lumsden. 2016. The McDonaldization of. Police-Academic Partnerships: Organisational and Cultural Barriers Encountered in Moving from Research on Police to Research with Police. *Policing & Society* 28 (1): 75–89.

Grierson, Jamie. 2020. Black People Five Times More Likely to Have Force Used on Them by Police. *The Guardian*, 17 December.

Hillyard, Paddy, Joe Sim, Steve Tombs, and Dave Whyte. 2004. Leaving a 'Stain Upon the Silence': Contemporary Criminology and the Politics of Dissent. *British Journal of Criminology* 44 (3): 369–390.

HMIC. 2009. *Adapting to Protest—Nurturing the British Model of Policing*. London: HMIC.

Hobbs, Dick. 1988. *Doing the Business: Entrepreneurship, the Working Class, and Detectives in the East End of London*. Oxford: Clarendon Press.

Home Affairs Committee. 2021. The Macpherson Report: Twenty-Two Years on—Third Report of Session 2021–22. https://committees.parliament.uk/publications/7012/documents/89144/default/. Accessed 24 April 2023.

Hudson, Barbara. 2011. Critical Reflection as Research Methodology. In *Doing Criminological Research*, ed. Pamela Davies, Peter Francis, and Victor Jupp, 328–344. London: Sage.

INQUEST. 2022. BAME Deaths in Police Custody. https://www.inquest.org.uk/bame-deaths-in-police-custody. Accessed 24 April 2023.

Jackson, Will. 2019. Researching the Policed: Critical Ethnography and the Study of Protest Policing. *Policing and Society* 30 (2): 169–185.

Jackson, Will, Joanna Gilmore, and Helen Monk. 2018. Policing Unacceptable Protest in England and Wales: A Case Study of the Policing of Anti-fracking Protests. *Critical Social Policy* 39 (1): 23–43.

Lee, John A. 1981. Some Structural Aspects of Police Deviance in Relations with Minority Groups: In *Organizational Police Deviance*, ed. Clifford Shearing. Toronto: Butterworth.

Loader, Ian. 2011. Where Is Policing Studies? *The British Journal of Criminology* 51 (2): 449–458.

Macpherson, William. 1999. *The Stephen Lawrence Inquiry: Report of an inquiry*. London: Stationary Office.

Manning, Peter. 2005. The Study of Policing. *Police Quarterly* 8 (1): 23–43.

McCulloch, Jude. 2016. Police, Crime and Human Rights. In *The Routledge International Handbook of Criminology and Human Rights*, ed. Leanne Weber, Elaine Fishwick, and Marinella Marmo, 323–332. London: Routledge.

McLanahan, Bill, and Avi Brisman. 2016. Police Violence and the Failed Promise of Human Rights. In *The Routledge International Handbook of Criminology and Human Rights*, ed. Leanne Weber, Elaine Fishwick, and Marinella Marmo, 334–341. London: Routledge.

McLaughlin, Eugene. 2007. *The New Policing*. London: Sage.

Nader, Laura. 1972. Up the Anthropologist—Perspectives Gained from Studying Up. In *Dell Hymes*, ed. Reinventing Anthropology, 284–311. New York: Pantheon Books.

Oppenheim, Maya. 2019. Police Accused of "Systemic Failure" to Protect Victims of Domestic Abuse and Sexual Violence. *The Independent*, 20 March.

Reiner, Robert, and Tim Newburn. 2008. Police Research. In *Doing Research on Crime and Justice*, eds. Roy D. King and Emma Wincup, 343–374. Oxford: Oxford University Press.

Scraton, Phil. 2007. *Power, Conflict and Criminalisation.* Abingdon: Routledge

Stubbs, Julie. 2008. Critical Criminological Research. In *The Critical Criminology Companion*, ed. Anthony Cunneen. Alexandria, NSW: Federation Press.

Vitale, Alex. 2017. For a Critical Criminology. Available at: https://www.versobooks.com/blogs/3434-for-a-critical-criminology. Accessed 21 September 2021.

Weber, Leanne, Fishwick, Elaine, and Marmo, Marinella. 2014. *Crime, Justice and Human Rights.* London: Palgrave.

Wright Mills, C. 1959. *The Sociological Imagination.* Oxford: OUP.

[illegible] 1972. Up the Anthropologist: Perspectives Gained from Studying Up. In Dell Hymes ed. Reinventing Anthropology, [illegible]. New York: Pantheon Books.

[illegible]

5

Criminology, Humanitarianism, and the Right to Life at the Border

Katja Franko

The right to life is one of the most fundamental human rights. 'Everyone's right to life shall be protected by law. No one shall be deprived of his life intentionally' declares Article 2 of the European Convention on Human Rights (ECHR). Similarly, Article 3 of the Universal Declaration of Human Rights declares: 'Everyone has the right to life, liberty and security of person'. The right to life is valuable not only for its own sake, but also because its effective protection is 'the prerequisite for the enjoyment of all other human rights and the content of which can be informed by other human rights' (Human Rights Committee 2019).

Yet, the right to life has attracted relatively scarce scholarly attention compared to some other human rights. In criminology, it has been mostly addressed in connection to the question of the death penalty

K. Franko (✉)
University of Oslo, Oslo, Norway
e-mail: katja.franko@jus.uio.no

L. Weber and M. Marmo (eds.), *A Research Agenda for a Human Rights Centred Criminology*, Palgrave Critical Studies in Human Rights and Criminology,
https://doi.org/10.1007/978-3-031-46289-4_5

(Hoyle 2022). The right to life is not absolute and the ECHR specifies several circumstances in which the intentional deprivation of life is permissible. The conditions of these limitations have been in several respects both unclear, contentious, and controversial, particularly when it comes to questions of abortion, assisted suicide, and euthanasia (Wicks 2010). These controversies may have been reasons behind reluctance to approach the issue. Moreover, the meaning of what 'life' is has often been interpreted to mean human life, an understanding which is challenged by a growing body of criminological scholarship addressing animal rights and speciesism (Sollund 2017).

Despite the controversy, the critical core of the right to life, which implies the prohibition of arbitrary killings by state agents and other actors, remains today as relevant as ever. The right to life goes at the very heart of the state use (and abuse) of power, not only in countries with autocratic systems of governance, but also in those usually described as liberal democracies. This has been forcefully exemplified in recent years with social movements such as the Black Lives Matter, which have brought attention to the loss of life of racial minorities due to arbitrary actions of state agents (Zimring 2020). The right to life is, therefore, not only a topical and emerging issue but carries a broad relevance to scholarly interests in how sovereign violence operates and how human rights can critically and more effectively address the lethal consequences of actions of state agents.

In this chapter, I will first look at one context in which these issues are played out in practice, namely, at the external borders of Europe, where human life is extremely precarious and where actions (and inactions) of border control agents have encountered intense criticism. At the time of writing of this chapter, 80 people are confirmed dead and 500 are missing after an overcrowded fishing boat capsized off the Greek coast. The tragedy has sparked an outrage across Europe and critical questions have been asked about the (in)actions of the Greek coast guard in preventing the accident (*Guardian* 2023). The chapter presents various actors and discourses that address these conditions of precariousness of human life at the border, particularly those operating within the field of humanitarianism. It then examines the convergences and tensions between the focus on humanitarianism and human rights. The chapter argues that the right to life and the protection of life is intrinsically connected to the question of global inequality and concludes by a reflection on what a criminological approach more attuned to achieving a more democratic system of governance, where *all* lives are worthy of state protection, might look like.

The Right to Life at the Border

The borders of the Global North have in the past two decades exerted an excruciating death toll on people on the move (Weber and Pickering 2011). Europe is by far the deadliest destination. As the International Organization for Migration (IOM) points out in a recent report (Black and Sigman 2022, p. 6):

> More than half of the 50,000 deaths documented during migration since 2014 have occurred within or en route to Europe, with 29,126 deaths or disappearances recorded within Europe and at its external borders, on sea routes in the Mediterranean and Atlantic, as well as at land borders such as the Greece-Türkiye border.

The situation has attracted considerable critical interest by researchers, journalists, and activists alike. It may seem a paradox that a political community that praises itself for its respect for human rights is also unable (or unwilling) to create institutional arrangements that would protect human life at the border (Aas 2011). The right to life imposes both a positive obligation on states to put in place an appropriate legal and administrative framework to protect life, as well as to abstain from certain actions in order to prevent the loss of life (Harris et al. 2014). Some scholars have pointed out that such obligations should also move beyond the prevention of death to include protection of human dignity (Joseph 2019).

A question arises then, how do European states and the EU itself operationalize these obligations, if the results are so tragic in terms of human consequences? Issues of border control are one of the prerogatives of state sovereignty and are operationalized by border control forces of member states and Frontex, the European Border and Coast Guard Agency.[1] In my own research on Frontex, I have discovered that the agency has a complex and ambivalent relationship with human rights (Aas and Gundhus 2015; Franko 2020). While human rights are present at the discursive level of the agency's self-presentation, border guard officers seldom explicitly mention human rights (although some do express humanitarian sentiments toward migrants) (Aas and Gundhus 2015).

Frontex, whose task is to support EU member states in the management of the EU's external borders, has been accused of complicity with individual member states of condoning and participating in so-called push backs that have directly resulted in the loss of life. In January 2021, a report by the United Nations High Commissioner for Refugees (UNHCR) established that the pushbacks are 'carried out in a violent and apparently systematic way. Boats carrying refugees are being towed back. People are being rounded-up after they land and then pushed back to sea. Many have reported violence and abuse by state forces' (UNCHR 2021; see also Cortinovis 2021). Although these incidents have been well documented by journalists and human rights activists, they have not been sanctioned by the courts. As Soliman (2021, p. 235) points out, 'attempts to define non-assistance as an international crime rely on concepts such as intent and responsibility which would be difficult to establish in a court of law, making prosecution problematic'.

The situation migrants find themselves in can be described as one of humanitarian borderlands, which are also defined by perceptions of jurisdictional messiness (Franko 2022). The messiness stems from the fact that borders are regulated in a piece-meal approach, and that the rules of engagement are relatively ill-defined and allow for the interaction between very diverse sites, actors, and types of movement (De Witte 2022). This in-between nature of borderlands enables the playing of jurisdictional games between various actors, which then creates possibilities for the avoidance of responsibility and tacit acceptance of violations of rights. Former Frontex director, LeMonde (2022) has, for example, stated the following:

> Between the imperative not to allow people to cross irregularly and the other, the principle of non-refoulement (which forbids pushbacks) as

everyone in need of protection has the right to asylum, how should we act?/…/ No one can give me the answer. We're schizophrenic.

Leggeri's statement is telling not only as an example of messiness at the border, but also because it reveals how migrants' rights are in direct conflict with the control objectives of the authorities. Not only Frontex, but also other state authorities are increasingly framing irregular migration as a question of criminalization (Franko 2020). Migrants trying to cross the border are often defined as 'illegal' and states are putting in place increasingly severe measures to deter those helping them to cross the border irregularly. This means that not only networks of human smugglers, but also humanitarian actors trying to save lives at sea are subjected to penal measures (ICJ 2022).[1]

The responsibility for the loss of life at the border is, therefore, either placed on criminal(ized) actors, and framed as a question of crime (Franko 2020), or defined as a question of 'death by nature' (Schindel 2022). Sovereign violence thus operates not only through actions and inactions of state agents, but also 'through the abandonment and exposure of migrants to the elements and therefore the production of a zone of mere biological survival, while accountability chains are concealed' (Schindel 2022, p. 428). The right to life at the border is challenged both by passivity and inaction of state actors, as well as by active prosecution and criminalization of actors who are willing to offer help.

Another way of framing the question is to suggest that sovereign border control regimes are perpetuating structural violence (Weber and Pickering 2011). And since this type of violence is difficult to capture and bring to accountability by using the language of criminalization, the framework of harm (and zemiology) could provide an alternative. The language of harm brings focus on how to prevent death rather than punish the perpetrators (Soliman 2021). In the case of Frontex, introducing a harm-based approach would mean that the agency and its critics should move from trying to pin criminal responsibility on individual actors and focus instead on reducing the harm produced at the border

[1] https://fra.europa.eu/en/publication/2023/2023-update-ngo-ships-sar-activities

(Soliman 2021). This approach might then reduce the systematic indifference to border deaths, making the reduction of mortality a central concern for the agency.

In a recent study I conducted on the public communication strategies employed by Frontex, I discovered that migrant suffering, particularly death, hardly feature in them. Although more than 2,000 people were reported to have died yearly on sea routes to Europe, the agency used the words 'dead' or 'deadly' only twice in a two-year period. The words 'death' and 'drown' were not used at all (Franko 2021, p. 386). While focusing on presenting itself in a crime-fighting mode, the agency seems to be closing its eyes to death, echoing several of the strategies of denial, such as 'turning a blind eye' or 'looking the other way', described in Stanley Cohen's (2001) seminal work *States of Denial: Knowing about Atrocities and Suffering*. Another way in which knowledge about migrant mortality is being hidden by state actors is through the unwillingness to collect statistics about border deaths (Aas and Gundhus 2015). As we saw above, it is the International Organization for Migration that has been since 2014 collecting data about migrant mortality. Although Frontex collects a variety of data about border crossings and have the technical capabilities to see and record migrant mortality, they do not do so. The right to life is, therefore, not operationalized in state bureaucratic procedures. Like many other phenomena, human rights' violations need to be empirically documented in order to 'exist' in popular and political consciousness. As Andreas and Greenhill (2010, p. 1) point out: 'to measure something – or at least claim to do so – is to announce its existence and signal its importance and policy relevance'. The fact that European states are not collecting numbers about migrant mortality is, therefore, an expression of a lack of political will to acknowledge and to know the phenomenon.

Between Humanitarianism and Human Rights

In her critical analysis of the jurisprudence of the European Court of Human Rights, Marie Benedicte Dembour (2015) argues that much of migrants' suffering is left out of the account by the court—it is considered illegitimate and outside its area of concern. Although there have been important exceptions, the migrant is first and foremost defined as an alien rather than a subject of rights. The main focus of European institutions is to provide security and rights for their own citizens. This is also an apt description of how Frontex defines the issue of migrant mortality. And while human rights are defined precisely by their aspirations to universality, states actively derelict their responsibility to save the lives of non-citizens and increasingly leave this task to other actors. Humanitarian NGOs have thus in recent years become the most prominent actors conducting search and rescue operations in the Mediterranean, while the EU and its member states are scaling down their efforts (Carrera and Cortinovis 2019; Cuttitta 2020).

The case of the European Union shows that the protection of precarious life in various social and institutional settings has not primarily been framed as an issue of rights, but as a question of humanitarian governance. Criminology has, in the past decade, begun to actively engage with the field of humanitarianism, particularly within the field of studies of border control (see inter alia Bosworth 2017; Lohne 2020). Critical observers have pointed out that while humanitarian actors provide vital life-saving functions to populations that can rely on few other resources, there are also important tensions between humanitarianism and human rights.

In his seminal study, *Humanitarian Reason*, Didier Fassin (2012) points out that humanitarianism does not operate through the universalist language of rights but is instead structured by the discourse of emotion and morality. It draws on notions of compassion and care and, therefore, 'presupposes a relation of inequality' (Fassin 2012, p. 4; see also Ticktin, 2011). Similarly, Paolo Cuttitta (2018, p. 283) observes that although humanitarian assistance can be 'more inclusive than what human rights would require, it is posited as an act of grace rather than an enhancement of human rights'. Studies of humanitarianism point out its usefulness as a form of effective governance of disasters and as a form of 'care for distant strangers' (Pallister-Wilkins, 2020, p. 1). As such, it is often enhancing objectives of sovereign states rather than presenting an alternative form of thinking and solving social problems. In the context of migration and border control, Polly Pallister-Wilkins (2015, p. 65) argues that humanitarianism and policing should not be seen as two separate or competing practices but rather that there is a considerable level of overlap and convergence (see also Aas and Gundhus 2015). Although humanitarian actors use different language and strategies of claiming authority, they are also active participants in practices of immobilization and externalization of the border (Cuttitta 2018).

One empirical example of the complex nature of humanitarianism that is being played out is a recent trend toward juridification of 'vulnerability' in the EU context. As Luc Leboeuf (2022, p. 14) points out, it has 'become fashionable, in the EU policy discourse on asylum and migration, to emphasize the need to protect 'vulnerable' migrants and refugees'. The trend has resulted in some concrete legal developments and bureaucratic identification of specific positions of 'vulnerability' that require state action. However, vulnerability is a fuzzy legal concept, which rather than increasing access to rights 'may also feed a vulnerability competition, as asylum applicants will feel the need to portray themselves as more vulnerable than others to secure their chances at obtaining access to protection' (Leboeuf 2022, p. 14).

The Right to Life in a World of Inequality

The example of Frontex shows how populations on the move, who are defined as alien, are, at best, seen as deserving humanitarian sentiments of compassion, rather than of real equality and rights. The notion of universal rights is difficult to achieve for populations who fall outside the sphere of state sovereign protection (Haddad 2003) and have the overburdened and unpredictable system of humanitarian assistance as their only recourse. Even when it comes to the most fundamental human rights, such as the right to life, Northern states fail to take adequate actions to protect populations in precarious situations. How then can we start to imagine a more democratic approach to the protection of human life? Human rights scholars and activists have argued that human rights and humanitarian law that apply to deaths which occur in conflict and humanitarian disaster should be applied to border deaths to protect the rights of families to know the fate of their relatives (Grant 2011). States should take active steps to acknowledge the legal relevance of lives lost in migration journeys.

The fact remains, nevertheless, that we live in a world marked by enormous inequalities in terms of protection of life. These inequalities divide not only various groups of migrants and citizens, but also various groups of citizens. There are dramatic differences particularly between countries in the Global North and the Global South in terms of how protected the lives of their inhabitants are. For example, while homicide rates in Europe are 3.0 per 100,000 population, in contrast, the homicide rate in the Americas is 17.2 victims per 100,000 population, the highest recorded in the region since reliable records began in 1990 (UNODC 2019). 'What state are you a citizen of?' is, therefore, a crucial question to ask in terms of the right to life as numerous states lack crucial capabilities to protect their citizens. In Latin America, the high levels of violence have propelled large populations to move in search of more secure living environments. Global security inequalities are thus also important drivers of mobility as inhabitants of insecure states move in search of more secure environments. However, what is important to note is not only the state inability to offer protection for these populations, but that state agents themselves often represent one of the main security threats to the population (Willis 2015). And while affluent citizens of insecure countries may be able to purchase private security protections, poor, and racialized populations fall prey to organized criminal groups and (or in collusion with) corrupt state agents.

How then can criminology address this global security inequality? One of the first steps to take would certainly be to expand our awareness of how global inequalities shape the unequal protection of life and why some lives matter more than others (Franko 2021). The large majority of criminological scholarship is produced in countries of the Global North. And while we have seen growing focus on the precarious conditions at the border, as well as global North–South divisions (see inter alia Carrington et al. 2016), a challenge remains that much of our data, research funding and hence definitions of research problems are tied to the state and its sphere of interests. This intimate connection to the state takes off a critical edge from research and often makes it, as Nils Christie observed almost three decades ago, quite trivial (Christie 1997). (State) Power and scientific knowledge are intertwined and tied together in a variety of ways (Foucault 1980). This means not only that (affluent) states often lack interest in obtaining knowledge about vulnerability and violations of rights of certain groups, such as migrants, but also that there is a large number of states who lack the capacity to record and collect data about threats to life of their inhabitants.

The growing field of border criminology has created a considerable body of empirical and theoretical insights into the treatment of migrant populations, particularly by states in the global North. However, we need a better conceptual, methodological and theoretical apparatus for understanding the unequal protection of life at the global level and in Southern contexts. Our knowledge of migration journeys and control regimes in the global South, and threats to life in these contexts, is far scarcer. Consequently, we also have less advanced theoretical and empirical understanding of threats to life in these contexts, particularly illicit organized sources of violence and the 'dirty togetherness' between the state and illicit actors (Willis 2015). Phenomena, such kidnapping of migrants, which is far more frequent in Global South contexts, remain poorly examined (although see Yohannes 2023; Slack 2015). Also our understanding of sovereignty is often premised on a model most frequently found in countries of the global North.

A question, therefore, needs to be asked: how can we think about security of human life when the state and its agents (in collusion with sources of organized violence) present one of the main threats to life, and when notions of rights and human rights make little sense with no one to enforce them? How can we think about securing people from states and in insecure states, when we are used to thinking about states as main providers of security as 'public good' (Loader and Walker 2007)? Is humanitarianism with its uneven and unequal provision of help, and inability to deliver rights, the best option? Or should we be braver in thinking about smaller, bottom-up modes of organization, which could be based on alternative ways of social inclusion? Regardless of chosen practical solutions, criminology as a discipline should take decisive steps in trying to shed light not only on the security inequalities that exist globally, but also the inequalities of knowledge about insecurity that underpin them. Savoring 'a more cosmopolitan imaginary' (Braithwaite 2021) may therefore be a first step on the way, followed by sustained efforts toward building more democratic knowledge structures. Currently, much of knowledge about migrants' rights is still produced by Northern academics, NGOs, and activists. The language of rights is deeply anchored in the notions of legal and democratic governance and the public sphere. Scholars promoting epistemologies from the South have suggested that critical theory should move closer to the new emancipatory movements and abandon the established (Eurocentric) notions of the public sphere (de Santos 2012). There is no doubt that existing legal and accountability mechanisms have proven to be very slow in addressing and responding to border deaths.

In July 2022, the European Court of Human Rights (ECtHR) concluded in *Safi and Others v. Greece* that, in an incident in which a migrant boat sank in the eastern Aegean Sea in 2014, national authorities had not done all that could reasonably be expected of them to prevent the loss of lives. Eleven people drowned in the incident. This is the first time that the ECtHR applied this positive obligation, flowing from Article 2 of the ECHR (FRA 2023, p. 149). It remains to be seen how (and if) the judgment will have an impact on the daily realities of the right to life at the borders.

Note

1. https://frontex.europa.eu/.

References

Aas, K.F. 2011. A Borderless World? Cosmopolitanism, Boundaries and Frontiers. In *Cosmopolitan Justice and Its Discontents*, ed. C. M. Bailliet and K.F. Aas. Routledge.

Aas, K.F., and H.I. Gundhus. 2015. Policing Humanitarian Borderlands: Frontex, Human Rights and the Precariousness of Life. *British Journal of Criminology* 55 (1): 1–18.

Andreas, P. and Greenhill, K.M. (eds.) 2010. Sex, Drugs and Body Counts: The Politics of Numbers in Global Crime and Conflict. Cornell University Press.

Bosworth, M. 2017. Penal Humanitarianism? Sovereign Power in an Era of Mass Migration. *New Criminal Law Review* 20 (1): 39–65.

Black, J., and Z. Sigman. 2022. 50,000 Lives Lost During Migration: Analysis of Missing Migrants Project Data 2014–2022. IOM GMDAC. Available at: https://missingmigrants.iom.int/sites/g/files/tmzbdl601/files/publication/file/2022%2050k%20deaths.pdf.

Braithwaite, J. 2021. Glimmers of Cosmopolitan Criminology. *International Criminology* 1: 5–12.

Carrington, K., R. Hogg, and M. Sozzo. 2016. Southern Criminology. *British Journal of Criminology* 56 (1): 1–20.

Carrera, S., and R. Cortinovis. 2019. Search and Rescue, Disembarkation and Relocation Arrangements in the Mediterranean. Sailing Away from Responsibility? *CEPS Paper in Liberty and Security in Europe* No. 2019-10, June 2019.

Cohen, S. 2001. *States of Denial: Knowing about Atrocities and Suffering*. Polity.

Cortinovis, R. 2021. Pushbacks and Lack of Accountability at the Greek-Turkish Borders. 2021–01 CEPS Paper in Liberty and Security in Europe. Available at: https://www.ceps.eu/ceps-publications/pushbacks-and-lack-of-accountability-at-the-greek-turkish-borders/

Christie, N. 1997. Four Blocks Against Insight: Notes on the Oversocialization of Criminologists. *Theoretical Criminology* 1 (1): 13–23.

Cuttitta, P. 2018. Delocalization, humanitarianism, and human rights: The Mediterranean border between exclusion and inclusion. *Antipode*, 50 (3): 783–803.

Cuttitta, P. 2020. Search and Rescue at Sea, Non-governmental Organisations and the Principles of the EUs External Action. In *20 Year Anniversary of the Tampere Programme: Europeanisation Dynamics of the EU Area of Freedom,*

Security and Justice, ed. S. Carrera, D. Curtin, and A. Geddes, 123–144. Florence: European University Institute.

Dembour, M.-B. 2015. *When Humans Become Migrants: Study of the European Court of Human Rights with an Inter-American Counterpoint*. Oxford: Oxford University Press.

de Santos, B.S. 2012. Public Sphere and Epistemologies of the South. *Africa Development* XXXVII (1): 43–67.

de Witte, F. 2022. Here be Dragons: Legal Geography and EU Law. *European Law Open*, 113.

Fassin, D. 2012. *Humanitarian Reason: A Moral History of the Present*. University of California Press.

Foucault, M. 1980. *Power/Knowledge: Selected Interviews and Other Writings 1972–1977*. In ed. C. Gordon. Pantheon Books.

FRA. 2023. Fundamental Rights Report 2023. European Union Agency for Fundamental Rights, Luxembourg. Available at: http://fra.europa.eu/sites/default/files/fra_uploads/fra-2023-fundamental-rights-report-2023_en_0.pdf (viewed on 30 June 2023).

Franko, K. 2020. *The Crimmigrant Other: Migration and Penal Power*. London and New York: Routledge.

Franko, K. 2021. The two-sided spectacle at the border: Frontex, NGOs and the theatres of sovereignty. *Theoretical Criminology*, *25*(3), 379–399.

Franko, K. 2022. 'See no evil': Towards an analytics of Europe's legal borderlands. *European Law Open*, *1*(1), 131–134.

Grant, S. 2011. Recording and Identifying European Frontier Deaths. *European Journal of Migration and Law* 13 (2): 135–156.

Guardian. 2023. Greece Shipwreck: Up to 100 Children Were Below Deck, Survivors Say, 15 June 2023. Available at: https://www.theguardian.com/world/2023/jun/15/greece-refugee-shipwreck-rescuers-scour-sea-for-survivors (viewed on 28 June 2023).

Haddad, E. 2003. The Refugee: The Individual Between Sovereigns. *Global Society* 17 (3): 297–322.

Hoyle, C. 2022. Death Penalty. In *Elgar Encyclopedia of Human Rights*, ed. C. Binder, M. Nowak, J.A. Hofbauer, and P. Janig. Edward Elgar Publishing.

Human Rights Committee. 2019. International Covenant on Civil and Political Rights, General Comment No. 36, Article 6: Right to Life. Available at: https://docstore.ohchr.org/SelfServices/FilesHandler.ashx?enc=6QkG1d%2FPPRiCAqhKb7yhsrdB0H1l5979OVGGB%2BWPAXhNI9e0rX3cJImWwe%2FGBLmVrGmT01On6KBQgqmxPNIjrLLdefuuQjjN19BgOr%2FS93rKPWbCbgoJ4dRgDoh%2FXgwn (viewed on 28 June 2023).

Harris, D.J., M. O'Boyle, E. Bates, and C. Buckley. 2014. *Law of the European Convention on Human Rights*, 3rd ed. USA: Oxford University Press.

ICJ. 2022. Criminalization of Humanitarian and Other Support and Assistance to Migrants and the Defence of Their Human Rights in the EU. Briefing Paper by the International Commission of Jurists. Available at: https://www.icj.org/wp-content/uploads/2022/04/Criminalization-paper-22-04-2022.pdf (viewed on 28 June 2023).

Joseph, S. 2019. Extending the Right to Life Under the International Covenant on Civil and Political Rights: General Comment 36. *Human Rights Law Review* 19 (2): 347–368.

Leboeuf, L. 2022. 'The Juridification of "Vulnerability" Through EU Asylum Law: The Quest for Bridging the Gap Between the Law and Asylum Applicants' Experiences. *Laws* 11 (3): 45.

LeMonde. 2022. Frontex boss Leggeri resigns from EU border control agency, viewed on December 7, 2023 at: https://www.google.com/url?sa=t&rct=j&q=&esrc=s&source=web&cd=&ved=2ahUKEwj6rr_epv2CAxUhYPEDHZYtBYYQFnoECBQQAQ&url=https%3A%2F%2Fwww.lemonde.fr%2Fen%2Finternational%2Farticle%2F2022%2F04%2F29%2Ffrontex-boss-leggeri-resigns-from-eu-border-control-agency_5981965_4.html&usg=AOvVaw0CA7zZS_xcWvBB7jYkdkMV&opi=89978449

Loader, I., and Walker, N. (2007). *Civilizing security*. Cambridge University Press.

Lohne, K. 2020. Penal Humanitarianism Beyond the Nation State: An Analysis of International Criminal Justice. *Theoretical Criminology* 24 (2): 145–162.

Pallister-Wilkins, P. (2015). The humanitarian politics of European border policing: Frontex and border police in Evros. *International Political Sociology*, 9 (1): 53–69.

Pallister-Wilkins, P. (2020). Hotspots and the geographies of humanitarianism. *Environment and Planning D: Society and Space*, 38 (6): 991–1008, first published online January 25, 2018.

Schindel, E. 2022. Death by 'Nature': The European Border Regime and the Spatial Production of Slow Violence. *EPC: Politics and Space* 40 (2): 428–446.

Slack, J. 2015. Captive Bodies: Migrant Kidnapping and Deportation in Mexico. *Area* 38 (3): 271–277.

Soliman, F. 2021. States of Exception, Human Rights, and Social Harm: Towards a Border Zemiology. *Theoretical Criminology* 25 (2): 228–248.

Sollund, R. 2017. Causes for Speciesism: Difference, Distance and Denial. In *Transnational Environmental Crime*, 75–96. Routledge.

Ticktin, M. 2011. *Casualities of Care*. University of California Press.
UNHCR. 2021. UNHCR Warns Asylum Under Attack at Europe's Borders, Urges End to Pushbacks and Violence Against Refugees. Press Release. Available at: https://www.unhcr.org/news/news-releases/unhcr-warns-asylum-under-attack-europes-borders-urges-end-pushbacks-and-violence
UNODC. 2019. Global Study on Homicide: Homicide trends, patterns and criminal justice response. United Nations Office on Drugs and Crime. https://www.unodc.org/documents/data-andanalysis/gsh/Booklet2.pdf.
Weber, L., and S. Pickering. 2011. *Globalization and Borders: Death at the Global Frontier*. Basingstoke: Palgrave Macmillan.
Wicks, E. 2010. *The Right to Life and Conflicting Interests*. USA: Oxford University Press.
Willis, G.D. 2015. *The Killing Consensus: Police, Organized Crime, and the Regulation of Life and Death in Urban Brazil*. The University of California Press.
Yohannes, H.T. 2023. Refugee Trafficking in A Carceral Age: A Case Study of the Sinai Trafficking. *Journal of Human Trafficking* 9 (1): 33–47.
Zimring, F.E. 2020. Police Killings as a Problem of Governance. *The ANNALS of the American Academy of Political and Social Science* 687 (1): 114–123.

6

The Promise and Pitfalls of Human Rights in Immigration Detention

Andriani Fili and Mary Bosworth

Introduction

Despite their enforced elusiveness, as successive governments have restricted research access, information about detention centres in Greece is not in short supply (Amnesty International 2010; Bhui et al. 2019). International and national human rights organisations have monitored and reported on detention conditions for far too many years. With limited academic literature on immigration detention in the country (Fili 2013, 2023 [forthcoming]; Bosworth et al. 2018), these reports have been the key source of knowledge about these sites (Amnesty International 2010, 2012; Human Rights Watch 2008; Medécins Sans

A. Fili (✉) · M. Bosworth
University of Oxford, Oxford, UK
e-mail: andriani.fili@crim.ox.ac.uk

M. Bosworth
e-mail: mary.bosworth@crim.ox.ac.uk

L. Weber and M. Marmo (eds.), *A Research Agenda for a Human Rights Centred Criminology*, Palgrave Critical Studies in Human Rights and Criminology,
https://doi.org/10.1007/978-3-031-46289-4_6

Frontières 2010, 2014; Pro Asyl 2007, 2012; Border Violence Monitoring Network 2023; Mobile Info Team 2023). The severity of the issues uncovered by these monitoring missions cannot be brushed aside. Over and over again, they reveal that everyday life inside Greek immigration detention centres is cruel and inhumane. Conditions are degrading and structurally violent; the dignity and human rights of people, including that of children, within them, cannot be guaranteed and safeguarded.

Evidence from these reports has been cited in multiple determinations of human rights violations by Greek courts and in the European Court of Human Rights (ECtHR). Between 2001 and 2015 alone, the ECtHR ruled at least 55 times that Greece had breached Article 3, which prohibits torture, and inhuman or degrading treatment or punishment (Xenakis and Cheliotis 2018). However, given that Greece has one of the poorest records of ECHR signatory states in implementing the judgements of the Court, the impact of such judgements and the millions of euros in fines they have generated, has been minimal. Instead, successive Greek authorities have managed to deflect criticism and remained indifferent to demands for change, maintaining repressive border control measures in rather than human rights protection and the rule of law (Fili 2023 [forthcoming]). In doing so, they have not acted alone. As we will show, (international) NGOs and other human rights defenders have provided discursive legitimation to entrenched state practices.

Drawing on over five years of research with organisations in Greece from the National Preventive Mechanism (NPM), with its official mandate to monitor human rights protections in all forms of custody, to independent activist organisations, this article seeks to explain how this situation has evolved, why human rights organisations and protections have been so ineffective and what could be done differently. The chapter draws on in-depth interviews with more than 70 experienced (I)NGO practitioners, researchers, journalists, academics and activists as well as additional research on conditions in detention and the nature of human rights-based monitoring within detention centres in Greece (on the former, see Fili 2023 [forthcoming]; on the latter: Bhui et al. 2018, 2019; Bhui and Bosworth 2020). Engaging with critical literature on human rights protections and our ongoing work in immigration detention, we critically assess the limited impact of human rights protections on border control policies in Greece and set out a series of factors that undermine their effects. To bring matters to life, we use a selection of anonymised testimonies from legal and civil society practitioners as well as fieldnotes. We end with a consideration of the role for academic research in illuminating human rights violations in places of detention and in generating improved accountability.

Human Rights in the Literature

As a European Union member state, Greece is bound by international human rights agreements and legal standards. Immigration detention there, as it is throughout the continent, is situated within wider immigration and asylum law and practices which dictate that deprivation of liberty should be a measure of last resort and that people are entitled to procedural safeguards. In 2014, Greece signed the Optional Protocol to the Convention Against Torture and other Cruel, Inhuman or Degrading Treatment or Punishment (OpCat), which created National Preventive Mechanisms (NPMs) (Bhui et al. 2018). Greece's detention sites are also regularly visited by international monitors and there is a strong presence in the country of local and international NGOs, all of which champion human rights. Human rights protections are, in other words, written into the nation's system of migration control and play a role in its everyday operation. However, as the next section will demonstrate, the impact of these protections and the organisations that champion them, has been extremely limited. Instead, the Greek police, which manages detention centres, remains sacrosanct, and attempts to challenge their practices and behaviour have foundered. To better understand such matters, we turn first to the literature on human rights and border control, which sets out the promise of such legal frameworks. Then we move on to accounts in border criminology which identify the pitfalls, before drawing on our long-term empirical research in Greece.

For Dutch legal scholar Galina Cornelisse, human rights protections disrupt assumptions about territorial sovereignty that inhere in border control. Whereas 'existing human rights adjudication proves inadequate

... when the national state wishes to enforce its sovereign claims against those who have allegedly violated its territorial boundaries', the universal protections of human rights legislation, she suggests, allow for a wider and more inclusive approach to belonging (Cornelisse 2010, p. 315). Human rights in the immigration detention context can function as what she describes as 'destabilisation rights', ensuring that full legal scrutiny is applied to claims that the national state presents as predominantly based on its territorial sovereignty. Costello (2012) and Marin and Spena (2016) put forward similar viewpoints.

By contrast, Gyollai and Amatrudo (2019, p. 436) take a more critical view, pointing out that, '[i]n order to neutralise human rights claims, the state needs only to find a reason to deport', because the 'right to have rights' (Arendt 1951) depends on citizenship (Dembour and Kelly 2011). While Snacken and van Zyl Smit (2009) celebrate human rights protections in Europe, they overlook the implications of this reality for immigration detainees. More recently, Spalding (2022) has demonstrated how the European Court of Human Rights (ECtHR) has effectively constructed a 'two-tier system', in which human rights are applied and interpreted to offer a lesser protection in immigration cases than in other contexts. This approach, which echoes the 'abnormal justice' and 'bordered penality' identified by Katja Franko (2020), has entrenched and normalised discrimination against non-citizens, undermining the universalistic principles of the European Convention on Human Rights (ECHR).

While these authors acknowledge that it is not easy to mobilise human rights in support of migrants, they insist on their value in analysing, exposing and challenging the treatment of irregular migrants and detainees. By contrast, when border criminologists have considered human rights, they have usually been more circumspect. For example, Bosworth and Vannier (2016) point to the difficulties that detainees face in exercising rights in detention and question the value of such protections if they cannot be accessed. Similarly, Majcher et al. (2020) argue that since the onset of the 'refugee crisis' in 2015, the EU legislation has led to the adoption of laws and practices that disregard fundamental rights and standards. In the Greek context, Fili (2023) shows that a range of human rights defenders inside the country's facilities have allowed detention to go unchallenged and also to thrive, by prioritising their own organisation's survival at the expense of advocating for radical change inside detention. This approach has often delivered discriminatory and violent consequences for the very people they are meant to protect. Overall, these critiques place more emphasis on empirical evidence and lived experience of detainees, and less on putative legal protections. As a consequence—and faced with ample evidence of the poor treatment of detained migrants—they raise profound questions about the impact of human rights protections in a system where 'many of the fundamental protections guaranteed by law are observed only in the breach' (Bosworth et al. 2021).

Defending Human Rights in Immigration Detention

The relationship between organisations like Medicins San Frontier (MSF) and the United Nations High Commission for Refugees (UNHCR), and the Greek authorities is key in understanding the scope and challenges of human rights monitoring in practice. For, as with others, we have found that immigration detention in Greece, 'operates through and with the support of the international human rights regime' (Morris 2016, p. 51). Niki, a member of an international human rights institution was very clear:

> INGOs have a complex structure, what is raised [as an issue] every time is a matter of choice depending on the circumstances…As an INGO you can't go and say I'm going to do this, because then you substitute the state. This is national sovereignty. The critical point is if the law has been broken. This is the beginning and end of an intervention. (Interview, Athens, 2018)

Another former member of an INGO agreed. When preparing a report on the conditions in detention facilities in the Evros region, she and colleagues spent considerable time debating the extent to which they could denounce the detention system as a whole, rather than simply outlining the degrading treatment inside them. 'It's a governmental policy', she pointed out. 'It's like going out there and saying that prisons are wrong. You cannot challenge a policy' (Interview, Athens, 2018).

This apparent acceptance of the status quo does not and cannot address the root causes of harmful detention conditions. It further diverts energy and focus away from building oppositional movements for change. Matters are compounded by the organisational form of these international bodies, the politics of their knowledge production and the micropolitics of their management, all of which are deeply tied to their makeup and efforts for financial viability. Together, they limit their capacity for more critical or reflexive views, rendering their interventions 'timid and undecisive' (Schaub 2013, p. 10). Frequently disconnected from the struggles of those inside, such groups tend to emphasise polite reformism and quiet diplomacy. This mechanism of quiet diplomacy, though successful at times, has not produced a significant change in the way detention is implemented in Greece. Nor has it held many accountable for the gross human rights violations the same organisations have identified (Flynn 2012).

The Greek NPM is meant to play a key role in preventing torture and ill-treatment together with the two supranational bodies which also have a mandate to visit detention sites in Greece: the UN Subcommittee on Prevention of Torture and other Cruel, Inhuman or Degrading Treatment or Punishment (SPT) and the 'European Committee for the Prevention of Torture and Inhuman or Degrading Treatment or Punishment' (CPT). This human rights framework, and the laws that enshrine it, is meant to prevent ill-treatment and to deter future occurrences through prosecution and sanction. In line with this optimistic reading of this framework, Bhui and Bosworth (2022) have argued that 'the fact that NPMs exist as part of the mechanisms that can prevent ill treatment of those in custody should be celebrated, and the struggle to help them achieve their purpose continued' (Bhui and Bosworth 2022, p. 654). Yet, as our research highlights, there is scant evidence that these mechanisms have been effective in Greece.

The Greek NPM was established in 2014, as part of the Greek Ombudsman. Three years later, in 2017 state funds were allocated for inspections and to employ and train inspectors. It remains small, with no more than 15 members of staff to visit all the custodial institutions in Greece, including 7 pre-removal centres, numerous police stations and more than 30 prisons. Staff continue to bear responsibility for additional tasks as part of the Ombudsman office, like receiving and responding to complaints, monitoring of removal procedures and investigating the arbitrary behaviour of law enforcement officials. Under these conditions, it is perhaps unsurprising, that NPM monitoring reports appear only sporadically, if at all. Their dissemination strategy is focused on publishing annual special reports, which summarise the main findings of all their inspections that year, yet these too, are often delayed (The Greek Ombudsman 2018a, b).

According to the NPM, it is the national police who determine whether the government accepts their recommendations. While some detention managers tried to implement their suggestions, few took action. A meeting we observed with the senior director of Athens' main detention centre, Petrou Ralli, in September 2018, was typical. The director did not consider this session to be part of a monitoring visit but merely as a way for him to complain to the NPM about funding. Whereas maintaining good working relationships with the authorities may appear to be a good practice, having casual conversations with the directors of the centres over coffee undermines their ability to raise their findings and press for solutions (Birk et al. 2015). As Dimitris, a member of the Greek NPM blatantly put it 'We can't be very displeasing. We have a gentlemen's agreement with the police' (Fieldnotes, Athens, 2018). Through this informal agreement between honourable men (Campbell 1964), the NPM and the Hellenic police have made their association dependent on the fulfilment of spoken or unspoken obligations, an arrangement that limits the obligation of the NPM to hold the government to account.

In our research, we have found that the benefits offered by human rights protections are not always clear, even to those defending them at courts. Greek NGO lawyers we have interviewed, for instance, often have little faith in bringing about systematic change through litigation. Evgenia, who had years of experience in representing immigrants at court, spoke for many when we asked her about available legal actions: 'I don't think there is a mechanism that is able to change the way the police work. They are somewhat autonomous and only interventions from very high up can bring change. Whatever the rest do is just beating the air' (Interview, Athens, 2018). And indeed, the evidence is clear: most cases of alleged police ill-treatment are not criminally prosecuted, and very few of those which make it to court result in any kind of disciplinary sanctions. Given the extensive evidence of police brutality, this situation raises questions about the complicity of the judicial system in fostering a culture of impunity (Papapantoleon 2014; Bosworth et al. 2021; Fili 2023). However, it also destabilises the centrality of the rule of law in bringing tangible results in human rights protections (Anagnostou 2014).

Is There Hope for Human Rights in Immigration Detention?

One practical criticism that can be levelled at institutions that aim to monitor and protect human rights inside detention facilities is that they point out to detention staff and managers what they already know, doing little to help the change process, and return months or years later to report the same failings. In the meantime, the detention authorities have not implemented recommended changes because they lack motivation, money, knowledge or capability. This state of affairs increases cynicism towards these organisations from government and civil society, and undermines their utility. In Greece, this unvirtuous circle is in full flow, and lends a depressing inevitability to our findings.

Despite all the evidence against the Greek detention system, members of the government or the police are quick to dismiss any negative comments. When a journalist asked about a report that described inhumane conditions in detention centres and police stations back in 2013, then Minister of Public protection, Mr Dendias, replied 'I want to say first and foremost that NGOs and Amnesty International do their job. And their job is to denounce. What we do, is investigate what they say. But I don't have the sense that the latest report from Amnesty International claims what you are mentioning' (Bamiatzis 2013). In a similar vein, the Director of the Petrou Ralli detention centre assured us that there had been no monitoring of the centre whatsoever. 'For several years there have been no reports on the centre and the previous ones did not make specific claims to any problems. We are ok' (Interview, Petrou Ralli detention centre, 2018), he declared as he laid back on this chair, disregarding or totally ignorant of repeated critical findings about the centre (Fili 2023 [forthcoming]). Such statements of denial (Cohen 2001), help cover up the, often intentional, failure of human rights protections behind bars. If those at the receiving end of criticisms of human rights violations ignore such concerns, is there any hope for change?

We suggest that a first step is to engage in broader research about these institutions that aim to protect individuals against human rights abuses. This work should not merely contain evidence on their effectiveness or even the impact of human rights treaties on state behaviours (Carver and Handley 2016). Rather, it should focus on how these institutions perform their duties, gather information and engage with the authorities and other organisations. Research projects should also address issues of transparency and trust. In other words, it is vital to unpack 'the extent of non-state actors involved in performing state functions and critically assessing the implications of human rights-based policies on detention's expansion' (Morris 2016, p. 66).

Immigration detention centres across the world are opaque places, rooted in emerging assemblages of bordered forms of penality, with prison-like, overcrowded and unhygienic conditions. Those who live inside them experience high levels of anxiety, depression and post-traumatic stress disorder, while confined and long after their release (Bosworth 2016). These accounts need to be documented. However, to reform or even dismantle the system is not an easy task.

As Kelly (2009) has argued, human rights monitoring all too often 'displaces the discussion of the causes and consequences of violence in favour of a focus on the systems that are supported to monitor cruelty', to the extent that 'measurements, monitoring, and prevention are in danger of becoming merged' (Kelly 2009, p. 777). Paying particular attention to state reporting of compliance with the Convention Against Torture to the Committee Against Torture, he suggested that the process of monitoring can depoliticize conceptions of violence: 'Human rights indicators become confused with human rights … [while] structural inequalities that produce torture are downplayed' (Kelly 2009, p. 779). Broader questions about the purposes of detention and the effects they have on people are beyond the scope of their investigations. By individualising systemic problems, and focusing on the minutiae of cases in an inquisitorial forum, monitoring, however unintentionally, all too often leaves the practice of detention itself uncontested.

In his paper on the unintended consequences of promoting human rights in detention, Flynn (2012) takes a similar view, arguing that attempts to reform immigration detention without also seeking to restrict use of detention, may lead to 'kinder and gentler' regimes, while extending the harmful outcomes created by immigration detention. He advises that any campaign aimed at reforming immigration detention 'must have as an integral component working to constrict that country's detention activities' (Flynn 2012, p. 3). To take this approach further, we ask, does the scale of atrocity need to be so (exceptionally) awful as to merit condemnation of human rights violations? If the system were slightly more humane or more in line with human rights norms, would it mean that detention would automatically become more legitimate? What is more, does appealing to protecting inviolable rights, such as the right against arbitrary detention or the right to dignity automatically risk providing a normative cover to an unhealthy detention system? Rather than advocating for humane forms of detention and uncritically accepting the universality and neutrality of human rights discourses and strategies that merely aspire to improve detention, why are we not trying to shake its foundations?

Conclusion

In this chapter, we have documented the relationship between the culture of violence inside Greek immigration detention centres and those human rights-based organisations that are supposed to prevent harm, and investigate and punish its perpetrators. In exploring these relationships, we have identified a series of processes that have functioned to protect, legitimise and exonerate the Greek detention system. We are not refuting the independence of these actors, but rather we point out their 'bare bones' approach to their institutional mandates, all too often resorts to questionable alliances between them and the authorities (Grenfell and Caruana 2022). This quiet, reformist approach has inadvertently contributed to Greece not meeting its international obligations to protect individuals against human rights abuses on its soil. While putting people through such atrocities as those described in numerous reports cannot be solely explained by a simplistic reference to Greek authorities' malicious intentions or disregard people's humane standards altogether, we argue that the safeguards built into social systems that uphold compassionate behaviour, renounce cruelty and protect human rights have been in the Greek case absent or scarcely found. Against this setting, detained people in Greece are left to fend for themselves.

Under these circumstances, what role is there for academic research or expertise? As academics, we should not give up on the relevance of empirical evidence. So, even as research access to immigration detention becomes further constrained, and the impact of our work more tenuous, we must continue to insist on studying the system and its impacts directly, in order to have material to challenge the politicisation of human rights and reform agendas that have acquired such mainstream visibility. Second, as we have argued in this chapter, we must be prepared to innovate, widening the scope of our research, shifting the focus away from governments to other institutions that are purported defenders of human rights inside detention. This body of research, in line with border criminology scholars who emphasise lived experience as opposed to rights-centred analyses, should have a key and common aim, to bring to life the perspectives of different actors inside detention. Only by studying their interaction can we fully grasp the intricacies of working against but also within the system. Third, we need to reach out to others who have been managing similarly bleak political landscapes for longer. To build a world without harmful policies and agendas, we cannot work in silos. We can only do so in solidarity with each other.

References

Amnesty International. 2010. *Greece: Irregular Migrants and Asylum-Seekers Routinely Detained in Substandard Conditions*. London: Amnesty International.

Amnesty International. 2012. *Greece: The End of the Road for Refugees, Asylum-Seekers and Migrants*. London: Amnesty International.

Anagnostou, D. 2014. Law and Rights' Claiming on Behalf of Minorities in the Multi-level European System. In *Rights and Courts in Pursuit of Social Change: Legal Mobilisation in the Multi-level European System*, ed. D. Anagnostou. London: Hart Publishing.

Arendt, H. 1951. *The Origins of Totalitarianism*. New York: Schocken Books.

Bamiatzis, S. 2013. Δένδιας: Η Αμυγδαλέζα Είναι από τα Πιο Σύγχρονα Στρατόπεδα στην Ευρώπη [Dendias: Amygadleza Is One of the Most Modern Camps in Europe]. News247, 11 July. https://www.news247.gr/politiki/dendias-i-amygdaleza-einai-apo-ta-pio-sygchrona-stratopeda-stin-eyropi.6217730.html. Accessed 11 September 2018.

Bhui, H.S., and M. Bosworth. 2020. Human rights protections and monitoring immigration detention at Europe's Borders. *European Human Rights Law Review* 6 : 640–654.

Bhui, H.S., and M. Bosworth. 2022. Human Rights Protections and Monitoring Immigration Detention at Europe's Borders. *European Human Rights Law Review* 6: 640–654.

Bhui, H.S., A. Fili, and M. Bosworth. 2018. *Monitoring Immigration Detention at the Borders of Europe: Report on a Pilot Project in Greece, Hungary, Turkey and Italy, 2016–2017*. Oxford: Centre for Criminology. https://www.law.ox.ac.uk/sites/default/files/migrated/project_report_final_1.pdf.

Bhui, H.S., A. Fili, and M. Bosworth. 2019. *Monitoring Immigration Detention at the Borders of Europe: Report on Immigration Detention Monitoring in Turkey and Greece*. Oxford: Border Criminologies. https://www.law.ox.ac.uk/sites/default/files/migrated/monitoring_immigration_detention_at_the_borders_of_europe_compressed.pdf.

Birk, M., G. Moritz, D. Long, R. Murray, and W. Suntinger. 2015. *Enhancing Impact of National Preventive Mechanisms. Strengthening the Follow-Up on NPM Recommendations in the EU: Strategic Development, Current Practices and the Way Forward*. Vienna: Ludwig Boltzmann Institute of Human Rights. https://www.bristol.ac.uk/media-library/sites/law/hric/2015-documents/NPM%20Study_final.pdf. Accessed 11 September 2018.

Border Violence Monitoring Network. 2023. Dark Rooms, Degrading Treatment and Denial: The Use of Violence in Greece's Pre-removal Detention Centres. https://borderviolence.eu/reports/detention-violence-greece/.

Bosworth, M. 2016. The Impact of Immigration Detention on Mental Health: Literature Review. In *Review into the Welfare in Detention of Vulnerable Persons: A Report to the Home Office by Stephen Shaw*. London: HMSO, CM 9186.

Bosworth, M., and M. Vannier. 2016. Comparing Immigration Detention in Britain and France: A Matter of Time? *European Journal of Migration & Law* 18 (2): 157–176.

Bosworth, M., A. Fili, and S. Pickering. 2018. Women and Border Policing at the Edges of Europe. *Journal of Ethnic and Migration Studies* 44 (13): 2182–2196.

Bosworth, M., F. Esposito, and A. Fli. 2021. Accessing Justice from Immigration Detention in Greece and Italy. In *Rule of Law: Strategies, Experiences, and Interpretations*, ed. B. Faedda, 177–186. Vicenza: Ronzani Editore.

Campbell, J.K. 1964. *Honour, Family and Patronage: A Study of Institutions and Moral Values in a Greek Mountain Community*. Oxford: Clarendon Press.

Carver, R., and L. Handley. 2016. *Does Torture Prevention Work?* Liverpool: Liverpool University Press.

Cohen, S. 2001. *States of Denial. Knowing About Atrocities and Suffering*. Cambridge: Polity Press.

Cornelisse, G. 2010. *Immigration Detention and Human Rights: Rethinking Territorial Sovereignty*. Leiden: Martinus Nijhoff Publishers.

Costello, C. 2012. Human Rights and the Elusive Universal Subject: Immigration Detention Under International Human Rights and EU Law. *Indiana Journal of Global Legal Studies* 19 (1): 257–303.

Dembour, M.-B., and T. Kelly, eds. 2011. *Are Human Rights for Migrants? Critical Reflections on the Status of Irregular Migrants in Europe and the United States*. Abingdon: Routledge.

Fili, A. 2013. The Maze of Immigration Detention Greece: A Case Study of the Athens Airport Detention Facility. *Prison Service Journal* 205: 34–38.

Fili, A. 2023, forthcoming. *Mapping Resistance in Immigration Detention*. Abingdon: Routledge.

Flynn, M. 2012. On the Unintended Consequences of Human Rights Promotion on Immigration Detention. Graduate Institute of International and Development Studies. https://www.google.com/url?sa=t&rct=j&q=&esrc=s&source=web&cd=&cad=rja&uact=8&ved=2ahUKEwjIs7v9tPXsAhXfQEEAHRHOBTsQFjABegQIBBAC&url=https%3A%2F%2Fwww.

globaldetentionproject.org%2Fwp-content%2Fuploads%2F2016%2F06%2FFlynn_Discussion_Paper_v4.pdf&usg=AOvVaw3vX1uMea2lQtx9_NK4QU05. Accessed 5 July 2020.

Franko, K. 2020. *The Crimmigrant Other: Migration and Penal Power*. Abingdon: Routledge.

Grenfell, L., and S. Caruana. 2022. Are We OPCAT Ready? So Far, Bare Bones. *Alternative Law Journal* 47 (1): 54–59.

Gyollai, D., and A. Amatrudo. 2019. Controlling Irregular Migration: International Human Rights Standards and the Hungarian Legal Framework. *European Journal of Criminology* 16 (4): 432–451.

Human Rights Watch. 2008. *Stuck in a Revolving Door: Iraqis and Other Asylum Seekers and Migrants at the Greece/Turkey Entrance to the European Union*. New York: Human Rights Watch.

Kelly, T. 2009. The UN Committee Against Torture: Human Rights Monitoring and the Legal Recognition of Cruelty. *Human Rights Quarterly* 31 (3): 777–800.

Majcher, I., M. Flynn, and M. Grange. 2020. *Immigration Detention in the European Union*. Cham: Springer.

Marin, L., and A. Spena. 2016. Introduction: The Criminalization of Migration and European (Dis)Integration. *European Journal of Migration and Law* 18 (2): 147–156.

Medécins Sans Frontières. 2010. *Migrants in Detention: Lives on Hold*. Athens: MSF.

Medécins Sans Frontières. 2014. *Invisible Suffering: Prolonged and Systematic Detention of Migrants and Asylum Seekers in Substandard Conditions in Greece*. Athens: MSF.

Mobile Info Team. 2023. "PRISON FOR PAPERS": Last Resort Measures Used as Standard Procedure. Researching Pre-removal Detention Centres on Mainland Greece. https://www.mobileinfoteam.org/detention.

Morris, J. 2016. *In the market of morality: International human rights standards and the immigration detention 'improvement' complex*. In Conlon, C. and Hiemstra, N. (eds.) Intimate Economies of Immigration Detention: Critical perspectives. London: Routledge.

Papapantoleon, C. 2014. The Judiciary. In *Mapping Ultra-Right Extremism, Xenophobia and Racism Within the Greek State Apparatus*, ed. D. Christopoulos. Brussels: Rosa Luxemburg Stiftung.

Pro Asyl. 2007. *The Truth May Be Bitter but It Must Be Told: The Situation of Refugees in the Aegean and the Practices of the Greek Coast Guard*. Frankfurt/Main: Pro Asyl.

Pro Asyl. 2012. *Walls of Shame: Accounts from the Inside: The Detention Centres of Evros*. Frankfurt/Main: Pro Asyl.

Schaub, M. 2013. Humanitarian Problems Relating to Migration in the Turkish-Greek Border Region: The Crucial Role of Civil Society Organisations. Research Resources Paper for COMPAS, University of Oxford. https://www.compas.ox.ac.uk/2013/humanitarian-problems-relating-to-migration-in-the-turkish-greek-border-region-the-crucial-role-of-civil-society-organisations/.

Snacken, S., and D. van Zyl Smit. 2009. *Principles of European Prison Law and Policy: Penology and Human Rights*. Oxford: Oxford University Press.

Spalding, A. 2022. *The Treatment of Immigrants in the European Court of Human Rights: Moving Beyond Criminalisation*. Oxford: Hart Publishing.

The Greek Ombudsman. 2018a. OPCAT—National Preventive Mechanisms Against Torture and Ill-Treatment: Annual Special Report 2016. https://www.synigoros.gr/resources/docs/opcat_2016_en.pdf. Accessed 12 June 2018.

The Greek Ombudsman. 2018b. OPCAT—National Preventive Mechanisms Against Torture and Ill-Treatment: Annual Special Report 2017. https://www.synigoros.gr/resources/opcat_2017_en.pdf. Accessed 12 June 2018.

Xenakis, S., and L. Cheliotis. 2018. Carceral Moderation and the Janus Face of International Pressure: A Long View of Greece's Engagement with the European Convention of Human Rights. *Crime, Law and Social Change* 70 (2): 37–56.

7

An Anticolonial, Abolitionist, and Feminist Lens to Interrogate Human Rights Penality

Silvana Tapia Tapia

Human Rights, Penality, and the Limits of Liberal Legalism

Brutal police practices, the hyper-surveillance of stigmatised and marginalised people, and the degrading living conditions in prisons and detention centres around the world are some of the urgent matters we face given the 'tough on crime' and 'zero impunity' discourses that continue to dominate around the globe. Recent cases of extreme carceral violence include harrowing riots in Ecuadorian prisons, which resulted in hundreds of people being tortured and killed (Human Rights Watch 2022), and prison policy in El Salvador, where deaths in custody, extreme overcrowding, torture, and arbitrary arrests have been denounced by former inmates and human rights organisations (Marcial Pérez 2023).

S. Tapia Tapia (✉)
Birmingham Law School, University of Birmingham, Birmingham, UK
e-mail: s.tapiatapia@bham.ac.uk

L. Weber and M. Marmo (eds.), *A Research Agenda for a Human Rights Centred Criminology*, Palgrave Critical Studies in Human Rights and Criminology,
https://doi.org/10.1007/978-3-031-46289-4_7

A significant portion of international human rights (IHR) instruments, guidelines, and case law have been conceived to limit state coercion, prevent the abuse of penal power, and uphold democratic principles (EEAS 2021; OAS 2001). However, IHR also contribute to strengthening the penal apparatus by incorporating criminal processes and imprisonment as central signifiers of justice. IHR bodies encourage and even compel states to criminalise, investigate, prosecute, and punish human rights violations. Moreover, I have used the terms 'rights-based criminal law' and 'rights-based penality' to show how due process principles and human rights mandates are used by progressive political actors, such as left-leaning feminists, to devise and justify the criminalisation of gender-based violence and hate crimes, among others (Tapia Tapia 2018, 2022a). Similarly, the terms 'coercive human rights' (Lavrysen and Mavronicola 2020; Pinto 2023) and 'human rights penality'[1] point at the role of IHR in mobilising penality, a broad discursive field that includes laws, institutions, and representations where imprisonment is an explicit or implicit end: in the horizon of human rights penality, carceral punishment and other forms of detention largely amount to the realisation of justice.

In this chapter, leveraging critical research in human rights, criminology, and law, and using the example of VAW, I contend that an anticolonial, abolitionist, and feminist lens is essential to undertake further investigations into the mechanisms through which human rights penality discursively shapes gender, violence, crime, and accountability. Such research is necessary because IHR can perpetuate the hegemonic and colonial legal order, including by framing violence against women (VAW) primarily as a penal issue (Tapia Tapia, 2023; Kapur 2018, chap. 3). All the while, penal systems have consistently failed to adequately address the material needs of victim-survivors while sidelining other modes of prevention and redress, and leaving the continuity of carceral violence unadressed.

Of course, we shall acknowledge that, as mentioned above, there are IHR instruments that aim at protecting incarcerated or detained persons. For instance, the United Nations (UN) General Assembly has adopted the Minimum Rules for the Treatment of Prisoners (Mandela Rules), the Body of Principles for the Protection of All Persons under Any Form of

Detention and Imprisonment, the Minimum Rules for Non-Custodial Measures (Tokyo Rules), and the Rules for the Treatment of Women Prisoners and Non-custodial Measures for Women Offenders (Bangkok Rules). Yet, as Loughnan and Caruana affirm in this volume, rights-based laws do not always deliver on their promise and reformist strategies may even re-legitimise and perpetuate violent systems.

Indeed, IHR standards for the treatment of incarcerated people are built on the pre-conceived legitimacy of imprisonment (Mavronicola 2015) and the assumption that carceral systems can be human-rights-compliant. Liberal legalism, which dominates in mainstream IHR and criminological disciplines (Douzinas 2013; Kapur 2018; Moore 2023), has 'solved' the paradox that incarceration violates fundamental freedoms (Dubber 2008) by producing axioms and rules that limit (but also implicitly justify) punishment. Potential abuses of state power are rebutted through rights-based principles and 'guarantees' such as due process, legality, proportionality, *ultima ratio*, and *non-bis in idem*[2] (Ferrajoli 2009). On that basis, the state responds to human rights violations through constitutional and democratic processes of criminalisation, prosecution, and punishment (Tapia Tapia 2022a, chap. 4), even though human rights violations are, in practice, systematically committed in spaces of confinement.

Elsewhere, I have shown that the theorisation of a minimalist and democratic criminal law in connection with human rights discourses has provided actors across the political spectrum with an avenue to conciliate their agendas with the resort to penality (Tapia Tapia 2022a, p. 4; Tapia Tapia and López Hidalgo 2022). Notably, some feminist sectors are invested in a 'constitutionalised' criminal law, limited by human rights, to address the gender bias inherent in legal systems and the issue of excessive state coercion, while also tackling VAW (Villagómez 2013; Heim 2019; Tapia Tapia 2022a, chap. 5). These are examples of a 'turn to rights' within the domain of criminal law.

At the same time, to complete a circle of sorts, critics have identified a 'turn to criminal law in human rights' (Engle 2015), which is driven by a normative consensus on fighting impunity (Engle, Miller, and Davis 2016). Indeed, anti-impunity is at the centre of campaigns to criminalise and prosecute gender-based violence (GBV) and VAW, encompassing offences such as trafficking, sexual assault, hate crimes, and domestic violence (Tapia Tapia 2018; Pinto 2022; Lamble 2013; Pérez and Radi 2020). These endeavours have influenced legislative projects in IHR, international criminal law, and domestic criminal law (Ní Aoláin 2014; Halley et al. 2006). For instance, the Belem do Pará and the Istanbul conventions, adopted within the Organisation of American States and the Council of Europe respectively, contain explicit directives to criminalise and punish VAW, which have been taken up in domestic legislations in Latin America and Europe.

Indeed, for many feminists, criminalising VAW amounts to a political act of recognition of wrongness and harm, with valuable expressive power and a potential to produce social change (Gotell 2015; Schneider 2000; Heim 2019). However, others have denounced the systemic re-victimisation of victim-survivors by the penal system and its inadequacy to prevent and halt VAW (Snider 1998; Maier 2008; Goodmark 2021). For example, in conducting empirical research on Ecuador's specialised criminal courts for VAW, I observed high attrition rates that were related to the complainants' withdrawal from the proceedings after a negative experience during the criminal trial, while protective measures were generally ineffective (Tapia Tapia 2021). All this, in a context where budget cuts for shelter homes and services are reoccurring (Primicias 2022). Furthermore, criminal law reform can be showcased as an indicator of the state's commitment to counteract VAW by adopting measures endorsed by IHR bodies (UNIFEM 2003). In turn, 'progress' in the sphere of criminal law may obscure the state's failure to provide survivors with tangible protection and remedies (Bedford and Tapia Tapia 2021).

In addition to denouncing inadequate responses for victim-survivors, counter-hegemonic feminisms are concerned that penality targets people who are already subject to stigma and surveillance—not only perpetrators, but also victim-survivors who end up persecuted by the system (Johnson 2012; French 2013; Sudbury 2002; Richie 2012; Aguirre Salas et al. 2020; Goodmark 2021). Because penal violence contributes to the persecution and dispossession of people of colour, migrants, queer folk, impoverished communities, etc. (Cradle Community 2021; Day and McBean 2017; Coba Mejía 2015; Aguirre Salas 2019), feminist critiques of the penal apparatus are re-crafting anti-carceral work and penal abolition. Some prefigure a world without prisons and do address sensitive matters, including responding to sexual violence without penal force, by promoting community-accountability, re-centring social and economic needs, focusing on healing, and developing a transformative justice (Cradle Community 2021; Day and McBean 2017; Fulchiron 2017; Lamble 2011; Taylor 2018).

Adding to this radical work, I contend that dismantling penal violence and rethinking social responses to systemic injustice requires an examination of human rights penality as an element of the colonial and liberal legal order. A key challenge, in my experience, is that colonial legality is self-referential and presents law as having the remedies for the very problems it causes, usually through successive reforms that rely on the theoretical self-correcting nature of law. For instance, in Ecuador, the procedural hurdles caused by the criminalisation of VAW in 2014 (Tapia Tapia 2018) were addressed through a new law for the eradication of VAW in 2018, and then by additional reforms to the penal code in 2019 (Bedford and Tapia Tapia 2021). Nevertheless, femicides are on the rise (Fundación Aldea 2022) and VAW persists (INEC 2019). The idea that the threat of punishment discourages aggressors from offending is not grounded on substantial empirical evidence but continues to sustain penal strategies in a circular fashion: if the expected result (deterrence) falls short, more law reform is proposed, while the doctrine itself is not questioned. Disrupting this cycle requires a gaze from outside of the colonial paradigm to avoid falling back into the law's own rationalisation of the violence it produces. As Carol Smart (1989) famously argued, critical feminists should not merely address the discrepancy between law and reality but also scrutinise the assumption that law is capable of resolving deep-seated social issues.

In view of the above, I reckon that an anticolonial and feminist critique shall dispute the colonial universality of liberal legalism and the conflation between penality and justice that underlies IHR, to transform feminist anti-violence work. In the next section, I propose a research agenda to develop an anticolonial feminist critique of law, rights, and penality, aiming at producing a framework to envision justice beyond the confines of the penal system.

The Colonial Hegemony of Penality: A Feminist, Anticolonial, and Abolitionist Agenda for Criminology and Human Rights Research

Considering the challenges of human rights penality, some undertakings I regard as essential for a research agenda are: tracing how global governance agencies' discourses on gender equality incorporate human rights and penality; mapping the relationship between human rights penality and the decline of non-penal (including socio-economic) approaches to gender justice in law and policymaking; foregrounding the praxes of abolitionist feminists and counter-carceral movements and exploring their engagements/ruptures with human rights; and assessing the pitfalls and setbacks that human rights penality presents to efforts to counteract carceral violence.

The proposed themes arise from various concerns. For example, how do many governance agencies (not only the state but also NGOs, international organisations, international financial institutions, and private corporations) encourage penality in connection to gender and human rights while contributing to perpetuating structural inequalities and economic violence? Also, although feminist anti-carceral work is flourishing and proliferating, there is a long way ahead before non-penal models of justice are considered by policymakers and mainstream academia. Furthermore, a deeper awareness and self-reflection within IHR scholarship is needed regarding the paradox of feeding penal narratives while attempting to counter carceral violence. Next, I reflect on the conceptual frameworks that may be useful to embark on such projects.

Studies on the connections between colonialism and penality are not new (Aliverti et al. 2023). However, there is a growing drive, in contemporary post-colonial, decolonial, and Southern criminological perspectives, to identify and mitigate the omissions of 'metropolitan thinking' (Carrington et al. 2015) by fostering a diverse approach to research. This requires acknowledging the unequal power relations embedded in the production, organisation, and validation of knowledge. To advance these goals, I propose a conceptual framework to interrogate human rights penality by linking hegemony and colonialism. Framing human rights penality as a liberal-legal discourse that is hegemonic (Carvalho 2022; Wills 2014; Litowitz 2000) and colonial (Tapia Tapia, 2023; Quijano 2000; Rivera Cusicanqui 2010; Sattar 2019; Kapur 2018) enables critical accounts of its prevalence, as well as strategies to resist the violence it exerts upon 'subalternised' people.

The concepts of hegemony and colonialism can also reveal how carceral discourses thrive, while insights from other (non-carceral) worldviews are displaced. Ever since the invasion of the Americas, imperialist enterprises have imposed and maintained moral and legal frameworks based on race, gender, and class hierarchies, which have permitted selective criminalisation and punishment (Moore 2023; Tapia Tapia 2016; Lugones 2007; Sattar 2019). Penality, as a colonial device, has universalised imprisonment and marginalised approaches such as those of indigenous systems, to which incarceration is not central (Bracco Bruce 2022; Tapia Tapia 2016; Tapia Tapia and López Hidalgo 2022). The purported objectivity and universality of legal knowledge in reality exerts ontic and epistemic violence: worlds without prisons are not allowed to exist or even be imagined, and justice without carcerality is (presented as) impossible to exist, to be known, taught, or practised. If colonialism denies the existence of other worlds, dismantling the 'penal commonsense' is a priority for an anticolonial emancipatory agenda.

Similarly, studying colonialism and hegemony can elucidate how penality traverses the political spectrum and multiple geographies, with differentiated impacts. Global governance agencies posit penal systems, under the rule of law, as constitutive of democracy and justice; however, this could enable a representation whereby non-compliance with human rights becomes a matter of 'civilisation', especially in the Global South. In this manner, the failure of the carceral system to deliver on its promises regarding prevention, protection, and redress, does not lead to questioning penality as such; rather, it is seen as a fault that can be overcome if the 'least civilised' societies behave like the most 'democratic' ones. In other words, the liberal mirage of the benign prison, the fair criminal trial, or the responsive and sensitive police, are not only legal but also civilizational projects. In response, a decolonial lens can dismantle the seemingly inevitable association between criminal punishment, development, and democracy.

In addition, projects to 'southernise' and decolonise criminology can be radicalised by empirically tracing the histories of anti-carceral work in the Global South, to foreground currently displaced non-juridical approaches to violence and conflict. These may be based on worldviews that exceed the possibilities of Western liberalism and academic thinking by centring embodiment, interdependence, relationality, the materiality of life, mutual aid, community-building, resource redistribution, and healing (Orellana Matute 2021; Kapur 2018; Spade 2020; Fulchiron 2017).

Several of the ideas above emerge from my encounters with anti-carceral activism. Ongoing research in that context has shown me that grassroots collectives acting against both carceral and gender-based violence, such as *Mujeres de Frente* in Ecuador and Sisters Uncut in the United Kingdom, do not typically use mainstream human rights language. They tend to regard IHR as an elite discourse that produces little material change and does not reflect the needs and demands of the most impoverished and stigmatised groups. At the same time, however, some collectives and communities *do* use IHR tools and vocabulary strategically. For instance, they engage with socio-economic rights, often to challenge the monopolisation of resources by the elites and demand that the state provides the minimum material conditions to sustain life, such as access to decent housing (Tapia Tapia 2022b). Importantly, these uses of human rights language are usually devoid of a carceral dimension, which suggests that, in turn, human rights penality could debilitate strategic and subversive uses of human rights that address the materiality of life from the perspective of communities that are hyper-policed and criminalised.

My purpose in this chapter has been to outline some underexplored debates at the intersection of penality and human rights, using the case of VAW, and signposting ways to challenge dominant legal and criminological framings. I have proposed an abolitionist feminist lens, informed by the concepts of hegemony and colonialism, to interrogate the penal enterprise. The hegemonic legality that authorises the colonial penal order harms people inside, outside, and around prisons, despite the existence of IHR instruments and guidelines on humane treatment and the limits of coercive power. Moreover, said guidelines may paradoxically be contributing to legitimising and universalising penality, while carceral violence is regarded as incidental, or a matter of 'underdevelopment', rather than an effect of colonial violence and structural power imbalances. The hegemonic equation between imprisonment and justice operates at the cost of displacing non-carceral worldviews and establishing a particular paradigm as inevitable and definitive.

In response, we should disassemble the hegemonic colonial order by unmasking ontic and epistemic colonialism and its effects on the ground. An anticolonial and abolitionist feminist agenda needs to fracture legalism and penality to combat what Rivera Cusicanqui (2010, p. 29) terms 'the masculine and lawyerly aspects of the juridical process'. Centring the experience of those who suffer law's violence, and ethically supporting their knowledge production, is key to creating emancipatory research and praxis.

Acknowledgements A portion of the arguments presented in this chapter were developed thanks to research funded by the Leverhulme Trust, under the Early Career Fellowships scheme. I am grateful to the collectives and activists that have participated in this project, especially *Mujeres de Frente*, *Coredores Migratorios*, *Fundación Dignidad*, *CDH Guayaquil*, *Vivir Libre*, and *Alianza Contra las Prisiones.*

Notes

1. The term was first used in a workshop to which I was invited, entitled "Human rights penality: the next decade", supported by the Modern Law Review, held in Birmingham on March 25, 2022, and organised by Natasa Mavronicola, Mattia Pinto, and Steven Malby.
2. *Ultima ratio* refers to the use of criminal law as a last resort, once other possibilities of conflict resolution and other areas of law have been exhausted. *Non-bis in idem* mandates that no legal action can be instituted for the same cause more than once, that is, no one can be judged twice for the same crime.

References

Aguirre Salas, Andrea. 2019. *Incivil y criminal: Quito como escenario de construcción estatal de la delincuencia entre los decenios 1960 y 1980*. Quito: Universidad Andina Simón Bolívar.

Aguirre Salas, Andrea, Typhaine Léon, and Nadia Soledad Ribadeneira González. 2020. Sistema Penitenciario y Población Penalizada Durante La Revolución Ciudadana (2007–2017). *URVIO - Revista Latinoamericana de Estudios de Seguridad* (27) (April): 94–110.

Aliverti, Ana, Carvalho Henrique, Anastasia Chamberlen, and Máximo Sozzo, eds. 2023. *Decolonizing the Criminal Question. Colonial Legacies, Contemporary Problems*. Oxford: Oxford University Press.

Bedford, Kate, and Silvana Tapia Tapia. 2021. Specialised (In)Security: Violence Against Women, Criminal Courts, and the Gendered Presence of the State in Ecuador. *Latin American Law Review* (7): 21–42.

Bracco Bruce, Lucia. 2022. *Prison in Peru. Ethnographic, Feminist and Decolonial Perspectives*. Cham: Springer.

Carrington, Kerry, Russell Hogg, and Máximo Sozzo. 2015. Southern Criminology. *The British Journal of Criminology* 56 (1): 1–20.

Carvalho, Henrique. 2022. Dangerous Patterns: Joint Enterprise and the Culture of Criminal Law. *Social & Legal Studies* (August). https://doi.org/10.1177/09646639221119351.

Coba Mejía, Lisset. 2015. *Sitiadas: la criminalización de las pobres en Ecuador*. Quito: Flacso Ecuador.

Community, Cradle. 2021. *Brick by Brick: How We Build a World Without Prisons*. Maidstone: Hajar Press.

Day, Aviah Sarah, and Shanice Octavia McBean. 2017. *Abolition Revolution*. Las Vegas: Pluto Press.

Douzinas, Costas. 2013. The Paradoxes of Human Rights. *Constellations* 20 (1): 51–67.

Dubber, Markus Dirk. 2008. Criminal Police and Criminal Law in the Rechtsstaat. In *Police and the Liberal State*, ed. Markus D. Dubber and Mariana Valverde, 92–109. Police and the Liberal State. Stanford, CA: Stanford University Press.

EEAS. 2021. Human Rights and Democracy at the Core of EU External Action. European Union External Action. https://www.eeas.europa.eu/eeas/human-rights-and-democracy-core-eu-external-action_en.

Engle, Karen. 2015. Anti-impunity and the Turn to Criminal Law in Human Rights. *Cornell Law Review* 100 (5): 1069.

Engle, Karen, Zinaida Miller, and D.M. Davis, eds. 2016. *Anti-impunity and the Human Rights Agenda*. Cambridge: Cambridge University Press.

Ferrajoli, Luigi. 2009. *Diritto e ragione. Teoria del garantismo penale*. Rome: Laterza.

French, Jan Hoffman. 2013. Rethinking Police Violence in Brazil: Unmasking the Public Secret of Race. *Latin American Politics and Society* 55 (4): 161–181.

Fulchiron, Amandine. 2017. Actoras de Cambio En Guatemala: Poner El Cuerpo y La Vida de Las Mujeres En El Centro de La Justicia. In *Género y Justicia Transicional. Movimientos de Mujeres Contra La Impunidad*, ed. Irantzu Mendia Azkue, Gloria Guzmán Orellana, and Iker Zirion Landaluze, 65–112. Spain: Universidad del País Vasco.

Fundación Aldea. 2022. Femicidios en Ecuador. Realidades ocultas, datos olvidados e invisibilizados. Fundación Aldea. https://nube.fundacionaldea.org/index.php/s/nBmMbDQdoM9JzLY/download.

Goodmark, Leigh. 2021. Gender-Based Violence, Law Reform, and the Criminalization of Survivors of Violence. *International Journal for Crime Justice and Social Democracy* 10 (4): 13–25.

Gotell, Lise. 2015. Reassessing the Place of Criminal Law Reform in the Struggle Against Sexual Violence. In *Rape Justice: Beyond the Criminal Law*, ed. Anastasia Powell, Nicola Henry, and Asher Flynn, 53–71. London: Palgrave Macmillan.

Halley, Janet, Prabha Kotiswaran, Hila Shamir, and Chantal Thomas. 2006. From the International to the Local in Feminist Legal Responses to Rape, Prostitution/Sex Work, and Sex Trafficking: Four Studies in Contemporary Governance Feminism. *Harvard Journal of Law & Gender* 29: 335–423.

Heim, Daniela. 2019. La estrategia punitiva ante las violaciones de los derechos humanos de las mujeres. El caso del femicidio. In *Feminismos y política criminal, una agenda feminista para la Justicia*, ed. Ileana Arduino, 51. Buenos Aires: INECIP.

Human Rights Watch. 2022. Ecuador: Gang Control of Prisons Enabled Massacres. Human Rights Watch, July 19. https://www.hrw.org/video-photos/interactive/2022/07/28/ecuador-gang-control-prisons-enabled-massacres.

INEC. 2019. Encuesta Nacional Sobre Relaciones Familiares y Violencia de Género Contra Las Mujeres - ENVIGMU. November. https://www.ecuadorencifras.gob.ec/documentos/web-inec/Estadisticas_Sociales/Violencia_de_genero_2019/Principales%20resultados%20ENVIGMU%202019.pdf.

Johnson, Holly. 2012. Limits of a Criminal Justice Response: Trends in Police and Court Processing of Sexual Assault. In *Sexual Assault in Canada: Law, Legal Practice and Women's Activism*, ed. Elizabeth A. Sheehy, 613–634. Ottawa: University of Ottawa Press.

Kapur, Ratna. 2018. *Gender, Alterity and Human Rights: Freedom in a Fishbowl*. Cheltenham: Edward Elgar.

Lamble, Sarah. 2011. Ten Reasons to Dismantle the Prison Industrial Complex Through Queer/Trans Analysis and Action. In *Captive Genders. Trans Embodiment and the Prison Industrial Complex*, ed. Eric A. Stanley and Nat Smith, 235–265. Oakland: AK Press.

Lamble, Sarah. 2013. Queer Necropolitics and the Expanding Carceral State: Interrogating Sexual Investments in Punishment. *Law and Critique* 24 (3): 229–253.

Lavrysen, Laurens, and Natasa Mavronicola, eds. 2020. *Coercive Human Rights: Positive Duties to Mobilise the Criminal Law Under the ECHR*. Oxford: Hart Publishing.

Litowitz, Douglas. 2000. Gramsci, Hegemony, and the Law. *Brigham Young University Law Review* 2000 (2): 515–552.

Lugones, María. 2007. Heterosexualism and the Colonial/Modern Gender System. *Hypatia* 22 (1): 186.

Maier, Shana L. 2008. 'I Have Heard Horrible Stories …': Rape Victim Advocates' Perceptions of the Revictimization of Rape Victims by the Police and Medical System. *Violence Against Women* 14 (7): 786–808.

Marcial Pérez, David. 2023. The Rampant Abuse in El Salvador's Prisons: 'They Beat Him to Death in the Cell and Dragged Him Out Like an Animal'. *El País*, March 26. https://english.elpais.com/international/2023-03-26/the-rampant-abuse-in-el-salvadors-prisons-they-beat-him-to-death-in-the-cell-and-dragged-him-out-like-an-animal.html.

Mavronicola, Natasa. 2015. Crime, Punishment and Article 3 ECHR: Puzzles and Prospects of Applying an Absolute Right in a Penal Context. *Human Rights Law Review* 15 (4): 721–743.

Moore, J.M. 2023. Abolition and (De)Colonization. Cutting the Criminal Question's Gordian Knot. In *Decolonizing the Criminal Question. Colonial*

Legacies, Contemporary Problems, ed. Ana Aliverti, Carvalho Henrique, Anastasia Chamberlen, and Máximo Sozzo, 37–52. Oxford: Oxford University Press.

Ní Aoláin, Fionnuala. 2014. Gendered Harms and Their Interface with International Criminal Law. *International Feminist Journal of Politics* 16 (4): 622–646.

OAS. 2001. Inter-American Democratic Charter. Organization of American States. http://www.oas.org/charter/docs/resolution1_en_p4.htm.

Orellana Matute, Pablo. 2021. Alternative Global Entanglements: 'Detachment from Knowledge' and the Limits of Decolonial Emancipation. *Millennium* 49 (3): 498–529.

Pérez, Moira, and Blas Radi. 2020. Gender Punitivism: Queer Perspectives on Identity Politics in Criminal Justice. *Criminology & Criminal Justice: The International Journal of Policy and Practice* 20 (5): 523–536.

Pinto, Mattia. 2022. Discursive Alignment of Trafficking, Rights and Crime Control. *International Journal of Law in Context* 19: 122–142.

Pinto, Mattia. 2023. Coercive Human Rights and the Forgotten History of the Council of Europe's *Report on Decriminalisation. The Modern Law Review* (February). https://doi.org/10.1111/1468-2230.12793.

Primicias. 2022. Casas de acogida hacen cuentas para operar con menos recursos públicos. Primicias, April 27. https://www.primicias.ec/noticias/sociedad/casas-acogida-mujeres-reduccion-presupuesto/.

Quijano, Aníbal. 2000. Colonialidad Del Poder y Clasificación Social. *Journal of World-Systems Research* XI (2): 342–386.

Richie, Beth E. 2012. *Arrested Justice: Black Women, Violence, and America's Prison Nation.* New York and London: New York University Press.

Rivera Cusicanqui, Silvia. 2010. The Notion of 'Rights' and the Paradoxes of Postcolonial Modernity: Indigenous Peoples and Women in Bolivia. *Qui Parle* 18 (2): 29–54.

Sattar, Adnan. 2019. *Criminal Punishment and Human Rights: Convenient Morality*, 1st ed. Abingdon: Routledge.

Schneider, Elizabeth M. 2000. *Battered Women and Feminist Lawmaking*. New Haven and London: Yale University Press.

Smart, Carol. 1989. *Feminism and the Power of Law*. London: Routledge.

Snider, Laureen. 1998. Towards Safer Societies: Punishment, Masculinities and Violence Against Women. *The British Journal of Criminology* 38 (1): 1–39.

Spade, Dean. 2020. *Mutual Aid: Building Solidarity During This Crisis (and the Next)*. London: Verso Books.

Sudbury, Julia. 2002. Celling Black Bodies: Black Women in the Global Prison Industrial Complex. *Feminist Review* 70 (1): 57–74.

Tapia Tapia, Silvana. 2016. Sumak Kawsay, Coloniality and the Criminalisation of Violence Against Women in Ecuador. *Feminist Theory* 17 (2): 141–156.

Tapia Tapia, Silvana. 2018. Feminism and Penal Expansion: The Role of Rights-Based Criminal Law in Post-neoliberal Ecuador. *Feminist Legal Studies* 26 (3): 285–306.

Tapia Tapia, Silvana. 2021. Beyond Carceral Expansion: Survivors' Experiences of Using Specialised Courts for Violence Against Women in Ecuador. *Social & Legal Studies* 30 (6): 848–868.

Tapia Tapia, Silvana. 2022a. *Feminism, Violence Against Women and Law Reform: Decolonial Lessons from Ecuador*. Social Justice. Abingdon: Routledge.

Tapia Tapia, Silvana. 2022b. "Extreme Violence, Prisons, and the Prospects of Anti-carceral Human Rights – Part 2." Birmingham Law School Research Blog, December 12. https://blog.bham.ac.uk/lawresearch/2022/12/extreme-violence-prisons-and-the-prospects-of-anti-carceral-human-rights-part-2/.

Tapia Tapia, Silvana. 2023. Human Rights Penality and Violence Against Women: The Coloniality of Disembodied Justice. *Law and Critique*. https://doi.org/10.1007/s10978-023-09355-4.

Tapia Tapia, Silvana, and Sebastián López Hidalgo. 2022. Colonialidades legales: la constitucionalización de la justicia indígena y la continuidad del discurso judicial hegemónico en Ecuador. *Revista Derecho del Estado* (52) (April): 299–331.

Taylor, Chloe. 2018. Anti-carceral Feminism and Sexual Assault—A Defense: A Critique of the Critique of the Critique of Carceral Feminism. *Social Philosophy Today* 34: 29–49.

UNIFEM. 2003. *Not a Minute More: Ending Violence Against Women*. New York: Kumarian Press.

Villagómez, Gayne. 2013. La Revolución Ciudadana y Las Demandas de Género. In *El Correísmo al Desnudo*, ed. Juan Cuvi, Decio Machado, Atawallpa Oviedo, and Natalia Sierra, First, 53–69. Quito: Montecristi Vive.

Wills, Joe. 2014. The World Turned Upside Down? Neo-liberalism, Socioeconomic Rights, and Hegemony. *Leiden Journal of International Law* 27 (1): 11–35.

8

Human Rights for Southern Criminology: Neoliberal Colonialism and Rights from Below

Pablo Ciocchini and Joe Greener

Introduction

Human rights have become the Western-centric vantage point for understanding global injustice and its possible countermeasures (Supiot 2003). Global political elites have mobilized human rights to legitimize or delegitimize Governments as well as justify military interventions (Asad 2000). Notwithstanding their spurious uses and manipulation, there is consensus on their emancipatory potential (Supiot 2003). Even when

P. Ciocchini (✉)
National Scientific and Technological Research Council, La Plata, Argentina
e-mail: plc@liverpool.ac.uk

Institute of Legal Culture, National University of La Plata, La Plata, Argentina

J. Greener
Department of Sociology, Social Policy and Criminology, University of Liverpool, Liverpool, England, UK
e-mail: jgreener@liverpool.ac.uk

L. Weber and M. Marmo (eds.), *A Research Agenda for a Human Rights Centred Criminology*, Palgrave Critical Studies in Human Rights and Criminology,
https://doi.org/10.1007/978-3-031-46289-4_8

they may be viewed as undergirding imperialist aspirations of powerful states, rights discourses and efforts are attempts at hegemony-making with the potential for those lower down the political hierarchy to demand elites hold true to the values they declare (Woodiwiss 2012). The two most essential values that contemporary human rights embody—the protection of individual freedom and the recognition that everyone is equally valuable (Benton 2006)—could arguably mitigate widespread violence at the hands of state power and corporations experienced in many societies in the Global South.

Despite their relevance, human rights approaches arguably convey depoliticized messaging which places the focus on the state, and particularly on its failure to prevent abuses, without foregrounding communities' role in ensuring the rights of its members or the different political and economic interests that are behind violence in peripheral regions. In this chapter we argue that Southern criminological approaches to human rights should place the structural conditions which shape abuses whilst seeking to offer a critically led analysis of the limitations and opportunities of the prevailing human rights corpus. This moves away from both the postcolonial school's (Connell 2007) and dominant Southern criminology (Carrington et al. 2016) concerns with seeing decolonization as primarily an epistemological project (Ciocchini and Greener 2021), contending that the inclusion of marginalized voices in knowledge creation and discourse, on its own, has far-reaching and radical potential. We suggest that connecting the socio-economic dynamics that result in barbarism sheds light on both the causes of human rights abuses but also highlights important omissions and preferences in the ascendant rights discourse. Our Southern criminological approach to studying and critiquing rights seeks to foreground the political and economic conditions which fashion rights and rights abuses in the Global South, identifying the connection between the structural violence experienced in societies and the contemporary unequal global capitalist order that perpetuates it (Ciocchini and Greener 2021, 2022; Dix-Carneiro and Kovak 2023). This requires identifying the role Western countries, multinational corporations (MNCs) and international financial institutions (IFIs), such as the International Monetary Fund (IMF) and the World Bank, play in implementing policies that produce mass poverty

(Hickel 2016; Patnaik and Patnaik 2021). It also analyses the dominant narratives which frame rights discussions, which seek to tell simple stories of mistreatment and its appropriate solutions. These discourses often perpetuate simplistic conceptualizations of savagery and victimhood (Mutua 2002), subverting from more politically charged action aimed at societal transformation.

In the following section, we examine the pitfalls of established human rights discourse practice, noting their frequent incapacity to account for the fact that the realization of rights is embedded within complex global politics and their tendency to attribute the causes of abuses to simplistically understood acts of 'savagery' (Mutua 2002). We advocate for a more politicized approach that acknowledges the economic and political circumstances that give rise to these abuses, rather than solely focusing on the prevention of harms. After our initial conceptual critique of legalisitic and liberal conceptions of human rights, we present two case studies which illustrate the need for more expansive notions of rights and their grounding in multifaceted relational strucutures. Firstly, we recount the arguments made in what is now a relatively large body of thought critiquing 'new abolitionist' activism and its claim that one of the primary, contemporary threats facing many in poorer countries is modern slavery (Brace and O'Connell Davidson 2018; O'Connell Davidson 2015). The endorsement of the Modern Slavery construction by Governments, Non-governmental organizations (NGOs) and even corporations reveals the pitfalls of delinking forms of unfreedom from their structural roots and viewing them in terms morally founded 'bad' acts. Secondly, we turn to examine the state-organized and sanctioned violence during the 'war on drugs' in the Philippines. Rather than being primarily rooted in institutional corruption or totalitarian rule, the emergence of Duterte's regime needs to be situated in complex politics of legitimacy-seeking and power consolidation amidst failing neoliberal development projects. Both discussions reveal that global unequal strucutures of wealth are central in shaping the capacities for individuals to live in safety from state or corporate violence or reside in contexts where they are empowered to exercise their capacities to freedom, eliding simple legalistic responses to abuses.

Human Rights: Abstract Idealizations and Concrete Possibilities

The dominant human corpus is a posser for various principles established in Western classical Enlightenment philosophy from the seventeenth and eighteenth centuries. There are, at essence, two main claims in such conceptions of rights. Firstly, the primary moral imperative is the freedom of the individual person and, secondly, that all individuals have inherent equal value, and are necessarily worthy of respectful treatment (Benton 2006). Following this, the necessary role of political systems is viewed to be clearing any potential hindrances to autonomous action. Each citizen's freedom and liberty, if they are to have their rights facilitated according to the Enlightenment account, rests on achieving a society where individuals are not permitted to impose harm on another person and securing and reproducing the field of autonomous action is held as the primary political philosophy. However, the historical victory for capitalism was that many of the principles of 'freedom', 'liberty' or 'equality', came to be accepted as the freedom and liberty to own property. As described by Marx (1843) in *On the Jewish* Question, the radical liberalism of universal freedom becomes a kind of egoistic individualism, legitimizing property relations, with liberty understood as simply the right to live in security to do what one wishes with the fruits of their labour. For Marx, market societies rest on a particular effacement of 'spiritual and material' (1843: N/A) questions and powers to direct the condition of life in the community from politics. The political sphere becomes separate to societal questions.

For Benton, 'radical sceptics' of rights reject individualism and instead emphasize collective collaboration in the capacity to set and accomplish life-objectives. Rights are collectively 'won'—they emerge from interdependencies and co-operative actions to create and defend social contexts where rights are possible. Or, as Benton puts it, personal autonomy is innately a social fact, as it 'is an achievement made possible only where the developing individual has the interpersonal, emotional-relational, cultural-linguistic, social structural and material-ecological conditions of life that sustain and favour it' (2006, p. 23).

This assertion of the imbrication between the social facts of a context and the tangible liveability of rights is where our thinking around developing Southern perspective in criminology lies: the challenge is that human rights, according to its dominant stated principles, is an abstract appeal to a universally enjoyed set of freedoms and protections which are not only clearly *absent* in every society, but also need to stretch far beyond those more easily codified through legal doctrines or statements of intent.

Mutua (2002) argues that inscribed within ascendent human rights discourse is the appeal to the rule of law as the primary guarantor of stability, which is not only Western-centric but depoliticizing as it foregrounds an abstracted and top-down approach to political change. The common practice is a Western-led imposition of a narrow set of reforms as the desired path on which all societies should advance towards freedom and security. The limited scope in which human rights corpus promotes openness regarding intensive discussion of what liberty, solidarity and even wealth looks like, undermines their political radicality.

Mutua sees contemporary human rights endeavours directed at Global South societies are often defined by 'savages-victims-saviours (SVS)' (2002, p. 10) metaphor, conveying a particular story about which actors are behind human suffering whilst also indicating the potential interventions for preventing and undoing brutalities. The *savage*, in the hegemonic human rights corpus, is the corrupted and evil state that is authoritarian and mindlessly punitive. Critically, the depiction focuses on illiberal and traditional culture, barbaric and outmoded, committed to various horrifying practices, such as child labour, female genital mutilation, forced marriage or fierce labour relations.

The *victim*, on the other hand, is often depicted as a defenceless and wretched figure, fundamentally innocent and lacking any agency to challenge and confront the savage forces baring down on them. This is a critical part of the problem with the SVS metaphor: the victim is not only wholly 'good' but additionally incapacitated to challenge inequity without the help of external human rights corpus. The *saviour* is the human rights corpus with the dominant players being the United Nations, International Non-Governmental Organizations

(INGOs), charitable organizations and the complex web of multinational Western-led organizations such as the World Health Organization, International Monetary Fund, International Labour Organization and too many others to mention. These, for Mutua, are vehicles for the true saviour which is a certain liberal conception of freedom, freedom from the 'state, tradition, and culture' (2002, p. 11). Ultimately, this is a Eurocentric and bourgeois conception of freedom, rather than a serious attempt to struggle with what collective emancipation might look like in diverse social contexts.

Mutua (2002) builds a critique of human rights practice as it is mobilized for understanding the nature of social problems and social justice in the Global South. The primary contention is that it casts differing actors as either civilized or uncivilized, reasserting a longstanding imperialist that Western intervention can be understood as cultural and economic cultivation. Human rights imagine a kind of one-size-fits-all approach: that liberal capitalism offers the single best model for development. Human rights language often appeals to certain doctrines, but often without further interrogation of what they mean on the ground or how they might be concretely fulfilled. Arguably there is a kind of top-downism, in that external INGOs, multinational organizations or foreign governments often produce dissections of the relevant human rights abuses and propose a series of 'policy solutions'. Issues of power, and in particular the inherent racialized inequality of the world system, where supply chain capitalism, dollar hegemony and military might are deployed to secure and reproduce imperialist flows of wealth, are largely excluded from prevelent human rights discourse.

In *Cosmopolitan Dystopia*, Phillip Cunliffe (2020) takes the critique of human rights even deeper by suggesting that it became a central pillar in a Western-led global politics of interventionism. Human rights activities, such as military intervention in the name of protecting populations from their own regimes, bringing war criminals to trial, setting standards of civil liberties, deploying sanctions against countries' Governments and shaping transnational security policy towards the elimination of supposed threats, were all embedded in the shift towards globalization. Such actions were implemented through legal and policy frameworks which sought to undermine the more radical potential of nationally based liberation struggles with its direct appeal to utopianism. Human rights, in practice, as Cunliffe argues, heralded a 'liberalism of fear' (2020, p. 7) where the limit of politics is the application of incremental and small transformations within existing and dominant notions of development. For these reasons, the image of cosmopolitanism in the human rights discourse becomes a conduit for de-politicization: all that can possibly be achieved are measures to mitigate or prevent humanitarian crises, politics which seek to seriously reshape societies at their core are off the table. Herein lies the dystopic nature of contemporary Western-led cosmopolitanism, as Cunliffe (2020) sees it: a system where consistent war and perpetual securitization is justified on the basis of a singular conception of liberalism rather than an embrace of self-determination.

Casting an eye at the dominant concerns of the major contemporary human rights institutions reveals some of these limitations. Dominant human rights organizations have a proclivity towards investigations and activist work on criminal justice matters and civil liberties, rather than focusing on grander appeals to universal liberty and wealth development. Scrutinizing Human Rights Watch's last few years of reports shows that the general trend is documenting cruelties and offering policy solutions to the various harms occurring in particular Global South locations. This includes, by way of example, reports of oppression of protestors in Cuba (Human Rights Watch 2022a); unlawful detention in Uganda (2022b); and the health crisis in prisons in Pakistan (2022c): all serious brutalities with rights' organizations engaging in important work to expose. Yet, what lacks from this analysis is an ability to join up these different cases with the global economic order. This reflects Russell Jacoby's (1999) writings on the cultural disavowal of universality in politics: there is a tendency towards analysing the locally situated and pluralism of particularity. A kind of 'case-by-case' analysis which never stretches towards universal depictions of global justice, either in terms of the diagnosis of the problem or the potentiality of democratic solutions.

What emerges from these critiques of the human rights corpus is a complex picture. Many scholars, note the importance of developing politics based on universal objectives and accept that human rights, even the most Western-centric versions, bring an appeal to totalized human emancipation. Nevertheless, we can see that in practice, there is often a diversion towards undermining universality through a focus on pluralistic and localized scrutiny of human rights abuses. Perhaps more importantly, there is sidestepping and undermining of self-determination. Human rights narratives and activities are largely Eurocentric in their institutionalized form, and fail to put global inequality centrally as a founding reason for the often deeply exploitative and impoverished life conditions in the Global South. The subsequent two discussions develop two analyses of human rights abuses with the intention of situating them outside the explanations of savagery and culture, grounding analysis in how shifting patterns of political and economic structures in the Global South shape the possibilities of victimhood and agency. The first section reveals how contemporary constructions of modern slavery, a now well institutionally accepted human rights abuse, mis-conceptualize the experiences and driving forces of working conditions in the Global South, in particular failing to foreground neoliberal globalization as a central force shaping working life in the Global South. After that we discuss Duterte's 'war on drugs', noting that it cannot be explained as totalitarian 'savagery'. The ascendency of Duterte and the politics of moralization arise in the context of failed development. More importantly, the 'savagery' narrative often deployed to understand the Philippine case erases the resistance movements against Duterte's power abuses.

'Modern Slavery' and Work in the Global South

There has been a widespread resurgence of slavery abolitionism—or 'New Abolitionism'—being led by a number of high-profile NGOs, including Anti-Slavery International, Walk Free and Free the Slaves. As Free the Slaves state, they are 'dedicated to alerting the world about slavery's global comeback and to catalyse a resurgence of the abolition movement' (Free the Slaves 2023, N/A). A core basis of these organizations is a claim that there has been a resurrection of slavery conditions on a global scale. Walk Free's (2016) research in putting together the

Global Slavery Index puts global slavery at 40.3 million, comprising of a number of categories including forced labour involving various means of coercion and deception such as labouring through debt bondage, forced marriage and human trafficking.

Brace and O'Connell Davidson (2018) note that in order to maintain the story of the resurgence of modern slavery and the justification for new abolitionism, it involves a complex and selective inclusion of certain forms of domination whilst excluding others. For instance, whilst state-organized forced labour in certain countries is counted as modern slavery (Venezuela and North Korea being notable examples), heavily coerced labour occurring in prisons in Western states is excluded. There is also a lack of specificity concerning what should be counted as modern slavery with a whole host of practices that are not necessarily easily conceptualized as slavery becomes subsumed within the category of 'modern slavery'. For instance, the mandate from the special Rapporteur on contemporary states that 'forms of slavery includes but is not limited to issues such as: traditional slavery, forced labour, debt bondage, serfdom, children working in slavery or slavery-like conditions, domestic servitude, sexual slavery, and servile forms of marriage' (The Office of the High Commissioner for Human Rights, 2023, N/A).

Following similar constructions as those stated by Mutua (2002), modern slavery's underlying causes are constructed as lying within 'savagery': backward cultures, predatory gangs and evil employers, limiting or altogether excluding discussion of the complex structural forces which shape coercion and freedom underpinning systems of oppression. No doubt the modern slavery discourse correctly notes the continued existence of severe repression, but whether they can be primarily explained with reference to a simplistic criminological construction of predatory practices is a different question. O'Connell Davidson (2006), to take one apposite example, argues that trafficking policies and policing practices reproduce a simplistic story of victimized women and girls, coercively moved across borders, and forced into sex work by transnational gangster organizations against their will. Looking at three brothels in London, O'Connell Davidson uncovers a considerable diversity of working conditions and employment relations defined by differing degrees of employer control over those selling sex. Many of those working in the establishment are not easily described as 'pure' victims, but rather have come to the sex industry due to a range of other constraints and difficulties. Many people across the Western world find themselves participating in sex work because it is one of the few available subsistence opportunities for those with restrictive immigration statuses. The same study also revealed that in the course of policing raids of prostitution establishments, authorities sought to distinguish between 'innocent victims' and 'guilty sex workers/illegal migrants' (O'Connell Davidson, 2006: 15), and therefore deterimining who was worthy of assistance and who should be deported or criminalized.

Okyere's (2019) account of child labour in artisanal mining in Ghana, again, reveals that trafficking and modern slavery discourses cannot account for complex socio-political dynamics which lead to engagement in extremely difficult forms of work. The reality is that artisanal mining comes to prominence in the course of corporate legitimacy-seeking as the direct result of land dispossession. The children in Okyere's study do not fit the bill of school drop-outs or coerced victims as specified in 'Child Slavery' narratives or the International Labour Organization's Worst Forms of Child Labour agenda. Children were consentingly participating in artisanal mining to help their family, access education and work towards future opportunities. Employment relations, as Okyere describes, was not one of conniving adults exploiting vulnerable minors, but rather the 'site was populated by adults and children collaborating in an attempt to scrape out a living on the margins of society in the face of mutual hardships arising locally from the loss of lands and nationally from decades of enforced austere socio-economic reforms' (2019, p. 243). There are, in fact, human rights approaches to child labour that recognize the economic violence imposed by global inequality, such as the African Movement of Working Children and Youth or Bhima Sangha in India (Van Daalen and Hanson 2016). These organizations arguably seek to empower children by recognizing their agency.

New abolitionism seeks to draw a tight distinction between those who can be considered as objects of victimhood, and identified within the slavery category, or freely and contractually consenting subjects. This ultimately obscures the fact that the structures of domination that define economic life arise from specific contextual social and political conditions; conditions which shape both the possibilities to exercise agency in pursuing life-objectives but also often push people to 'choose' to engage in harsh, degrading or stigmatizing work. Through certain constructions of modern slavery as the result of evil gangs and outmoded cultures, it obfuscates the critical function of state policies and their failure, international intervention and global inequality in shaping the forms of compulsion to engage in work and the types of prevailing labour relations.

Duterte's 'War on Drugs', the Ruins of Neoliberal Development and the Moralization of Poverty

The 'War on Drugs' in the Philippines conducted by state-sponsored forces has resulted in more than 12,000 deaths (Human Rights Watch 2020). Despite its manifest illegality, it was frequently lauded by former president Rodrigo Duterte in his public speeches (Curato 2017). Western states and NGOs, such as Amnesty International (2017) and Human Rights Watch (2020), were fast to condemn those atrocities. Furthermore, there was an attempt to prosecute Rodrigo Duterte before the International Criminal Court (Al Jazeera 2023). Nevertheless, Duterte ended his period in office with a high approval rating amongst the Filipino population and without any serious repercussions at the international level (Parrocha 2022). For all the evidence presented by local and international human rights NGOs and journalists, there have been only a few isolated legal cases against police officers involved in the killings (Reuters 2022).

The human rights activists' narrative on Duterte's war on drugs focused on raising awareness of the violence perpetrated by state forces (Human Rights Watch 2020; Amnesty International 2017). It sought to galvanize support amongst the international community to pressure the Filipino government. This approach reproduced colonial logics in which Filipinos were presented either as barbaric, with the state visualised as a vehicle for violence latent in the culture, or helpless victims. Meanwhile the international community was constructed as the champions of protection. In this account, state brutality, isolated from any other economic or political interest than Duterte's charismatic appeal, is essentialized as a local cultural trait that needs to be suppressed by replacing backward values with Western liberal ones.

Moving away from approaches that reproduce the idea of a 'barbaric' culture, a critical Southern criminological approach seeks to uncover the structures that fuels the violence experienced under the 'war on drugs' and the potential resistances of the Filipino people. Therefore, the analysis should start to identify how state-sponsored violence is related to the failure of the political elite to build hegemony. The failure to build hegemony can be traced back to monetary and structural adjustment economic policies implemented in the Philippines since the American colonial period, which continued after independence under IMF mediation (Thompson and Slayton 1985; Abocejo 2014; Lumba 2022). These policies were aimed at supporting the requirements of neo-colonial accumulation strategies, particularly to prevent excessive wage increases in the Global South (Patnaik and Patnaik 2021). Income deflation policies imposed the privatization of public services, removal of labour protections and severe cuts to the state's budget in the Philippines. Their impact is brutally manifested in the extreme social inequality that shapes urban life in Manila (Garrido 2019). Politically, these policies prevented the political elite from making meaningful concessions to the working class to gain their consent (Joseph 2002). Consequently, they hindered the development of a national political project by local elites, forcing them to resort to coercion to maintain social order and reinforcing their neo-colonial legitimacy dependence on the international community. Duterte and his campaign emerged amidst the ruins of structural adjustment policies. The campaign capitalized on the neoliberal morality promoted by World Bank policies in the Philippines, blaming the 'undisciplined' poor for the failure of development (Kusaka 2017). State violence mobilizes lower and middle-class frustrations against the most vulnerable sectors of society, undermining attempts to foster class solidarity. Therefore, the violence is not the result of a cultural trait or some backward traditions, but of the economic policies imposed by global and local elites. But, to dispel the 'savage-victims' colonial dichotomic labels, it is also important to recognize that the Filipino people did not accept passively such violence. Though there was a significant level of support for Duterte's unleashed violence, there were also groups in the community denouncing and resisting the campaign. Notably examples were Catholic activist (Willis 2019) and socialist political organizations such as *Laban ng Masa* (Struggle of the Masses) (Makalintal 2018) rallying against the campaign. This shows a much more complex social dynamics shaping the state-sponsored violence than the liberal human rights approaches. It is only in exposing the interests behind the state violence and the communities raising against it, that we could promote an empowering human rights approach.

Conclusion

The often-simplistic stories central to dominant human rights corpus and its orientation towards abstraction sets a major barrier to its own radical potential. Rather than locating political action with a bottom-up and lived political praxis, it suggests that the job of ensuring liberty and preventing harm can be left to aloof global institutions, legalistic codifications and NGOs. This elides the significant importance of the global and transnational currents which are always underneath many of the conditions of life in poorer societies. Arguably, the mainstream human rights corpus has remained insensitive to both this point, and the even broader point that rights are essentially a lived thing, materially founded in the institutions, economic opportunities and political systems that prevail within a given society (Benton 2006). What unites some of our critiques presented here is that human rights, in its dominant liberal formulation, can work to obscure the real political issues at the heart of harm, violence and criminality. As we suggested, human rights tend towards particularism in terms of identifying particular abuses and constructing them as relatively isolated phenomena. Through the discussion on new abolitionist constructions of 'modern slavery', we sought to demonstrate that brutalizing working conditions prevalent across the globe are imagined as outside the project of liberal capitalist development, when in truth they exist firmly inside. People who engage in these forms of work are often exercising agency, albeit in conditions of constraint and structurally founded limitations. In the Philippines, we showed that a political regime with a commitment to gross violations against its own population can be understood through failures to embed stable economic development. Morally based understandings for social disorder problems took hold in a context of ongoing impoverishment.

In many ways, the issue of human rights and its tensions and contradictions, reflect broader-based, foundational problems in thinking through the problems and opportunities of modernity. Todd McGowan characterizes modernity as the 'promise of universal emancipation' (2020, p. 1), where humanity has undergone a world historical questioning of any naturalistic justifications for inequity. The idea that some groups are innately deserving of greater levels of status and prestige has been radically brought into question. Yet, despite a historically widespread recognition that 'race', nation, sexuality, dis/ability or gender cannot offer justifiable grounds for constructing inequalities is a clear reality contrary to this. Some groups maintain greater sway over influencing the economy, social relations and even the dominant modes of interpretation just as it is central to capitalist modernity that many other communities are subject to economic insecurity, cultural marginalization and the threat of bodily harm.

Southern criminology is inevitably also a relatively insignificant player in terms of achieving greater realization of human rights. Nonetheless, there are a number of insights that can be garnered from the discussion in this chapter. Understanding the intrinsic connections between the structures of the global economy and its shaping of access to wealth and resources, such as jobs, freedoms, material goods and welfare, is the starting point for analysing people's experiences of crime and violence. The kinds of labour relations, decisions to engage in criminality and forms of crime control that communities are subjected to often have their foundations in failed development projects and unequal transnational economic processes. We traced the roots of Duterte's state-led war on drugs as rooted in the unfolding of failed development through IMF structural adjustment and the political void this left in the Philippines. We also critiqued the seemingly 'honest' human rights agenda being developed by the abolitionist movement against modern slavery and its failure to engage in the complexities of structure and agency regarding economic life in the Global South in particular. Both discussions also reveal problems with what Mutua (2002) describes as the 'savages-victims-saviours' allegory which drives much human rights practice.

References

Abocejo, Ferdinand T. 2014. The Impact of International Monetary Fund (IMF) Structural Adjustment Policies (SAP) on the Philippines. *Recoletos Multidisciplinary Research Journal* 2 (1). https://ejournals.ph/function/reader1/read2/web/reader.php?id=uploads%2Farchive%2FRMRJ%2FVol.+2+No.+1+%282014%29%2FArticles%2F03_Abocejo.pdf&di=9458. Accessed 26 June 2023.

Al Jazeera. 2023, January 27. ICC to Resume Investigation into Philippines's Deadly Drug War. https://www.aljazeera.com/news/2023/1/27/icc-to-resume-investigation-into-philippiness-deadly-drug-war. Accessed 26 June 2023.

Amnesty International. 2017, February 4. Philippines: Duterte's 'War on Drugs' is a War on the Poor. https://www.amnesty.org/en/latest/news/2017/02/war-on-drugs-war-on-poor/. Accessed 26 June 2023.

Asad, Talal. 2000. What Do Human Rights Do? An Anthropological Enquiry. *Theory & Event* 4 (4) https://www.muse.jhu.edu/article/32601.

Benton, Ted. 2006. 'Do We Need Rights? If So, What Sort?' In *Rights: Sociological Perspectives*, ed. L. Morris, 21–36. London: Routledge.

Brace, Laura, and Julia O'Connell. Davidson. 2018. Slavery and the Revival of Anti-slavery Activism. In *Revisiting Slavery and Antislavery: Toward a Critical Analysis*, ed. L. Brace and J. O'Connell Davidson, 3–34. Switzerland: Palgrave Macmillan.

Carrington, Kerry, Russell Hogg, and Máximo. Sozzo. 2016. Southern Criminology. *British Journal of Criminology* 56: 1–20.

Ciocchini, Pablo, and Joe Greener. 2021. Mapping the Pains of Neocolonialism: A Critical Elaboration of Southern Criminology. *British Journal of Criminology* 61 (6): 1612–1629.

Ciocchini, Pablo, and Joe Greener. 2022. Regimes of Extreme Permission in Southeast Asia: Theorizing State-Corporate Crime in the Global South. *British Journal of Criminology*. https://doi.org/10.1093/bjc/azac091.

Connell, Raewyn. 2007. *Southern Theory: The Global Dynamics of Knowledge in Social Science*.

Cunliffe, Phillip. 2020. *Cosmopolitan Dystopia: International Intervention and the Failure of the West*. Manchester: Manchester University Press.

Curato, Nicole. 2017. Politics of Anxiety, Politics of Hope: Penal Populism and Duterte's Rise to Power. *Journal of Current Southeast Asian Affairs* 35 (3): 69–89.

Dix-Carneiro, Rafael and Brian K. Kovak. 2023. *Globalization and Inequality in Latin America*. https://www.andrew.cmu.edu/user/bkovak/LACIR_globalization_Dix_Carneiro_Kovak.pdf Accessed 26 June 2023

Free the Slaves. 2023. About Us. https://freetheslaves.net/about-us/. Accessed 14 June 2022.

Garrido, Marco. 2019. *The Patchwork City: Class, Space, and Politics in Metro Manila*. Chicago: University of Chicago Press.

Hickel, Jason. 2016. The True Extent of Global Poverty and Hunger: Questioning the Good News Narrative of the Millennium Development Goals. *Third World Quarterly* 37 (5): 749–767. https://doi.org/10.1080/01436597.2015.1109439.

Human Rights Watch. 2020. *World Report*, "Philippines." www.hrw.org/world-report/2018/country-chapters/Philippines. Accessed 26 June 2023.

Human Rights Watch. 2022a. Prison or Exile Cuba's Systematic Repression of July 2021 Demonstrators. https://www.hrw.org/report/2022/07/11/prison-or-exile/cubas-systematic-repression-july-2021-demonstrators. Accessed 26 June 2023.

Human Rights Watch. 2022b. "I Only Need Justice" Unlawful Detention and Abuse in Unauthorized Places of Detention in Uganda. https://www.hrw.org/report/2022/03/22/i-only-need-justice/unlawful-detention-and-abuse-unauthorized-places-detention. Accessed 26 June 2023.

Human Rights Watch. 2022c. "A Nightmare for Everyone" The Health Crisis in Pakistan's Prisons. https://www.hrw.org/report/2023/03/29/nightmare-everyone/health-crisis-pakistans-prisons. Accessed 26 June 2023.

Jacoby, Russell. 1999. *The End of Utopia: Politics and Culture in an Age of Apathy*. New York: Basic Books.

Joseph, Jonathan. 2002. *Hegemony: A Realist Analysis*. Routledge.

Kusaka, Wataru. 2017. *Moral Politics in the Philippines: Inequality, Democracy and the Urban Poor*. Singapore: National University of Singapore Press.

Lumba, Allan E.S.. 2022. *Monetary Authorities: Capitalism and Decolonization in the American Colonial Philippines*. Durham: Duke University Press.

Makalintal, Joshua. 2018. The Challenges of Building a United Resistance in Duterte's Philippines. *Waging Nonviolence*. https://wagingnonviolence.org/2018/03/united-resistance-duterte-philippines/ Accessed 26 June 2023.

Marx, Karl. 1843. *On The Jewish Question*. https://www.marxists.org/archive/marx/works/1844/jewish-question/

McGowan, Todd. 2020. *Universality and Identity Politics*. New York: Columbia University Press.

Mutua, Makau. 2002. *Human Rights: A Political and Cultural Critique*. Philadelphia: University of Pennsylvania Press.

O'Connell Davidson, Julia. 2006. Will the Real Sex Slave Please Stand Up? *Feminist Review* 83: 4–22.

O'Connell Davidson, J. 2015. *Modern Slavery*. London: Palgrave.

Okyere, Samuel. 2019. Moral Economies and Child Labour in Artisanal Gold Mining in Ghana. In *Revisiting Slavery and Antislavery: Toward a Critical Analysis*, ed. L. Brace and J. O'Connell Davidson, 231–262. Switzerland: Palgrave Macmillan.

Parrocha, Azer. 2022. Duterte's end of term high rating 'rarity' in PH pres'l politics, *Philippine News Agency*. https://www.pna.gov.ph/articles/1172012. Accessed 26 June 2023.

Patnaik, Utsa and Prabhat Patnaik. 2021. *Capital and Imperialism*: Monthly Review Press.

Reuters. 2022. Philippines Court Delivers Rare Conviction of Police Officer for Drugs War Violations. https://www.reuters.com/world/asia-pacific/philippines-court-delivers-rare-conviction-police-officer-drugs-war-violations-2022-11-24/. Accessed 24 November 2022.

Supiot, Alain. 2003. The Labyrinth of Human Rights: Credo or Common Resource? *New Left Review* 21: 118–136.

Thompson, Mark, and Gregory W. Slayton. 1985. An Essay on Credit Arrangements Between the IMF and the Republic of the Philippines: 1970–1983. *Philippines Review of Economics and Business* 21 (1–2): 59–91.

Van Daalen, Edward and Karl Hanson. 2016. Can Campaigns to Stop Child Labour be Stopped? https://www.opendemocracy.net/en/beyond-trafficking-and-slavery/can-campaigns-to-stop-child-labour-be-stopped/. Accessed 26 June 2023.

Walk Free. 2023. Global Slavery Index. https://www.walkfree.org/global-slavery-index/. Accessed 14 June 2022.

Willis, Adam. 2019. The Catholic Rebels Resisting the Philippines' Deadly War on Drugs. *The Guardian*. https://www.theguardian.com/world/2019/jul/18/philippines-rodrigo-duterte-war-on-drugs-catholic-church. Accessed 26 June 2023.

Woodiwiss, Anthony. 2012. *Asia, Enforceable Benevolence and the Future of Human Rights, Sociology*.

The Office of the High Commissioner for Human Rights. 2023. Special Rapporteur on Contemporary Forms of Slavery. https://www.ohchr.org/en/special-procedures/sr-slavery. Accessed 14 June 2022.

9

Actioning the Human Rights Agenda and Issues of Access to Justice

Danielle Watson, Julie Berg, and Lamese Laponi

Introduction

The Universal Declaration of Human Rights, proclaimed by the United Nations General Assembly in Paris on 10 December 1948, identifies 'access to justice' as a fundamental human right. Though it has been almost 85 years since the establishment of 'access to justice' discourses (Galanter 2010) and its prominence as a global priority (Watson and Berg 2022), existing definitions and understandings of access to justice

D. Watson (✉)
School of Justice, Queensland University of Technology, Brisbane, Australia
e-mail: danielle.watson@qut.edu.au

J. Berg
School of Social and Political Sciences, University of Glasgow, Glasgow, Scotland, UK
e-mail: Julie.Berg@glasgow.ac.uk

L. Laponi
Tuvalu Police Service, Funafuti, Tuvalu

L. Weber and M. Marmo (eds.), *A Research Agenda for a Human Rights Centred Criminology*, Palgrave Critical Studies in Human Rights and Criminology,
https://doi.org/10.1007/978-3-031-46289-4_9

continue to be limited and exclusionary, in that they either fail or struggle to capture justice mechanisms beyond the scope of Western systems or those grounded in indigenous ideologies primarily present in Global South contexts. Mainstream descriptions, though significantly expanded to include nongovernmental justice mechanisms, retain elements of earlier references to accessing state judicial institutions recognised within Western governance frameworks and legislature adopted, adapted or imposed in non-Western contexts (Farrow 2013). Such proliferation of legalistic inscriptions in access to justice discourses creates a neat, convenient and narrowed lens with which to view and interpret what justice looks like, while also creating recommendations about what needs to be rectified to action the prescribed justice agenda.

When we examine issues of access to justice against a human rights agenda backdrop, individual versus community justice, state versus non-state justice mechanisms and mainstream versus marginalised perspectives on access, justice and access to justice (among others) add further descriptive complexities to be navigated. If we also consider resolution practices such as those preferred in rural or remote non-Western contexts, which challenge predominant justice narratives that acknowledge and situate courts and judicial systems at the forefront of resolving matters, we are exposed to ideas which prompt us to reconsider how we perceive justice and consider alternatives to one-size-fits-all ideas about not only how we think about access to justice but also the applicability of the human rights agenda to contexts outside of its general design and conceptualisation. Discourses premised on a notion of quality legal assistance continue to be problematic, especially in instances where justice mechanisms do not conform to Western standards of operation or take place outside of established state models. In contexts where what it means to access justice does not align with a foreign prescribed formula, a common practice has been to seek to 'remodel' the existing system to allow for international uniformity, as opposed to an expansion of our understanding of such systems as alternative models to be considered in the development of universal discourses. The forms in which this 'remodelling' may take place could include for instance, state-building endeavours (usually donor-funded) whereby state infrastructure is developed for the purposes of replacing existing systems. It may also include a subsuming or merging of traditional or non-state systems into state-centric systems, and/or the extraction of ideological aspects of the non-state into state systems, such that these become appendages to the state infrastructure (such as diversion or restorative justice programmes within the courts for instance). Very often this remodelling leaves a tangible gap in justice provision in terms of the transition to newly formed state systems which may be problematic in terms of, among other things, not being seen as a legitimate avenue for those seeking justice (Schärf and Nina 2001).

Accessing justice in many contexts is more complex than drawing on a universal playbook to select from a list of legally actionable and practical options. Here we draw reference to accessing justice in non-Western contexts to show the limits of the human rights agenda in the face of indigenous ideologies. We position consciousness and mobilisations as critical to an understanding of the sphere within which justice is practised and accessed. We expand on access to justice discourses by unpacking contextual realities that go beyond discussions about access to state institutions and understandings bound by non-contextualised statutory frameworks. Non-Western contexts are referenced to highlight the criticality of understanding the nature of non-state regimes and how they interface with state regimes, recognising and understanding non-state forms of justice as critical to an understanding of how justice is accessed, and rethinking conceptualisations of access to justice.

Rethinking Understandings of 'Access' and 'Justice'

Non-Western contexts bring to the forefront gaps in conceptualisations of access and justice. 'Access' in mainstream discourses makes mention of an aggrieved or victim of an act legislated as criminal in nature. 'Justice' in such instances relates specifically to the course of action taken to remedy or respond to the wrong done to the aggrieved. Such an understanding is individualistic and premised on notions of individual guilt and punishment. While such understandings are articulated in the legislation of most colonised countries, there are instances where no action by the state or an action contrary to upholding an individual's human rights are deemed the most appropriate option and deemed depictive of justice in action (see Howes et al. 2021). For example, an individual being exiled from their home in a rural outlying South Pacific Island because of their religious choices or a victim of domestic violence being silenced because of the impact of the possible legal outcome on the family or community, provides insight into who is recognised as the victim, who is worthy of justice and how what justice looks like is impacted by context. Such examples also raise questions about what circumstances, actions or inactions represent justice in action.

Unlike formalistic general indicators of justice tied to notions of just distribution as outlined in state laws and specific to an individual or group action legislated as a societal manifestation of dysfunction, justice as enforced by non-state actors in Western contexts is often viewed as illegitimate, frowned upon or loosely described as vigilantism and unsanctioned acts which violate human rights—specifically the right to state justice. Examples of such actions may include a woman being forced to marry someone who violates her in an attempt to restore her family honour, thus making 'just' amends for the wrong committed in the eyes of the community, or individuals kneeling in front the homes of persons they may have wronged and subjecting themselves to public beatings as a form justice. Other examples of cultural apologies, deemed cruel and inhumane by Western standards, can be found across the globe. In the absence of documentation regularising justice mechanisms that run parallel to state arms, the most accessible forms of justice are likely to be unrecognised or negatively categorised, co-opted or poorly understood because of their failure to adhere to 'universal descriptors' (Cappelletti 1993). There is also the perception that in the absence of regulations, there is a likelihood of differing justice outcomes based on the whims of local decision makers or powerful stakeholders. What it means to access justice in many non-Western contexts require an understanding of different variables—status, age, gender hierarchies, social expectations and operational patriarchal systems. This is to account for indirect access where persons require representation based on, for instance, their gender (see Watson et al. 2021). Therefore, in contexts where women are forbidden from entering spaces designated to making justice decisions for example, the power of representation and decisions about resolution is shifted away from an aggrieved female to a representative male. Also, police officers' absence or involvement in the actioning of non-state justice agendas raises questions about the contextual applicability of an imposed agenda and the possible impact of its actioning at the community level.

It is also necessary to consider how the challenges impacting access to state mechanisms or the perceived legitimacy of such systems impede if, how and for what purposes they are accessed. State and formal ordering systems tend to be well established in urban areas but less visible and accessible further away from central business districts. In multi-island jurisdictions or jurisdictions with large landmasses and rural settlements with limited state capabilities to provide access to justice mechanisms, accessing justice services is as difficult as it is costly (Sloan et al. 2021). Despite variances in form and effectiveness, informal community-based approaches to justice tend to be largely relied upon in the absence of alternatives. Perspectives on the desirability of state justice mechanisms in rural areas tend to diverge with powerful local stakeholders describing them as undesired and foreign while members of marginalised groups welcome ease of access to state justice mechanisms (Ahmad and Von Wangenheim 2021; Nandan 2020). Two issues are highlighted here: non-state mechanisms tend to be accessible and accessed in the absence of state justice mechanisms; however, accessing such mechanisms are in no way indicative of non-desire to access unavailable state justice mechanisms.

Re-imagining and Re-conceptualising Access to Justice

As mentioned, access to justice may not entail a one-size-fits-all approach given the contextual realities of formalised local systems. Yet, it has long been recognised that the developmental agenda is underscored by donors' ideological and political commitment to state-building (Baker 2010). For instance, consider Sustainable Development Goal 16, drawn from the United Nations 2030 Agenda for Sustainable Development and adopted by all UN member states in 2015 as the blueprint for peace and prosperity of all peoples, focused on promoting peaceful and inclusive societies which emphasises a rule of law approach (16.3) and a commitment to 'effective, accountable and transparent institutions' (16.6). This normative focus already precludes attention to non-institutional—but necessarily important—means of accessing justice in non-Western contexts.

There is also a tendency, as mentioned, to pathologise the non-state and plural systems (Berg and Shearing 2020). Yet it has long been shown within criminology that the sovereign state is a myth and the criminal justice system is itself a flawed system of justice (Garland 1996). Consider the long-standing evidence within criminological engagement of the failure of imprisonment, the defunding of police movements taking place across the globe, and the recognition of the harmful effects of the use and over-use of criminalised solutions to dealing with all manner of human deviance (Clear 2007; Haugh 2015).

The colonial roots of the criminal justice system in settler colonies have also been the subject of much attention, particularly its hegemonic nature, and its tendency to disproportionally criminalise certain racial and/or socio-economically disadvantaged groups causing more harm than good (Clear 2007; Kitossa 2020). Despite this, there remains a commitment to normatively equate state systems, especially policing, with 'the public good', yet—again—evidence suggests that in the right circumstances, non-state policing entities may be better at providing for the good of the public than the state (see Berg and Shearing 2018). The same is true for non-state justice systems, it has been shown in criminology that it is not necessarily the case that they will undermine human rights (see, for instance, Blagg 2016 and Froestad and Shearing 2007) and if they do, this should be considered within the broad continuum of justice responses to harm.

To reimagine and re-conceptualise access to justice and so too a human rights agenda, it is necessary to recognise the informality, plurality and hybridity of current justice mechanisms; to decolonise 'access to justice' and 'human rights'; and to rethink issues of 'reform'.

The Way Forward...

Recognising Informality, Plurality and Hybridity of Justice Mechanisms—A first step in engaging with access to justice and the human rights agenda is to identify and acknowledge *all* justice mechanisms operational within local contexts. It is to recognise the informality, plurality and hybridity of both state and non-state entities. This is not to say that these features have not been recognised already, particularly within the scholarship on non-state security and justice systems. For instance, it has long been recognised, empirically, that plurality in governance systems is a given—both within and outside of the state and within policing, security and justice arrangements (see Baker and Scheye 2007). There is a normative component to this, in terms of the argument that plural systems may be better suited to engage with the complex nature of old and new harms (see Berg and Shearing 2020). 'Informal' systems of ordering, too, have been recognised and researched within scholarship and policy circles (see Wojkowska 2006). So too has it been acknowledged that there may not be a distinction between 'state' and 'non-state', 'public' and 'private', 'formal' and 'informal' and the tendency to dichotomise them suffers from the same Western-centric normative tendencies outlined above (Abrahamsen and Williams 2008). More recent scholarship within security and justice circles has placed value on the acknowledgement of hybrid systems of governance to describe the complexity of governance arrangements in global and local settings and especially in situations where state systems are limited and where authority may come from various sources (Albrecht and Moe 2015; Luckham and Kirk 2012). Hybridity may mean one of two things: it may refer to a mix of state and non-state security and justice *services* that are provided or a complete *integration* of the state and non-state—not just a grafting or a co-operation, but a merging (Albrecht and Moe 2015; Luckham and Kirk 2012).

The challenge then is to engage with the 'messiness' of justice, in that systems of justice may be a fusion of state and non-state, formal and informal and constitute hybridised and pluralised systems. There may also be a continuum of policing and justice practices performed by the same entities—it is not always the case that policing and justice will be distinct or feature distinct institutions. However, there is a tendency within criminology to revert to dichotomised engagement with policing and justice systems and to neaten the messiness. Therefore, for instance, policing scholarship has focused much attention on how state and non-state entities network and how to improve their interlinkages and partnering (Baker 2010). The challenge has been to ensure that state and non-state partnerships or networks are aligned to democratic principles, good governance and/or the human rights agenda. However, this does not fully engage with issues of hybridity, informality, how state and non-state entities may coalesce, how local justice systems evolve over time and how tradition impacts on justice narratives. The challenge then is to empirically engage with the nature and extent of 'justice' in contexts of plurality and hybridity, and to withhold a normative starting point. This also requires a rethink of what constitutes 'justice' and whether or how human rights can be considered in complex systems—essentially what is needed is a decolonised starting point.

Decolonising 'Access to Justice' and 'Human Rights'—Criminology's past and present 'is deeply entangled with Western-centric and Northern ways of thinking' (Berg and Shearing 2021, p. 23) and has been accused of being complicit in perpetuating (neo)colonial, authoritarian and 'racist statecraft' in light of the failings of the criminal justice system and criminology's alignment to that system (Agozino 2019; Kitossa 2020, p. 9). Yet there have been several shifts within criminology to 'decouple criminological thinking and practice from its Western-centric conceptual roots' (Berg and Shearing 2021, p. 24; Watson and Kerrigan 2018) through decolonisation and engaging with indigenous systems of ordering, for instance.

Access to justice and the human rights agenda fits squarely within that decoupling process. Part of the process of decolonising is the establishment of platforms for reorientation towards change discourses or adaptations to reflect what is deemed appropriate for context. For instance, conceptualisations of 'human rights' and 'justice' have been critically reconsidered in non-Western contexts. Human rights has been described as a 'social imaginary' as an enactment, not just a legal or political doctrine, but it is a highly contested term as it is largely imagined in an individualistic way (Buur 2008, p. 571). This may go against communal and group-based approaches to dealing with harms and subsequent collective understandings of justice, summed up in the abstract notion of 'Ubuntu'. Ubuntu has been described in several ways but in relation to justice, it can be defined as a communalistic 'goal of justice as the restoration of victims of crime, the offenders, and the community as much as humanely possible' (Elechi 2020, p. 32) with the acknowledgement that an individual's suffering affects the whole community and where 'an individual has meaning and significance only in relation with others' (Elechi et al. 2010, p. 81). In other words, this approach does not necessarily buy into the individualistic, 'governing through crime' (Simon 2007), and static victim-offender dyad epitomised by the criminal justice system yet may be more attuned to human rights principles of dignity, harm reduction and access than criminal justice responses. This is to acknowledge the paradox of applying a human rights approach—on the one hand recognising its colonial underpinnings and Western origins, but on the other its potential value in setting a framework for access to justice; a suggested way forward is to 'reclaim them critically' (Barreto 2018, p. 486). Shifting discourses could both entail the acknowledgement of the dimensions of local justice mechanisms that come into conflict with the human rights agenda and a rearticulation of how human rights can have relevance in local, community-led or driven contexts.

Rethinking the Criminological Approach—A criminological approach which is criminal justice-centric and one which relies 'too heavily on Western theorizing' (Cunneen and Tauri 2019, p. 359) is not going to be able to engage with the contextual realities of justice and human rights in non-Western contexts where informal, hybrid systems may be the norm and where state justice systems may be inaccessible, ineffective and/or harmful. At the very least, conceptual tools of engagement need to be adapted, as outlined above, at the most, there needs to be an expansion and regularisation of non-state mechanisms. Methodologically too, a criminological approach benefitting a user-perspective and engaging with those affected the most by issues of access to justice will allow for a contextually relevant approach (Cunneen and Tauri 2019). However, there are already-existing frameworks that could be explored that may align with the issues outlined above. For instance, one approach is that of transformative justice which is most applicable to transitional or developing contexts and where the emphasis is on localism, addressing power inequalities and exclusion. In other words, it considers power relations and aims to address broader structural issues of discrimination and inequality, for instance, that impact marginalised and vulnerable communities (Gready and Robins). It also emphasises a 'shift in focus from the legal to the social and political, and from the state and institutions to communities and everyday concerns' (Gready and Robins 2014, p. 340). Overall, it could be a way in which to rearticulate the conditions of access to and of justice in unequal contexts and is in line with a broader call for reparative justice (as opposed to punitive, criminal justice) which too acknowledges the problem of power inequalities and the need to undo harm rather than punish offenders, in line with a communal approach to justice (Agozino 2021).

The actioning of the human rights agenda in non-Western contexts therefore requires purposeful reimagining, reframing and/or expansion of understandings and models of access to justice. Such a de-Westernising necessitates not only a rethinking within conventional criminological engagement but also a re-education of stakeholders from the Global North, and a true commitment to understanding justice mechanisms operational in non-Western contexts.

The challenge is also a political one, as articulated well by Baker (2010, p. 608) in describing situations of reform:

> Links with non-state actors will rarely be seen by governments as a perfect solution. State monopoly of provision offers an easier route to centralised control, co-ordination and service equality. It removes the necessity for the messy politics of dealing with many diverse and informal groups and determining just who is 'acceptable'.

The 'messiness' of governance practices on the ground is a real obstacle to both politically engaging with them and moral decisions about 'acceptability' in terms of ordering, usually informed by a human rights framework and Western-centric assumptions of value. Therefore, a reframing should not and cannot be informed by a regularisation agenda, but instead a commitment to rearticulating conditions of access to justice and establishing a platform for reorientation towards change discourses.

References

Abrahamsen, Rita, and Michael C. Williams. 2008. Public/Private, Global/Local: The Changing Contours of Africa's Security Governance. *Review of African Political Economy* 35 (118): 539–553.

Agozino, Biko. 2019. Humanifesto of the Decolonization of Criminology and Justice. *Decolonization of Criminology and Justice* 1 (1): 5–28.

Agozino, Biko. 2021. Reparative Justice: The Final Stage of Decolonization. *Punishment and Society* 23 (5): 613–630.

Ahmad, Jawad, and Georg Von Wangenheim. 2021. Access to Justice: An Evaluation of the Informal Justice Systems. *Liberal Arts and Social Sciences International Journal (LASSIJ)* 5 (1): 228–244.

Albrecht, Peter, and Louise Wiuff Moe. 2015. The Simultaneity of Authority in Hybrid Orders. *Peacebuilding* 3 (1): 1–16.

Baker, Bruce. 2010. Linking State and Non-state Security and Justice. *Development Policy Review* 28 (5): 597–616.

Barreto, Jose-Manuel. 2018. Decolonial Thinking and the Quest for Decolonising Human Rights. *Asian Journal of Social Science* 46: 484–502.

Berg, Julie, and Clifford Shearing. 2018. Governing-through-Harm and Public Goods Policing. *The Annals of the American Academy of Political and Social Sciences* 679 (1): 72–85.

Berg, Julie, and Clifford Shearing. 2020. Polycentric Security Governance and Sustainable Development in the Global South. In *The Emerald Handbook of Crime, Justice and Sustainable Development*, ed. J. Blaustein, K. Fitz-Gibbon, N. Pino, and R. White, 153–173. Bingley: Emerald Publishing Limited. ISBN 9781787693562. https://doi.org/10.1108/978-1-78769-355-520201011.

Berg, Julie, and Clifford Shearing. 2021. Criminology: Some Lines of Flight. *Journal of Criminology* 54 (1): 21–33.

Blagg, Harry. 2016. *Crime, Aboriginality and the Decolonisation of Justice*, 2nd ed. Sydney: Federation Press.

Baker, Bruce, and Eric Scheye. 2007. Multi-layered Justice and Security Delivery in Post-conflict and Fragile States. *Conflict, Security & Development* 7 (4): 503–528. https://doi.org/10.1080/14678800701692944.

Buur, Lars. 2008. Democracy & its Discontents: Vigilantism, Sovereignty & Human Rights in South Africa. *Review of African Political Economy* 35 (118): 571–584. https://doi.org/10.1080/03056240802569250

Cappelletti, Mauro. 1993. Alternative Dispute Resolution Processes Within the Framework of the World-wide Access-to-justice Movement. *The Modern Law Review* 56 (3): 282–296.

Clear, Todd. 2007. *Imprisoning Communities: How Mass Incarceration Makes Disadvantaged Neighborhoods Worse*. London: Oxford University Press.

Cunneen, Chris, and Juan Tauri. 2019. Indigenous Peoples, Criminology, and Criminal Justice. *Annual Review of Criminology* 2: 359–381.

Elechi, Oko O. 2020. *Mbari and Ubuntu in Indigenous Africana Criminologies from:* In *The Routledge Handbook on Africana Criminologies*, ed. B. Agozino, V. Saleh-Hanna, E. Onyeozili and N. P. Dastile, 32–40. Abingdon: Routledge.

Elechi, Oko O., Sherill Morris, and Edward Schauer. 2010. Restoring Justice (Ubuntu): An African Perspective. *International Criminal Justice Review* 20 (1): 73–85.

Farrow, Trevor. 2013. What is Access to Justice. *Osgoode Hall Law Journal* 51: 957.

Froestad, Jan, and Clifford Shearing. 2007. The Zwelethemba Model: Practicing Human Rights Through Dispute Resolution. In *Crime and Human Rights*, ed. S. Parmentier and E. Weitekamp, 193–214. Oxford: Elsevier.

Galanter, Marc. 2010. Access to Justice in a World of Expanding Social Capability. *Fordham Urban Law Journal* 37: 115.

Garland, David. 1996. The Limits of the Sovereign State: Strategies of Crime Control in Contemporary Society. *British Journal of Criminology* 36 (4): 445–471.

Gready, Paul, and Simon Robins. 2014. From Transitional to Transformative Justice: A New Agenda for Practice. *The International Journal of Transitional Justice* 8: 339–361.

Haugh, Todd. 2015. Overcriminalization's New Harm Paradigm. *Vanderbilt Law Review* 68 (5): 1191–1241.

Howes, Loene, Danielle Watson, and Lyndsay Newett. 2021. Police as Knowledge Brokers and Keepers of the Peace: Perceptions of Community Policing in Tuvalu. *Police Practice and Research* 22 (1): 745–762.

Kitossa, Tamari. 2020. Authoritarian Criminology and Racist Statecraft: Rationalizations for Racial Profiling, Carding and Legibilizing the Herd. *Decolonization of Criminology and Justice* 2 (1): 5–36.

Luckham, Robin and Thomas Kirk. 2012. Security in Hybrid Political Contexts: An End-user Approach (Justice & Security Research Programme Paper 2). London: Justice & Security Research Programme. https://eprints.lse.ac.uk/56358/1/JSRP_Paper2_Security_in_hybrid_political_contexts_Luckham_Kirk_2012.pdf. Accessed 24 April 2023.

Nandan, Tanvee. 2020. An Examination of the Effect of Informal Justice Systems Upon Women. *Journal of Indian Law and Society* 11: 88.

Schärf, Wilfried, and Daniel Nina. Eds. 2001. *The Other Law: Non-state Ordering in South Africa*. Juta.

Simon, Jonathan. 2007. *Governing Through Crime: How the War on Crime Transformed American Democracy and Created a Culture of Fear*. London: Oxford University Press.

Sloan, Tom, Sinclair Dinnen, and Mark Rowe. 2021. Access to Justice in Post-RAMSI Solomon Islands Part 2: Perceptions of Access to Justice.

Watson, Danielle, and Julie Berg. 2022. It's Time to Move Beyond a Western Understanding of Development: Are We Missing the Forest and the Trees?. In *Policy Forum*. Asia and the Pacific Policy Society (APPS). https://pacificsecurity.net/its-time-to-move-beyond-a-western-understanding-of-development/. Accessed 24 April 2023.

Watson, Danielle, and Dylan Kerrigan. 2018. Crime, Criminality, and North-to-South Criminological Complexities: Theoretical Implications for Policing 'Hotspot' Communities in 'Underdeveloped' Countries. *The Palgrave Handbook of Criminology and the Global South*, 611–632.

Watson, Danielle, Francis Boateng, and Toby Miles-Johnson. 2021. Legitimizing Policing Practices: A Study of Stakeholder Perceptions of Police Trustworthiness, Effectiveness and Relationship with the Community. *Police Practice and Research* 22 (1): 623–639.

Wojkowska, Ewa. 2006. Doing Justice: How Informal Justice Systems Can Contribute. UN Development Programme. *Oslo Governance Centre Report*. http://www.albacharia.ma/xmlui/bitstream/handle/123456789/30535/0280Doing_Justice__How_informal_justice_systems_can_contribute_(2007)7.pdf?sequence=1. Accessed 26 April 2023.

10

Developing a Kaupapa Māori Rights-Focused Research Agenda

Stella Black, David Burnside, Jessica Hastings, and Katey Thom

Positioning Ourselves as Contributors to This Book

We do not consider ourselves experts in domestic or international human rights, nor was our methodology initially driven by relevant United Nations Conventions or Declarations. Our project emerged from a collective sense of urgency that there was little appropriate system

S. Black (✉) · D. Burnside · J. Hastings · K. Thom
Auckland University of Technology, Auckland, New Zealand
e-mail: stella.black@aut.ac.nz

D. Burnside
e-mail: daveb@odyssey.org.nz

J. Hastings
e-mail: jessica.hastings@aut.ac.nz

K. Thom
e-mail: katey.thom@aut.ac.nz

L. Weber and M. Marmo (eds.), *A Research Agenda for a Human Rights Centred Criminology*, Palgrave Critical Studies in Human Rights and Criminology,
https://doi.org/10.1007/978-3-031-46289-4_10

response to the high incidence of mental distress and addiction experienced by people involved with the criminal justice system. This is highly represented within Māori in Aotearoa, replicating the challenges of other indigenous populations where basic human rights are denied through lack of access, participation, equity, and self-determination in devising solutions. We were committed to approaching our inquiry with an understanding of the colonised history of Māori cognisant of the impacts of the Pākehā legal system.

Introduction

This chapter describes our collaborative project aiming to create better support for people experiencing mental distress and/or addiction within criminal justice spaces in Aotearoa.[1] We explain our kaupapa Māori-led methodology and how this approach fosters a kaupapa Māori human rights-focused research agenda. We critically reflect on how our intentionally grounded processes in kaupapa Māori methodology might expand our thinking across a range of criminological contexts and support the objectives of human rights-centred criminology.

We first ground our work within the context of Te Tiriti o Waitangi as the foundation of the constitutional framework of Aotearoa before moving to make connections with international human rights. We then place our methodology in the distinct cultural context upon which our research practices were based. The remainder of the chapter illustrates this alternative approach in action and concludes with key factors to consider regarding research of this kind.

A Brief Background into Te Titiri o Waitangi / The Treaty of Waitangi and Tikanga Maōri

Te Tiriti o Waitangi and The Treaty of Waitangi established a formal agreement between the British and Māori. Te Tiriti o Waitangi is the Māori version signed by some rangatira (chiefs) in 1840, and this differs in meaning from the English version, called the Treaty of Waitangi. The latter was used by representatives of the Crown to distinguish the rights of Māori under Pākehā (European) laws. Māori, in contrast, signed the te reo version expecting, under Article Two, to retain tino rangatiratanga (self-determination) over their taonga (prized possessions), including their whenua (land) and right to self-govern. While Article One of te Tiriti Maori gave the Crown kawangatanga (governorship) of their own people the new British settlers, they did not cede sovereignty. Under both versions of the treaty, all people were to be afforded oritetanga, which provides equality and equity for both Māori and Pākehā.

While te Tiriti may have promised Māori some protections of their rights, from a constitutional perspective, it was a revolutionary act that consequently left Māori on the losing side (Brookfield 2013). Starting with the influx of settlers, new technologies, ideologies, beliefs, diseases, and the imposition of the Westminster legal system, tribal Māori lifestyles were quickly diminished, or completely banished. Different understandings of the Treaty articles, particularly regarding land ownership and sovereignty, have led to ongoing debates and legal challenges.

Over time, principles have emerged from the courts, which have been incorporated into policy and legislation (Came et al. 2023). Treaty principles have also been derived from the intentions, expectations, and spirit of the agreement (Te Puni Kōkiri 2001). The principles reaffirm the guarantee of Māori self-determination and mana motuhake (authority, sovereignty), as well as obligations of the Crown towards equity, active protection, options, and partnership for, and with, Māori. However, the framing and application of these principles by the Crown in policy and law remain heavily criticised.

Jackson, Mutu (2019), and Mikaere (2007) attest that te Tiriti provides a clear intent of the signatories, declaring their absolute sovereignty to govern themselves under the system of laws called tikanga. Simplistically, tikanga Māori is about doing the right thing and it traditionally helped regulate Māori society. Today, tikanga is described as a "system that includes laws, and legal traditions" that make it a distinctive Māori legal culture (Jones 2013, p. 32). The five key concepts of Māori legal traditions include these values-based imperatives:

- Whanaungatanga (relational obligations)

- Manaakitanga (duty to care and nurturing of relationships)
- Mana (sanctioned authority with limits)
- Tapu (sanctity and respect for the spiritual realm)
- Utu (balance and reciprocity) (Mead 2003; Jones 2013).

Nonetheless, the criminal justice system continues to operate according to Pākehā (European) systems of control and punishment, although the proposed inclusion of tikanga Māori under the Te Ao Marama initiative in our district courts offers a vision for the future (Taumaunu 2022).

As our project was focused on re-envisioning a holistic and inclusive system that would promote the voices of lived experience, we knew this had to be done in accordance with tikanga, as the first law of Aotearoa paid attention to the Treaty of Waitangi, however, international social movements for indigenous people who had lost their lands, social structures and supports, and loss of language resonated with Māori, and led to similar uprisings in Aotearoa. Te Tiriti o Waitangi then became a vital document for Māori to challenge the government on their tāngata whenua status and rights of citizenship.

Māori are entitled, under international human rights law, to the protection of their rights as indigenous peoples (Round 2019). Specifically, the United Nations Declaration for the Rights of Indigenous People (UNDRIP) offers a pathway for their concerns to be heard and a legal instrument to advance their aspirations (Wiessner 2011). Although the New Zealand government was slow to ratify the UNDRIP, it was eventually endorsed but identified it as an aspirational document (Johnstone 2011; Te Aho 2020). Although, non-binding our intermediate and highest courts have affirmed the status of UNDRIP in safeguarding the rights of Māori as indigenous people (Charters 2017). The value-oriented approach of UNDRIP differs from other human rights instruments by recognising the cultural nuances and worldviews of indigenous people, prioritising:

- Collective responsibility and access to resources as stewards
- Connection to the intangible and tangible realms

- Rights to self-determination through the demand and maintenance of cultural practices traditions, customs, rituals, knowledge, and attainment of artefacts (Wiessner 2011, p. 131).

The UNDRIP affirms the rights of indigenous people to tino rangatiratanga (self-determination), whenua (lands), taonga (precious resources), and cultural tikanga customs and values (Charters 2017). Te Tiriti also has provided a better legal mechanism for identifying indigenous rights via treaty breaches, negotiating settlements and resolutions through reparation or apologies (Round 2019; Walker 1990).

Both the Tiriti o Waitangi and the UNDRIP recognise an existing relationship between Māori and the Government, but as illustrated above, we are far from seeing an active partnership and slow to see an acceptance of indigenous rights. Domestic and international law are too slow to make an impactful difference for those caught up in the educational, health, financial, administrative, and legal systems. Te Tiriti protects the rights of Māori that continue to be utilised to hold the Government accountable for the ongoing breaches. The renaissance of te reo (Māori language) and focus on the maintenance of mātauranga Māori (ancient knowledge) has enabled iwi, hapu, and whānau to reclaim their individual and collective rights to tino rangatiratanga (self-determination). While domestic and international law may be useful, it is the pragmatic nature of tikanga that offers hope for a brighter future.

Te Tiriti, Tikanga Māori, and Our Rangahau (Research)

Our rangahau was intentionally focused on seeking positive solutions for Māori, as dictated by Māori. We grounded our research in seeing the indigenous rights reaffirmed in te Titiri o Waitangi for Māori and recognised in UNDRIP. This meant we utilised a kaupapa Māori research with tikanga leading our methodological approach, knowing this would be a tika (right) process for everyone. With *He Ture Kia Tika—Let the Law be Right* as our title, our rangahau was anchored in a rights-based kaupapa (purpose).

We started by looking at existing approaches to co-production used in mental health and addiction research premised on the principles of partnership, equal distribution of power, and commitment to building consumer leadership capacity (Carr and Patel 2016, Roper et al. 2018, Slay and Stephens 2013). We observed that this approach may help us shift from "doing to" to "being and doing with" in research (Kidd and Edwards 2016). We also reflected on Best's argument that recovery doesn't happen within people, it happens between people (Best 2016) and recognised that co-production does not just apply to service users, but also involves community groups, all working together towards identifying gaps and looking to implement solutions.

However, there remained critical factors to consider when using co-production in our research. Co-production can be used in a tokenistic way, seen as an abstract concept, and pay no attention to intersectionality (Humphreys and Grayson 2008, Roper et al. 2018, Rose and Kalathil 2019). Co-production writings can be unclear on the details of how to *do* co-production in a way that is attuned to power imbalances and diversity.

We took leadership from years of guidance provided by kaupapa Māori research. Co-production shares similar values to kaupapa Māori research in its aims to engage participants as experts in their own knowledge. However, kaupapa Māori research also disrupts the Pākehā hegemony and is actively political in its resistance to the ongoing colonisation of Māori (Mahuika 2008). Kaupapa Māori promotes Māori control, autonomy, power, and self-determination by highlighting the impacts of power, control, privilege, racism, and other social justice issues (Curtis 2016; Walker et al. 2006, Pihama 2004). This is not to say there is no place for non-Māori allies in kaupapa Māori research; however, this approach places the power and rights of indigenous Māori to challenge, question, and critique the control and benefits of Pākehā involvement (Mahuika 2008, Pihama et al. 2002, Smith 1999). Kaupapa Māori research must be beneficial for all Māori whānau, and hapori (community), not just those who participate in the research (Mahuika 2008; Walker et al. 2006).

We found kaupapa Māori research integral to guide our research and need to undertake intersectional rights-based research. We wanted to honour the diversity of voices in our research, and kaupapa Māori research led by our co-production rōpū actualised this aspiration.[2]

We have previously detailed the rationale development of our methodology and overall methods in accordance with a te Tiriti and tikanga-led pathway elsewhere (Thom, K., et al. 2022). In this chapter, we highlight our positive practices of engagement and co-creation of pūrakau (participant stories), made possible because of adherence to our Te Ara Tohu o He Ture Kia Tika (Te Ara Tohu) guidelines. We see Te Ara Tohu as an application of rights-based research according to te Tiriti and tikanga Maōri values. Below we described how these guidelines created distinct benefits, and sometimes challenges, through four illustrations, inclusive of our personal reflections: (1) tikanga haumaru—creating safe processes; (2) whakawhiti kōrero—exchanging narratives; (3) ngā tuhinga pūrākau—collaborative story writing; and (4) kia whakatika—doing the right thing.

1. **Tikanga Haumaru—Creating Safe Processes**

Participants came to our research either through hearing about our project online or were directly invited by members of our rōpū who have lived experience and/or support whānau who have experienced mental distress, addiction, and the criminal justice system. Prior familiarity and connection to participants built on trust were never taken for granted in this area of research that involved sharing sensitive and traumatic information. Stella observed the difference that shared experiences made in building trust in the process:

One observation I have made during the undertaking of these interviews is watching how Jess and Dave interact with whānau. Usually, they can connect immediately with whānau in the storytelling adding their own experiences, sharing the same feelings or similarities. That deep knowing from being there and having done that is evident during these exchanges, and I appreciate as an outsider/as an academic researcher the sense of "not knowing and not understanding." There is much to be said for "trusting the process of allowing the tohunga or expert of their experience to lead and/or navigate" these interactions. I have learnt humility is needed in taking a back seat to allow those who know best to share their stories (Stella).

Although it may have helped ease their uncertainty and fear about participating, we were careful to share further information to whakamana (empower) participants to know they could change their minds or say no. Thoroughly going over the information and consent forms strengthened our safety processes.

2. **Whakawhiti Kōrero—Exchanging Narratives**

During the first hui (meeting) with participants, we would start with whanaungatanga (building relationships). We would share ko wai tatou (who we are) and introduce the wider rōpū aided by a photo and brief text detailing the expertise represented in the rōpū. Kia mahaki means we were humble in our approach) when sharing this information with participants, but we did so with pride, rather than being whakahihi (arrogant) or showing off. This process of introducing the wider rōpū was important for whānau, so they knew who might see and hear their most intimate stories.

Mana motuhake (authority, sovereignty) means participants have the autonomy to decide whom they want to interview them. Participants were given several choices, including having one or two researchers with lived experience present or researchers identifying as Māori or a specific gender. Where possible we conducted the interviews in pairs, which provided the researchers with the opportunity to contribute to kōrero offering their own insights based on their lived experiences. This helped participants to feel at ease, and the kōrero tended to flow or trigger other thoughts when there was a shared understanding Jess describes the power of these moments:

> Many of the participants warmed up and began to open up more fully after we introduced ourselves, particularly if they related to something such as one of the researcher's places of birth or lived experiences of incarceration. Often there were heavy issues spoken about, sometimes we cried together, sometimes we laughed together but the spirit of unity and te ao Māori was always there. (Jess)

Conducting the interviews in pairs gave us the opportunity to debrief together after the interview. Bearing witness to some stories was significantly impactful. De-briefing became a crucial element of unloading some of the weighty stories we heard.

Te Ara Tohu guidelines outlined our need to whakamana participants, but we did this flexibly. Tikanga Māori would usually mean starting our kōrero (discussions) with karakia, prayer or an affirmation reading. Some participants led this process, while others preferred not to begin their interview this way. Also, when sharing our pepeha (recitation of genealogy) according to tikanga Māori processes of whanaungatanga, this was done in English or te reo Māori. We were cognisant that not all whānau participants knew their whakapapa or could share this in te reo Māori. We did not want our interactions to be a cause for their whakamā (shame or embarrassment).

Overall, the preparatory work towards creating a safe space and process aimed to ensure participants would feel empowered to share their stories, in their own time, and as they wanted. We were committed to making sure participants were well, after we left, and committed to a welfare check within a week after our hui. Based on feedback, our efforts were positively experienced:

I called [name removed] to see how she was and whether our interview had brought anything disturbing up for her… She thought it was sweet I was ringing to check up on her, and very appreciative. She shared that she had called her sponsor and other close whanau to help her deal with some of the issues that came up during the interview. She reflected on it… concluding she wanted to add more to her story (Stella).

3. Ngā Tuhinga Kōrero—Collaborative Story Writing

The process of co-creating each pūrākau with participants incorporated much of the tikanga values outlined above and an ongoing process of manaakitanga (active caring and nurturing). Our working relationship and interpretation of the stories were guided by Te Ara Tohu and centred on privileging the voice of each participant. The first step was choosing who would lead the writing of the story. While preference was given to the researchers that were present at the interview, in some cases, another researcher was found to be better suited given their lived experience or cultural knowledge. There were also pragmatic reasons that led to decision-making, such as the capacity of each member of our team. We always ensured, that the researchers present in the interview took the lead on communication with the participant.

The process of writing began with listening to the audio files and paraphrasing the context of each pūrākau (story). Upon completion of the first draft, this was circulated among the core team for comment and edits. We then met in person with participants to share a hard copy of their draft or shared this via email. The lead interviewer then made time to catch up with participants to obtain their amendments and photos or images that they wanted to be included in their story. Jess explained the safety of this process:

> The story-writing process has been unique, unifying, and collective. Each story is edited with each of our core team's creative and academic input. Lived experience also factors in and together we can give people a voice that is edited from all different aspects of life to bring together their individual stories. Allowing them to check the story and give informed consent also allows the participants the respect of choice they deserve; we are never sensationalising or abusing the gift we have been given, there is kindness and deep care in our methodology, which is intended to make everyone feel safe and free to communicate honestly. (Jess)

When the pūrakau had been carefully designed and packaged, the gifting back of each whanau pūrākau was the final, and often an emotional and appreciated, process in collaborative story writing.

4. **Kia Whakatika—Do Right**

In this final illustration, we further highlight the ways in which we strived to do right, "kia whakatika" throughout our research project. We regularly checked in with participants using the tikanga values of aroha, tapu, and pono (love, sacred restrictions, and integrity). This was done in the following ways:

- Our tika (right) processes meant we adapted to the needs of our participants, meeting them wherever they were and gently walking alongside them as they divulged their stories. We used a consent-in-stages approach, continually checking in. The fact that participants were able to decline participation in our research at any time was a mana (authority) enhancing process.
- We ensured we were conducting our research "kia tūpato" (using caution). Some participants were excited and passionate about the changes they had made and wanted to share their stories openly. In these cases, we carefully covered the disclosure scenarios, considering what might happen in the future if people were to read about their criminal past, and challenges with mental distress and/or addiction. At times, participants disclosed information about their immediate or wider whānau. We worked with them to de-identify some facts to protect those key relationships and anonymity.
- We also thought deeply about how we shared and gifted stories. For some whānau reading their stories was challenging, as it brought to the fore a lot of pain and regret. Tears were common throughout our research.
- Our staged consent process enabled whānau to amend or withdraw their pūrākau (story) at any time. We did so to honour their tino rangatiratanga (self-determination) and mana motuhake (autonomy, authority, sovereignty) status.

Discussion

A kaupapa Māori co-production research approach is not for the faint-hearted and uncommitted. It involves hard work and dedication in doing the right thing, "kia whakatika". This approach is resource intense, time-consuming, and involves a long-term commitment to engage with participants. We became accountable to our participants as if they are our whānau (family); we strived to reach a consensus after in-depth discussions among the core team and rōpū. The concept of kotahitanga (unity) was established at our first hui as a group of like-minded and social justice-focused practitioners and academics who envisaged a criminal justice system that better supported whānau experiencing mental distress and/or addiction. The safe environment that was created meant everyone could share their differing views and support each other in the continual learning process.

Our practices contribute new learnings for co-production research by rising to challenges of how this methodology had been used, already voiced in the literature (Humphreys and Grayson 2008, Rose 2019). We intentionally resisted privileging Westernised ideas. We chose a te ao Māori worldview to lead our approach that disrupted white privilege and prioritised the voices of those who are often marginalised. We intended to do this in a way that was respectful to diverse voices, with our Te Ara Tohu guidelines bridging both Māori and Pākehā spaces.

Whanaungatanga is integral to building relationships, relating to others, and collaborating with the community during research. We followed the core principles that have emerged from years of Kaupapa Māori research to guide us, including making time to gather advice on research questions and methodological design, ensuring consultation is face-to-face, laying bare who you are, moving through research with participants cautiously and most of all showing respect.

The safe space we created was enhanced by ensuring an intersectional team and design. Our co-production is grassroots; members of our team live and breathe te ao Māori and either work with or have experienced incarceration and community-based mental health and addiction support. We recognised the real value of lived experience as being not just something that could be measured by a qualification or quantified space of objective knowledge that met the standards of others. We allowed space for experiential and indigenous wisdom, free from judgement constraints. Those without lived experience in our rōpū were willing to take the back seat and trust the process. They recognised what it is to be an ally; to make the space, to recognise the rangatira (leader) voices of those who had intersectional experiences of race, gender, sexuality, mental distress, addiction, and criminal justice.

Ultimately, our methodology acknowledges that as researchers we are reliant on participants, and we need to understand our reciprocal responsibility that honours our part in producing meaningful outcomes. The gifting of pūrākau to whānau was a small measure that sometimes led to bigger, positive impacts in their lives. We recognise the responsibility for our research to become political and demand transformative change.

Conclusion

Our current legal system has done little to safeguard and protect the rights of indigenous people, many of whom make up the highest proportion of those apprehended, arrested, incarcerated, institutionalised, or in rehabilitation or recovery. There is a strong association that exists between unmet mental health and addiction needs, criminal offending, and re-offending. Compounding these needs, are the impacts of the continued colonisation of the indigenous people of Aotearoa and their basic human rights. The Eurocentric criminal justice system significantly contributes to the intergenerational trauma perpetuated on Māori through victimisation and (re)offending. Te Tiriti has been an effective legal instrument enabling Māori to highlight the breaches by the Government that keep them oppressed and in a perpetual cycle. The developments in our higher courts have affirmed the status of UNDRIP.

Law and policy changes are rarely formed with the input of those who have lived experience of the criminal justice system. Many of our participants viewed themselves as survivors of a war; a war on drugs; a war of oppression and marginalisation, where they were oppressed and punished, vilified; where they had no rights, or at least not the same rights as others in society. Many other indigenous populations, continue to be marginalised and denied the basic promise of access, participation, equity, and rights. This project, *He Ture Kia Tika,* is built on the premise that when we are seeking solutions, we need to listen to the people at the heart of the problems. This paper has detailed our creation of a kaupapa Māori co-production methodology, that we believe can help us realise these solutions.

Notes

1. The authors wish to acknowledge the funding received from the Borrin Foundation which made this research possible.
2. Four members of our co-production rōpū wrote this paper—Stella Black, David Burnside, Jessica Hastings, and Katey Thom— Stella Black, a wāhine of Māori (Ngāi Tūhoe, Whakatōhea, Te Whānau-a-Apanui, Ngāti Whakaue) descent; David Burnside, male and Jessica Hastings, a female, both have experiences of incarceration and identify as Pākehā; Katey Thom, who identifies as Pākehā (non-Māori) female. We all have varying personal and work-based experiences of mental distress and addiction. Wider rōpū are also referred to, including Shane White (Ngāti Tara Tawhaki Tokonui, Ngāti Ranginui, Ngāti Raukawa), Elaine Ngamu (Ngāti Porou), Brian McKenna (Pākehā), Jeremy Tumoana (Ngā Ariki Kaiputahi, Te Aitanga a Mahaki, Ngāti Porou and Tūhoe), Tracey Cannon (Pākehā), Debra Lampshire (Pākehā), Martin Burke (Pākehā and Ngāpuhi), Warren Brookbanks (Pākehā), Rob Tua (Ngāpuhi, Te Atiawa), Jason Haitana (Ngāti Tūwharetoa, Te Āti Haunui-a-Pāpārangi), Daniel Exeter (Pākehā), Thomas White (Samoan and British), Shelley Turner (Ngāti Rāhiri Tumutumu), and Khylee Quince (Ngāpuhi, Ngāti Porou), all representing diverse ethnicities and experiences of incarceration, mental distress, and addiction.

References

Best, D. 2016. Cutting Edge: Recovery as an Issue of Social Justice and Social Inclusion. Energy Events Centre, Rotorua, New Zealand: DAPPANZ.

Brookfield, Frederic. 2013. Morris. *Waitangi and Indigenous Rights: Revolution, law and legitimation.* Auckland University Press.

Came, Heather et al. 2023. Critical Tiriti Analysis: A Prospective Policy making tool from Aotearoa New Zealand. *Ethnicities* 0 (0). https://doi.org/10.1177/14687968231171651.

Carr, Sarah, and Meena Patel. 2016. Practical Guide: Progressing Transformative Co-production in Mental Health. *National Development Team for Inclusion*. Bath, England : 1–13.

Curtis, Elana. 2016. Indigenous Positioning in Health Research: The Importance of Kaupapa Māori Theory-informed Practice. *AlterNative: An International Journal of Indigenous Peoples* 12 (4): 396–410.

Charters, Clair. 2017. The Rights of Indigenous Peoples under International Law and their Domestice Relevance in Aotearoa New Zealand. In *International human rights law in Aotearoa New Zealand*, eds., M. Bedggood, K. Gledhill, & I. McIntosh, Wellington New Zealand: Thomson Reuters.

Humphreys, Ashlee, and Kent Grayson. 2008. The Intersecting Roles of Consumer and Producer: A Critical Perspective on Co-production, Co-Creation and Prosumption. *Sociology compass* 2 (3): 963–980.

Johnstone, N. (2011). Long-standing implications: The UNDRIP and New Zealand.

Jones, Carwyn. 2013. The Treaty of Waitangi Settlement Process in Māori legal History. PhD diss., Victoria University of Wellington. http://hdl.handle.net/1828/4488.

Kidd, Jacquie, and Gareth Edwards. 2016. Doing It Together: A Story from the Co-production Field. *Qualitative Research Journal* 16 (3): 274–287. https://doi.org/10.1108/QRJ-07-2015-0059.

Mahuika, Rangimarie. 2008. Kaupapa Māori Theory is Critical and Anti-colonial. *MAI Review* 3 (4): 1–16.

Mead, Hirini Moko. 2003. Tikanga Māori. *Living by Māori Values. Wellington: Huia.*

Mikaere, Ani. 2007. Tikanga as the First Law of Aotearoa. *Yearbook of New Zealand Jurisprudence* 10: 24–31.

Mutu, Margaret. 2019. 'To Honour the Treaty, We must First Settle Colonisation' (Moana Jackson 2015): The Long Road from Colonial Devastation to Balance, Peace and Harmony. *Journal of the Royal Society of New Zealand* 49 (sup1): 4–18. https://doi.org/10.1080/03036758.2019.1669670.

Pihama, Leonie et al. 2002. Creating Methodological Space: A Literature Review of Kaupapa Maori Research. *Canadian Journal of Native Education* 26 (1): 30.

Pihama, Leonie, et al. 2004. A literature Review on kaupapa Maori and Maori Education Pedagogy. *Prepared for ITP New Zealand by The International Research Institute for Maori and Indigenous Education (IRI).*

Roper, Cath, Flick Grey, and Emma Cadogan. 2018. Co-Production: Putting Principles into Practice in Mental Health Environments. Melbourne.

Synergy research. https://healthsciences.unimelb.edu.au/__data/assets/pdf_file/0007/3392215/Coproduction_putting-principles-into-practice.pdf.

Rose, Diana, and Jayasree, Kalathil. 2019. Power, Privilege and Knowledge: The Untenable Promise of Co-production in Mental "Health." *Frontiers in Sociology* 4 (2019): 57.

Round, Olivia, and Finkle, Jodi. 2019. Ensuring Indigenous Rights: New Zealand and UNDRIP. Honours thesis. Loyola Marymount University. https://digitalcommons.lmu.edu/honors-thesis/190.

Slay, Julia and Lucie Stephens. 2013. Co-production in Mental Health: A Literature Review. *London: New Economics Foundation* 4: 1–36.

Smith, Linda. 1999. Tuhiwai. *Decolonizing Methodologies: Research and Indigenous Peoples*. Zed Books.

Te Puni, Kōkiri. 2001. He Tirohanga o Kawa ki te Tiriti o Waitangi: A Guide to the Treaty of Waitangi as expressed by the Courts & the Waitangi Tribunal.

Te Aho, Fleur. 2020. Treaty settlements, the UN Declaration and Rights Ritualism in Aotearoa New Zealand. *UNDRIP Implementation: Comparative Approaches, Indigenous Voices from CANZUS*, 33–40.

Taumaunu, Heemi. 2022. Te Ao Marama: A vision for the District Court of New Zealand. *AUSTRALIAN LAW JOURNAL* 96 (2): 94–101. https://search.informit.org/doi/https://www.search.informit.org/doi/10.3316/agispt.20220308063136.

Thom, Katey, et al. 2022. He Ture Kia Tika/Let the Law Be Right: informing Evidence-based Policy through kaupapa Māori and Co-production of Lived Experience. *Evidence & Policy* 18 (2): 412–435. https://doi.org/10.1332/174426421X16432180922551

Walker, Ranginui. 1990. *Ka Whawhai Tonu Matou—Struggle Without End*. Auckland: Penguin.

Walker, Shayne, Anaru Eketone, and Anita Gibbs. 2006. An Exploration of kaupapa Maori Research, Its Principles, Processes and Applications. *International Journal of Social Research Methodology* 9 (4): 331–344.

Wiessner, Siegfried. 2011. The Cultural Rights of Indigenous Peoples: Achievements and Continuing Challenges. *European Journal of International Law* 22 (1): 121–140. https://doi.org/10.1093/ejil/chr007.

Williams, Joseph. 2013. The Harkness Henry lecture lex Aotearoa: An Heroic Attempt to Map the Maori Dimension in Modern New Zealand Law. *Waikato Law Review: Taumauri* 21: 1–34.

11

Queer Criminology Through the Lens of the Global South and Its Impact on Human Rights

George B. Radics

As one of the youngest fields in criminology, queer criminology in the last decade has made significant efforts to place LGBTQ identities at the center of criminological analyses. As a new field, Global South perspectives have always been considered and included in the debates; though, queer criminology theorizing has taken place mainly in Australia, the United Kingdom, the United States, and Canada. Additionally, over the past two decades, the United Nations has sharpened its focus on LGBTQ rights, denouncing acts of violence based on sexual orientation as early as 2003 and appointing an independent expert to report on LGBTQ human rights violations annually since 2016. But what definition of human rights are international organizations using? And what would happen if, as opposed to just including Global South perspectives, queer criminology was analyzed through the lens of the challenges in the

G. B. Radics (✉)
Department of Sociology and Anthropology, National University of Singapore (NUS), Singapore, Singapore
e-mail: radics@nus.edu.sg

L. Weber and M. Marmo (eds.), *A Research Agenda for a Human Rights Centred Criminology*, Palgrave Critical Studies in Human Rights and Criminology,
https://doi.org/10.1007/978-3-031-46289-4_11

Global South? Would the analysis look different? This chapter explores these questions.

The chapter will first review the history of the new field of queer criminology. It will begin by reviewing some of the most important work in the field in the last decade. It will next attempt to discuss tensions with the word 'queer,' who constitutes the 'Global South,' and what is the state of 'queer criminology' in the South. The remainder of the chapter will explore pertinent issues regarding criminology in the Global South that have an impact on human rights through three sections: (1) colonial laws and cultural wars; (2) police and religious violence in 'securitized' states; (3) elitist and biased courts and their transformative power in the South. The chapter will conclude with a section on how Global South queer criminology should advance, and by providing some final thoughts on how it can inform international human rights practices.

Queer Criminology in the North

Peterson and Panfil (2014) in the *Handbook of LGBT Communities, Crime, and Justice* provide a glimpse into how queer criminology grew in the last decade by discussing the challenges in presenting research on such topics at the annual American Society of Criminology (ASC) conference. They noted the difficulty in finding appropriate panels, assumptions being made about the content of the presentations, and the 'hodge podge' nature of queer criminological research being presented throughout the conference. Their edited volume can be seen as an important step in creating a more organized space to discuss queer criminology research—and their efforts have been successful, leading to a queer criminology division at the ASC in 2020. Even at the early stages, research on the Global South was part of the discussion. In the conclusion of their book, however, they were sensitive to how Global North terminology might not work in the Global South, noting that 'Western notions of 'gay' or 'transgender' may not be applicable in a 'global context' highlighting limitations they were aware of (Panfil and Peterson 2014, p. 559).

In the North, certain themes have emerged in the field of queer criminology. Woods (2015), in his mapping of the homosexual criminal identity in criminological research, argued that prior to the 1970s, LGBTQ people in Western countries were commonly labeled criminals, psychopaths, sinners, and perverts; while from the 1970s onwards, LGBTQ identities have been largely invisible in criminological studies. He goes on to discuss how recent studies that deal with queer populations have focused on specific areas of victimology: bias crime, intimate partner violence, and anti-LGBTQ bullying (Woods 2015, p. 132). In 2016, Buist and Lenning edited an important volume in 2016, with a second edition published in 2022, entitled *Queer Criminology*. Their impressive volume tended to focus on institutions, looking at laws, law enforcement, court rooms, and prisons.

A limitation of this growing field of queer criminology is the lack of Global South perspectives. Ball, Buist, and Woods (2014, p. 4) reiterate this concern in their *Critical Criminology* special issue where they argue, 'one important limitation of these contributions is the lack of discussions outside of the global North.' They add, 'while there is an international flavor to these contributions…these discussions primarily focus on 'Northern' concerns and contexts' (*ibid.*). Ball (2016, p. 250), in his critical work *Criminology and Queer Theory Dangerous Bedfellows?* also acknowledges the limitation of the field and writes:

> queer politics has a troubled and not yet fully developed relationship with (and productivity for) many, particularly those who do not experience particular forms of privilege (such as white privilege), indigenous people, and those outside of the Global North.

'Queer,' 'Criminology,' and the 'Global South'

Boaventura de Sousa Santos (2016, p. 18) describes the Global South as a 'metaphor for the human suffering caused by capitalism and colonialism on the global level, as well as for the resistance to overcoming or minimising such suffering' (Santos 2016, p. 18). Global South replaces 'developing' and 'third world' characterizations that define societies based on economic and social success, with the West as the standard (Radics and Ciocchini 2023). Thus, the term 'Global South' allows for a deeper and richer understanding of the neo-colonial and cultural pressures on nations outside of Europe, the United States, and Australia.

Some have argued that 'queer studies is a Euro-American centered academic project, authored by Western scholars' (Horton 2018, p. 173). The idea of 'queer' has also been criticized by some African scholars who see it as a neo-imperial concept (Matebeni et al. 2018). But not all who work on the Global South have rejected the term. Audrey Yue (2017, p. 21) introduced the idea of 'queer Asia as method,' that challenges 'astatic geographical sites' and more significantly 'reorients the flows, boundaries, and hierarchy of global queer knowledge production.' 'Queer,' which emerged in the Global North to challenge hetero-normative and binary thinking, is slow to become integrated into studies in the South, especially in regions where criminological scholarship has long been entangled with Northern scholarship and approaches, such as in African and Asian criminology (Agozino 2022; Liu 2018). In Latin America, criminology was highly influenced by critical criminology traditions of the 1970s, perhaps leading to a more progressive view toward 'queer' criminology.

Currently, no national criminology society (outside of the American Society of Criminology and the Australian New Zealand Society of Criminology) has formed a section or study group on LGBTQ or queer criminology. This is not to say that efforts are completely lacking in the South. The Chilean Society of Criminology in 2022 began soliciting articles for a special issue on queer criminology to be published in the Chilean journal *Política Criminal*. At the Asian Criminology Society annual meeting in 2017, a panel on queer criminology and a paper on 'Queer Criminology in the Global South' took place (Ball and Dwyer 2018). The Africa Criminal Justice Reform organization housed at the University of the Western Cape, South Africa, also provides numerous resources and a published presentation on LGBTQ issues.

Lastly, it is undeniable that there is resistance and skepticism to the human rights discourse in the Global South. As a site to colonialism, a battleground of the Cold War, and with nations deeply indebted due multi-lateral lending, it is only natural that 'universal values' and human rights can serve as a trigger in the South. Thus, in the following sections, as the chapter explores the issues, a queer criminology of the South should pursue moments in which the human rights discourse has failed, and points in which human rights mechanisms could intervene will be highlighted.

Queer Criminology and Human Rights in the Global South

For nations in the South, far from serving as a liberating and empowering institution, many times the state reproduced the same systems of oppression thrusted upon it as a colony and even after independence, abandoned citizens at the margins or overpoliced them (Radics and Ciocchini 2023). The colonial policy of necropolitics—or open violence against those who challenged authorities—became translated into the post-colonial state as national security doctrine (Mbembe 2009; Feierstein 2010). Queer criminology's focus on the criminalization of LGBTQ people, the way they are policed, and the role of the courts can help to understand securitization issues and its serious implications on human rights in the Global South.

Human rights in its modern form can be traced to the Charter of the United Nations (1948) which encourages 'respect for human rights and for fundamental freedoms for all without distinction.' Over the past two decades, the United Nations included sexual orientation in its General Assembly resolutions on extrajudicial, summary, or arbitrary executions (*see* United Nations A/RES/69/182; A/RES/67/168; A/RES/65/208; A/RES/63/182; A/RES/61/173; A/RES/59/197; A/RES/57/214). In 2011, the UN began to document discriminatory laws and acts of violence based on sexual orientation and gender identity expression (United Nations A/HRC/RES/17/19) and in 2016 appointed an independent to report annually on SOGI issues (United Nations A/HRC/RES/32/2). But to rely exclusively on the United Nations to uphold the rights of LGBTQ people across the world would be relying on a definition of human rights that is Eurocentric—with the West being depicted as the birthplace of modern conceptions of rights, freedom and liberty, and the

East as authoritarian, overly disciplined and a suffering from a lack of civil liberties (Radics and Ciocchini 2019). In fact, it is precisely the pressure placed on Global South nations through the UN and other external, Global North-based institutions that have caused a backlash in the Global South.

The remainder of this chapter will discuss themes in the South that make the study of crime and criminology different in the Global South. The three sections to be explored are: (1) colonial laws and cultural wars; (2) police and religious violence in 'securitized' states; (3) elitist and biased courts in the Global South.

Colonial Laws and Cultural Wars

One of the lasting consequences of colonization was the 'unnatural afterlife' of anti-sodomy and 'sex against the order of nature' laws that plagued much of the former-British colonies (Sanders 2009). Neil Cobb (2014, p. 296) in exploring anti-sodomy laws throughout the world states, 'just over half of the 76 remaining sodomy laws worldwide are found in sub-Saharan Africa; most such laws were introduced through colonial era penal codes, especially by the British.' Beyond just highlighting the fact that these laws were originally British, it helps to understand the motivations behind them at their inception.

Ann Stoler (1989, p. 646) discusses how many of the medical manuals provided to colonial officials before leaving for foreign posts warned them of how extended stays abroad could lead to 'over fatigue…individual and racial degeneration, of physical breakdown, of cultural contamination, and neglect of the conventions of supremacy and agreement about what they were.' Lenore Manderson (1997) argues that, particularly in colonial Malaya, men were considered morally and sexually lax, while Holden (2000) highlights how colonial leaders found the region as having a 'feminizing effect on men.' On these bases, I argue that anti-sodomy at their inception had the dual purpose instructing colonial wards of upright moral sexual manners, but also to protect Westerners from these wayward 'Eastern' practices (Radics 2013, 2014). In Singapore, the ironic 'afterlife' of Sect. 377A of the Penal Code (the law specifically prohibiting sodomy) saw conservative groups inverting the latter argument and asserting that the law protects Singapore from Western wayward values of gay marriage, the breakdown of the 'traditional family,' and toxic individuality. The inversion of the colonial rhetoric can be seen in other political moves in the post-colonial state, such as the Asian Values discourse, which has been used to stymie the advancement of human rights (Ngo et al. 2018). After the *Obergefell* opinion in the US granted gay marriage, the UN's Being LGBT in Asia project was forcefully ejected from Indonesia and was derided as part of 'proxy war' to conquer the country.

The East vs. West argument eventually manifests as the cultural wars being fought across the South. According to Patel (2023, p. 279) in 2009, the government, religious, and traditional leaders all depicted a *chinkhoswe* (a traditional matrimonial agreement) between a queer couple as un-African and un-Malawian because same-sex relationships are alien to the culture and are a 'Western phenomenon.' The couple was arrested and sentenced to 14 years in prison with hard labor for sex against the order of nature. They were only pardoned after UN Secretary Ban Ki Moon made an instructive visit, leading to debates on whether the president was 'correct to 'bow down to the West'' (Patel 2023, p. 277). India also had the same 'sex against the order of nature' provision, Sect. 377 of the Penal Code until 2013. Examining the lasting effect of Western laws on Indian society, Sneha Annavarapu (2014) highlights how the gender binary and entrenched patriarchy enforced by the law hid other forms of rape, such as the rape of those between the two ends of the gender spectrum, as well as women who rape women or men. Throughout most of the South, sexuality laws were not just meant to erase homosexuality, but trans people who played important religious and cultural roles were often demonized, criminalized, and erased through colonial criminal laws.

Police and Religious Violence in Securitized States

While much of the criminological attention on post-colonial violence has focused on racial, ethnic, or political minorities and the poor, little attention has been made on the impact on LGBTQ or queer people. For trans people who engage in sex work, their rights and sometimes lives are often seen as disposable. In Turkey, even efforts to 'modernize' their criminal law to join the European Union, move away from police violence against sex workers, and address human rights abuses, actually expose trans women sex workers to the overtly sexist court system and a policing that is more intense, pervasive, and insidious (Taşcıoğlu 2023). In Argentina, which has some of the most progressive laws in the world regarding LGBTQ rights, trans sex workers have experienced a long history of abuse from the police, and violence against them by police spiked during the COVID-19 lockdown (Aristegui et al. 2022). And in the Philippines, since 2010, the murder of at least 50 transgender or gender non-binary individuals has been recorded across the country (Gregorio 2023). The most notable case is that of Jennifer Laude who was murdered in 2014 by a US Marine whose sentence was cut short when President Rodrigo Duterte pardoned him in September 2020 (*ibid.*).

The state is not acting alone in the violence. Often the securitized state is justified by 'tradition,' morality, but most importantly, religion. In Asia, rapid economic growth led to Christian evangelicalism and an Islamic resurgence in the region (Chong 2011; Hefner 2010). Latin America, the region of the world with the most Catholics, has seen a surge in Pentecostalism—with these Protestants espousing more conservative views on homosexuality, contraception, and abortion (Gooren 2010; Pew 2014). According to van Klinken (2017, p. 1), 'the construction of a hegemonic, normative ideal of African heterosexual identity in postcolonial African societies is partly a continuation of the politics to regulate African sexuality initiated by missionaries and colonial administrators.'

Thus, when looking at the violence that many LGBTQ people face at the hands of the police, often the police's hand is forced by 'moral' citizens filing police reports or at the hands of these 'moral' citizens themselves. In Islamic countries, such as Brunei, draconian laws criminalizing sodomy, lesbian relations, and cross dressing can lead to caning and the death penalty (Radics 2021). Moderate Islamic countries like Malaysia are seeing a surge in politicians attacking LGBTQ rights to pander to the growing Islamic populace, often acting on anonymous, or sometime blatant, calls to raid gay bars or break up LGBTQ events—a strategy Weiss (2024) terms pink blocking.

Christianity also justifies police brutality against LGBTQ people or motivates personalized attacks on them. According to van Klinken (2013) in several African countries, the demonization of homoeroticism and same-sex relations is driven by an ideology of Pentecostal nationalism where the sexual purity of the nation is believed to be under the threat. In Latin America, years of progress regarding LGBTQ rights have led to a backlash, mainly led by Pentecostal Christians. These Christians have used the fundamentalist interpretations of the bible and a strategy that allows them to cast their anti-LGBTQ positions in more secular terms (i.e., family autonomy, defense of children) to expand their appeal beyond their traditional constituency (Corrales 2019, p. 196).

Elitist and Biased Courts

Lastly, beyond the laws, and the police who enforce them, the courts should arguably be the last line of defense: striking out laws that are unconstitutional or ending brutal police practices that contravene the law. Yet the courts, too, have their limitations. Historically, they have been used as mechanisms of control in many parts of the Global South, instructing unruly and immoral natives and immigrants in the civilized ways of the colonizer. Classism, elitism, and cultural politics become even more pronounced in judicial systems enforcing laws with foreign origins.

In my own work, I highlight how judges in colonial Singapore often used their position to emphasize citizens' responsibilities to the government and society at large, how men should take care of their wives and children, and how punishment was swift and harsh to deter others from violating the law (Radics 2014). Reiterating the role of courts in enforcing morality, in the numerous constitutional challenges to anti-sodomy law from 2010 to 2020, judges asserted that the rational purpose of the law was to protect 'Singapore's specific traditions regarding procreation and lineage' (Radics 2013, p. 90). When similar laws were challenged in India, Sheikh (2019) highlighted how part of the legal strategy in the Supreme Court challenge was to humanize LGBTQ people, since many judges believed that they had never met a gay person and often held inaccurate views and biases toward the LGBTQ community. Such biases can sometimes manifest as sheer ignorance, as seen in the High Court of Kenya which in 2019 upheld the law criminalizing consensual same-sex sexual activity, arguing that it is 'an effective method to contain the country's HIV epidemic.'

Courts can also come off as callous and prejudiced. In *Rommel Jacinto Dantes Silverio v. Republic of the Philippines* (G.R. NO 174689: October 22, 2007), Rommel Jacinto Dantes Silverio filed a petition to change her name and sex to Mely after she completed her sex reassignment surgery. The Supreme Court held that Mely's birth name did not prejudice her, even though there is a law on the books that allows for a name change when a birth name is deemed ridiculous, tainted with dishonor, difficult to pronounce, perpetually used, or to avoid confusion. In Turkey, the move to charge trans sex workers in court under a new set of laws led to several days of trial and exposure to the strict and bias attitudes of the judges. One woman interviewed stated, 'I saw the eye of the judge. I said 'Allah!' to myself, 'this is a very bad man. Completely. A homophobic man. It is so clear that he is looking to me with disgust' (Taşcıoğlu 2023, p. 241). She went on to add, 'when it comes to evidence, [The judge] tells [the witness] what to say. 'She was naked, wasn't she?' The judge says this, and the man replies 'Yeah'' (Taşcıoğlu, 2023, p. 242).

This is not to say that the courts are hopeless. It was the Ugandan Constitutional Court that struck down the 2014 Anti-Homosexuality Act, even if this was on a technicality and not on the merits of the law's unconstitutionality. In 2019, in *NGO Co-ordination Board vs. Eric Gitari & 5 Others*, the Kenyan Supreme Court held that the freedom of association is 'inherent in everyone irrespective of whether the views they are seeking to promote are popular or not' (¶70) and 'that just like everyone else, LGBTQ have a right to freedom of association which includes the right to form an association of any kind' (¶72). Lastly, in the *Navtej Johar V. Union of India*, the Court of Appeal wrote 'LGBT persons deserve to live a life unshackled from the shadow of being unapprehended felons' (¶21).

Creating a Global South Queer Criminology

For many decades, the definition of human rights has been dominated by Western jurisprudence and notions of personhood (Barreto 2018; Langlois 2017). A queer criminology from the Global South has the potential to broaden the scope of human experiences incorporated into the human rights discourse while also examining the way Global South nations react and resist to Global North LGBTQ definitions and protections. Thus, by examining issues as discussed in this chapter such as the legacy of colonial laws, the securitization discourse, and class elitism in the courts, queer criminology can begin to examine issues from a bottom-up approach, as opposed to forcing Global Northern frameworks onto the South.

Through deep contextualized studies bound together by thematic commonalities, studying criminal legalities in the Global South provides us with opportunities to develop new mechanisms and tactics to deal with our increasingly globalized world (Radics 2019). This is especially the case as North–South and South-South migration lends to the criss-crossing of cultures and peoples, creating for more multicultural societies. Queer criminology has over the past decade attempted to bring queer identities front and center, examining how LGBTQ people are treated by the courts, police, criminal justice system, and in the law (Peterson and Panfil 2014; Buist and Lenning 2016). More can be done, however, to explore queer criminology in the context of our multicultural world.

Going forward, queer criminology should focus on three themes. The first would be the challenges and pressures on queer communities in the Global South. Works that theorize through a commitment to, and engagement with, local communities in the Global South should be prioritized (*see* Chua 2014; Patel 2023; Gregorio 2023). Second, queer criminology should remain sensitive to issues that emerge out of reactions and responses to the West, or external pressures (*see* Ngo et al. 2018; Weiss 2023; Langlois 2017). Last, queer criminology should examine the ways in which queer experiences in the Global South can inform queer experiences in the North (*see* Ball 2016, 2018).

Conclusion

At the 2022 ILGA Asia conference, Victor Madrigal-Borloz, the UN Independent Expert on sexual orientation and gender identity, highlighted that during his term he would focus on two issues: religion and colonialism. I believe this is a step in the right direction. Going beyond the traditional rights and health agenda could allow human rights organizations to begin to understand the issues deep below the surface that are triggering negative responses when any sort of change is suggested, particularly with regard to LGBTQ rights. It can also help to dispel the myth the HIV/AIDS are purely an LGBTQ issue, or that LGBTQ rights are part of a 'proxy war' to conquer the South.

A more Global South-oriented queer criminology can help uncover these types of issues to prevent hostile and aggressive negative reactions to the human rights discourse. While there have been significant attempts to make criminology more globally inclusive through southern criminology, advances in the North pertaining to queer criminology can also play a role. As queer people in the South experience rights and the criminal justice system in a different way from queer people in the North, queer criminology should capture this.

Bibliography

Agozino, Biko, and Nontyatyambo Dastile. 2022. 'Criminology in Africa', in *The Oxford Handbook of the Sociology of Africa*, ed. R. Sooryamoorthy, and Nene Ernest Khalema. Oxford Academic.

Annavarapu, Sneha. 2013. Heteronormativity and Rape: Mapping the Construction of Gender and Sexuality in the Rape Legislations in India. *International Journal of Criminal Justice Sciences* 8 (2): 248–264.

Aristegui, I., Castro Avila, J., Villes, V. et al. 2022. 'Female Sex Workers and Police Violence during the Covid-19 Health Crisis in 2020–2021: Results from the EPIC Multi-country Community-based Research Program in Argentina.' *Harm Reduction Journal* 19 (139).

Ball, Matthew. 2016. *Criminology and Queer Theory: Dangerous Bedfellows?* London: Palgrave Macmillan UK.

Ball, Matthew, and Angela Dwyer. 2018. *'Queer Criminology and the Global South: Setting Queer and Southern Criminologies into Dialogue', Palgrave Handbook of Criminology and the Global South*. London: Palgrave.

Ball, Matthew, Carrie Buist, and Jordan Woods. 2014. 'Introduction to the Special Issue on Queer/Ing Criminology: New Directions and Frameworks.' *Critical Criminology*, 22 (1): 1–4.

Barreto, José-Manuel. 2018. 'Decolonial Thinking and the Quest for Decolonising Human Rights' *Asian Journal of Social Science*, 46 (4/5), 484–502.

Birdal, Sinan. 2019. 'The State of Being LGBT in the Age of Reaction: Post-2011 Visibility and Repression in the Middle East and North Africa,' in *The Oxford Handbook of Global LGBT and Sexual Diversity Politics*, ed. Michael Bosia, Sandra McEvoy, and Momin Rahman. Oxford Handbooks.

Buist, Carrie, and Emily Lenning. 2022. *Queer Criminology*. Milton: Taylor & Francis Group.

Chong, Terence. 2011. *The AWARE Saga: Civil Society and Public Morality in Singapore*. Singapore: NUS Press.

Chua, L. J. (2014). *Mobilizing Gay Singapore: Rights and Resistance in an Authoritarian State*. Temple University Press.

Cobb, Neil. 2014. 'Rethinking the "World Polity" Perspective on Global Sodomy Law Reform', in *Handbook of LGBT Communities, Crime, and Justice*, ed. Peterson, Dana, and Vanessa R. Panfil. New York: Springer.

Corrales, Javier. 2020. 'The Expansion of LGBT Rights in Latin America and the Backlash,' in *The Oxford Handbook of Global LGBT and Sexual Diversity Politics*, ed. Michael J. Bosia, Sandra M. McEvoy, and Momin Rahman, Oxford Handbooks.

Feierstein, Daniel. 2010. 'National Security Doctrine in Latin America: The Genocide Question,' in *The Oxford Handbook of Genocide Studies*, ed. Donald Bloxham, and A. Dirk Moses .

Gooren, H. 2010. The Pentecostalization of Religion and Society in Latin America. *Exchange* 39 (4): 355–376.

Gregorio, Veronica. 2023. 'Reaffirming Womanhood: Young Transwomen and Online Sex Work in the Philippines' in *Criminal Legalities and Minorities in the Global South*, ed. Radics, G.B., Ciocchini, P. Palgrave Socio-Legal Studies. Palgrave Macmillan.

Hefner, Robert. 2010. Religious Resurgence in Contemporary Asia: Southeast Asian Perspectives on Capitalism, the State, and the New Piety. *Journal of Asian Studies* 69 (4): 1031–1047.

Holden, Philip. 2000. *Modern Subjects/Colonial Texts: Hugh Clifford & the Discipline of English Literature in the Straits Settlements & Malaya, 1895–1907*. Greensboro, NC: ELT Press.

Horton, B.A. 2018. 'The Queer Turn in South Asian Studies?' or 'That's Over & Done Queen, On to the Next. *QED: A Journal in GLBTQ Worldmaking* 5(3), 165–180.

Lenning, Emily. 2018. Queer Criminology. *Oxford Bibliographies Online in Criminology*. https://doi.org/10.1093/OBO/9780195396607-0256.

Langlois, Anthony. 2017. Queer rights? *Australian Journal of International Affairs* 71 (3): 241–246.

Liu, Jianhong. 2018. 'The Asian Criminological Paradigm and How It Links Global North and South: Combining an Extended Conceptual Toolbox from the North with Innovative Asian Contexts' in *The Palgrave Handbook of Criminology and the Global South*, ed. Carrington, K., Hogg, R., Scott, J. and Sozzo, M. Palgrave Macmillan, New York.

Manderson, Lenore. 1997. Colonial Desires: Sexuality, Race, and Gender in Colonial Malaya. *Journal of the History of Sexuality* 7 (3): 372–388.

Matebeni, Zethu, Surya Monro, and Vasu Reddy. 2018. *Queer in Africa : LGBTQI Identities, Citizenship, and Activism*. Milton: Routledge.

Mbembe, Achille. 2009. *Necropolitics*. Durham: Duke University Press.

Ngo T.M Huong, Vu Cong Giao, Nguyen Minh Tam. 2018. 'Asian Values and Human Rights: A Vietnamese Perspective,' *Journal of Southeast Asian Human Rights*, 2 (1). June 2018 pp. 302–322.

Patel, Nigel T.M. 2023. 'A Queer Chinkhoswe: Re-imagining the Customary in *Criminal Legalities and Minorities in the Global South*, ed. Malawi' in Radics, G.B., Ciocchini, P. Palgrave Socio-Legal Studies. Palgrave Macmillan.

Peterson, Dana, and Vanessa Panfil. 2014. *Handbook of LGBT Communities, Crime, and Justice*. New York: Springer.

Pew Research Center. 2014. 'Religion in Latin America Widespread Change in a Historically Catholic Region.' *Report*. Nov. 13. https://www.pewresearch.org/religion/2014/11/13/religion-in-latin-america/.

Radics, George B. and Pablo Ciocchini. 2023. 'Law and Order,' in *Oxford Handbook on International Law and Development*, ed. Luis Eslava, Ruth Buchanan, and Sundhya Pahuja . London: Oxford.

Radics, George B. and Pablo Ciocchini. 2018. 'Introduction to Special Issue: Continuities and Ruptures in *Global North Legal Pressures on Global South Societies*,' 46 (4/5): 409–419.

Radics, George B. 2013. Decolonizing Singapore's Sex Laws: Tracing Section 377A of Singapore's Penal Code. *Columbia Human Rights Law Review* 45 (1): 57–99.

Radics, George B. 2014. Singapore: A 'Fine' City—British Colonial Criminal Sentencing Policies and its Lasting Effects on the Singaporean Corporal State. *Santa Clara Journal of International Law* 12 (3): 57–90.

Radics, George B. 2019. 'Conclusion' in *Criminal Legalities in the Global South: Cultural Dynamics, Political Tensions, and Institutional Practices*, ed. Pablo Ciocchini and George Radics. London: Routledge.

Radics, George B. 2021. Challenging antisodomy laws in Singapore and the former British colonies of ASEAN. *Journal of Human Rights* 20 (2): 211–227.

Sanders, Douglas. 2009. 377 and the Unnatural Afterlife of British Colonialism in Asia. *Asian Journal of Comparative Law* 4: 1–49.

Santos, B. 2016. 'Epistemologies of the South and the Future', From the European South: A Transdisciplinary Journal of Postcolonial. *Humanities* 1: 17–29.

Sheik, Danish. 2019. 'Privacy in public spaces: The transformative potential of Navtej Johar v. Union of India' in *Criminal Legalities in the Global South: Cultural Dynamics, Political Tensions, and Institutional Practices*, ed. Pablo Ciocchini and George Radics. London: Routledge.

Sozzo, Máximo. 2020. 'Public and southern criminologies: A possible encounter' in *Criminology and Democratic Politics.*, ed. Daems, T., & Pleysier, S. Routledge.

Stoler, Ann. 1989. On Cultural Hygiene: The Dynamics of Degeneration. *American Ethnologist* 16 (4): 634–646.

Taşcıoğlu, Ezgi. 2023. 'Circuits of Law: Everyday Criminalisation of Transgender Embodiment in Istanbul' in *Criminal Legalities and Minorities in the Global South*, ed. Radics, G.B., Ciocchini, P. Palgrave Socio-Legal Studies. Palgrave Macmillan.

United Nations. 1948. *The Universal Declaration of Human Rights*. New York: United Nations General Assembly.

van Klinken, Adriaan. 2013.'Gay Rights, the Devil and the End Times: Public Religion and the Enchantment of the Homosexuality Debate in Zambia,' *Religion* 43/4: 519–540

van Klinken, Adriaan. 2017. Queer Studies and Religion in Contemporary Africa: Decolonizing, Post-secular Moves. *The Scholar & Feminist Online* 14 (2): 1–2.

Weiss, Meredith. 2024. 'Scapegoating Queers: Pink-blocking as State Strategy' *Current Sociology*. In progress.

Woods, Jordan B. 2015. The Birth of Modern Criminology and Gendered Constructions of Homosexual Criminal Identity. *Journal of Homosexuality* 62 (2): 131–166.

Yue, Audrey. 2017. Trans-Singapore: Some Notes Towards queer Asia as Method. *Inter-Asia Cultural Studies* 18 (1): 10–24.

12

Are Victim Stories Human Rights Stories? Towards an Ethics and Politics of Listening and Seeing for Victimology

Sandra Walklate

Introduction

Victimology is an area of investigation whose raison d'etre is suffering (Walklate 2023). Whilst the different perspectives to be found within victimology make different claims as to the shape, form and knowledge they can reveal about such suffering, it nonetheless constitutes the common feature binding them together. This is the case, the ontological and epistemological challenges posed by the question of how it might be possible to 'know' another's suffering, notwithstanding (Wilkinson 2005). Whether attention is directed by the emergence of what Fassin and Rechtman (2009) labelled 'psychiatric victimology' or attention is directed by the foundational work of Mendelsohn and Von Hentig (wherein the origins of both positivist and radical victimology can be found), the victimological focus on suffering is self-evident. In parallel,

S. Walklate (✉)
University of Liverpool, Liverpool, UK
e-mail: S.L.Walklate@liverpool.ac.uk

L. Weber and M. Marmo (eds.), *A Research Agenda for a Human Rights Centred Criminology*, Palgrave Critical Studies in Human Rights and Criminology,
https://doi.org/10.1007/978-3-031-46289-4_12

it is also the case that the emergence of twentieth-century concerns with human rights was borne out of a recognition of specifically war-time suffering.

Yet, as the debates on human rights unfolded especially in the post-Second World War era, the human rights gaze muted the structural dimensions underpinning the suffering which had generated it in favour of adopting more general and generalisable principles (see Morrison 2021). The victim per se became lost. However, at the same time, the victim (especially of genocide) was central to shaping those debates. Thus, in some respects, the answer to the question posed in the title of this chapter is a simple 'yes'. Victim stories especially those of genocidal survival are human rights stories. However, in the decades since the parallel emergence of victimology and concerns with human rights, the answer to this question has become less clear. The purpose of this chapter is to trace the changing contours of these issues in order to understand why the answer to this question appears to be rather less straightforward in the twenty-first century than it did in the mid-twentieth century. An appreciation of these changing contours leads, in the first instance, to reviewing debates concerning the relationship or otherwise between victim needs and victim rights the role that positivist victimology has played in those debates.

Needs or Rights? The Dominance of Positivist Victimology

It was not until the United Nations Declaration of Basic Principles of Justice for Victims of Crime and Abuse of Power 40/34 (1985), which advocated for the 'compassionate and respectful treatment of victims by the police, prosecutors and courts, with emphasis placed on providing victims with information, assistance and compensation' (Mawby and Walklate 1994, p. 89), that victims as a group were specifically mentioned in relation to the question of rights. Commensurate with recommendations from the Council of Europe introduced at a similar time, these developments marked a significant moment in recognising the impact of crime on its victims. These initiatives also signified the inauguration of a victims' rights-based discourse within victimology and its cognate activities.

Since the 1980s, there has been a wealth of empirically informed material addressing the question of whether victims (of crime) have needs or rights and what the policy responses to such needs/rights might comprise. Goodey (2005, p. 130), for example, identifies a 'checklist of core rights', and in a similar vein, Waller (2010, Chapter 8) makes a case for the 'inalienable' rights of victims of crime. Notably, the lists compiled by Goodey (2005) and Waller (2010) implicitly refer to victims whose victimisation is known to the criminal justice system and/or other agencies and ultimately, whose capacity to be heard, is reliant on recognition by those agencies. Moreover, many of the 'rights' listed by each of them, whilst clearly supportive of a range of United Nations and Council of Europe declarations and statements of intent, are not in themselves necessarily claimable in law. They are not enshrined as legal rights. Even the most recent victims' rights strategy document (2020–2025), whilst expressing concerns about earlier policy implementation failures, itself fails to step outside of a victim-centred as opposed to a human-centred discourse (European Commission, 24th June 2020), further evidencing that the language of rights has become elided with calls for good practice.

Fast forward to the twenty-first century, many jurisdictions now operate with hybrid rights-based systems combining good practice directives with rights-based approaches some of which can be claimed in law. The recent work highlighted in the edited collection by Cox and Walklate (2022) speaks to such hybridity. The blurred boundaries between demands for good practice and claimable rights found within the work of commentators like Goodey (2005) and Waller (2010) have arguably contributed to the emergence of such hybrid models of justice. Moreover, despite the best efforts associated with the desire to improve practice with the victim in mind, the available evidence suggests that for many of the policies fitting under the heading of either good practice and/or rights, problems of implementation remain as acknowledged by inter alia the European Commission. The question also remains, given the historical contextual origins of victimology and its (unspoken) relationship with human rights, how it is that these concerns have unfolded in this way?

Part of the answer to this question lies in appreciating the dominance of positivist victimology.

Miers (1989, p. 3) was one of the first to define positivistic victimology. In essence, this body of work focused on individual pathology rather than collective responsibility in understanding the nature and extent of criminal victimisation was inevitably political. Morrison (2015) suggests that the dominance of positivism in both criminology and victimology needs to be understood in the context of the Cold War and the rise of North American intellectual, liberal imperialism. Morrison (2015) unashamedly evidences the powerful ways in which wars, particularly in the post-Second World War era, served as a conduit for the imperial ambitions of North American liberal democratic values (see also Walklate 2021).

The connections between these processes, the earlier Nuremberg Trials and liberal democratic understandings of human rights set the tone in which, within post-war victimology, sight was lost of its war-time/genocide origins. Concepts, such as victim proneness, victim culpability and victim precipitation, were applied to much more ordinary and everyday criminal experiences, such as burglary, murder and rape, denuded of their origins. That is until the (ongoing) Nuremberg Trials of the 1960s, specifically the trial of Adolf Eichmann. The silencing and then rediscovery of victims' voices, particularly as human rights voices, did not occur in a vacuum. For example, Bauman's celebrated book on *The Holocaust* (1989), in part, reflected his wish to make analytical sense of the biographical experiences of his wife, a Holocaust survivor. Yet, notably within the work of the victimologists, writing during and post these events, whose rationale for the establishment of victimology was informed by their own Holocaust experiences, barely receives a passing reference in Bauman's work. Of course in some respects, none of the social sciences had, up until this point, paid serious attention to The Holocaust. However, in the case of victimology, part of the explanation for this absence lies within the increasing embrace of positivism and the normalisation of the victim experience as equating with criminal victimisation as opposed to human rights victimisation: favouring the former agenda over the latter.

Importantly, in this positivistic embrace, suffering is taken to be given by the law with such suffering knowable and measurable in terms of the victimisation defined in law (Walklate, 2023, Chapter 2). This stands somewhat in contrast to the kind of suffering that carries with it the obligations to speak for those who did not survive—to ensure that they, and what they experienced, are never forgotten (Friedberg 2016). Put another way, as Valier (2004, p. 147) does, 'to be confronted with that which seemingly cannot be accepted *under any terms*, by anybody'. The positivistic victimological gaze in directing attention towards victims' criminal justice rights and/or needs served to silence the kind of suffering considered unacceptable under any terms. This silencing left a legacy, traces of which are to be found within twenty-first-century debates relating to listening to (victims') stories of suffering.

From a Victim Narrative to a Trauma Narrative

By the end of the 1960s, positivist victimology became pre-occupied with the development and refinement of the criminal victimisation survey. The deployment of this method quickly proliferated and produced a wide range of local, national and international survey-based data about crime and its victims. This work also spawned conceptual developments used to make sense of this data—concepts such as primary, secondary and indirect victimisation. Thus, victimhood, and its implicit concern with suffering, became stretched to include not only those directly affected by victimising experiences but also the wider community and society at large. In part, this stretching was intimately connected with the parallel growth and development of victim-centred organisations: the politicisation of the victim (Miers 1978). During the same historical time, Lasch (1979) notes a concomitant cultural shift in Western societies labelled by him as narcissism. In this move, victim-centred organisations also shifted from being concerned with the availability of appropriate support services for people going through difficult times to becoming a conduit for seeing the world through the prism of pain (Fassin 2012). McGarry and Walklate (2015) argue that these shifts are characterised by a move from what they have labelled a 'victim narrative' to a 'trauma narrative'.

To summarise: the victim narrative, largely informed by positivistic victimology, readily identified those groups of people on whom it was thought victimisation would take its greatest toll (the elderly, the frail, children and so on). However, as the concept of trauma took a different hold, initially it was deployed to make sense of how ordinary men could do extraordinary things, notably during the Vietnam War. Thus, through the recognition of post-traumatic stress syndrome and its concomitant embrace as rape trauma syndrome, the presence and influence of a trauma narrative grew. In this trauma narrative, facilitated by a culture of narcissism, everyone can be a victim (Furedi 2002). This narrative transposed the idea of people needing support when faced with difficult circumstances (like being a victim of burglary for example) into one in which the impact of those circumstances was, by definition, deemed to be traumatic. Under conditions of 'trauma creep' (Walklate 2016), being a victim and being traumatised are elided and assumed to be uniform and unifying experiences. Enter the increasing presence and power of victim stories, especially in the realm of policy.

The Narrative Turn in Victimology

If narrative criminology asks the question about offenders' motives and behaviour for harming people, narrative victimology is concerned with the experiences of being harmed. In centring *experiences* of harm, narrative victimology offers the potential to make sense of the victim's experience of suffering. It opens the door for the kind of in-depth and qualitative focus on suffering smoothed out by the measurement processes associated with positivist victimology. Placing the victim experience of suffering in the centre, narrative victimology frequently uses the victim's story as its source of data. Hence, narrative victimology does not focus on suffering as knowable through measurement but on how suffering is experienced and lived from the point of view of the victim (Rock 1998). This affords a space in which the voice of the victim can be heard in their own terms. This approach has some strengths as well as weaknesses.

In listening to victim stories, more conventional theoretical assumptions about experiences of and response to victimisation may not only be challenged and refined, they can also be disrupted and transformed. In addition, the practice of storytelling in and about suffering can also be therapeutic (Dichter et al. 2022). Indeed, this process can lend a coherence to experiences, when constructed by the victims themselves, in ways that might otherwise appear unthinkable and unimaginable to the researcher (Cook and Walklate 2019). Pemberton et al. (2018b) argue that narratives, in offering the opportunity for coherence and comprehensibility, enable victims to regain a sense of control over their own lives. As Pemberton et al. (2018a, p. 12) point out:

> The damage of victimisation can be understood as a narrative rupture, which endangers a sense of control and continuity of one's life story throughout time and with the social surroundings. The way victims attempt to make sense and meaning of their ordeal occurs in narrative modes of reasoning, while they adopt narrative means to regain agency and re-establish communion with their social context.

As just one example, the compelling autobiographical narrative of Brison (2002) adds some weight to this view. However, this focus on narratives and stories is not without its problems. This is especially the case when such stories are used as a means of informing policy (Meyers 2016; Wheildon et al. 2021): a phenomenon that has made its presence increasingly felt in the policy turn towards taking account of 'lived experience'. This turn has made its presence felt in several different ways. The focus here is primarily on its use in relation to violence against women as victim-survivors.

Stories and Lived Experience

It is arguably not until the beginning of the twenty-first century that 'lived experience' began to feature within the policy formation process. This kind of approach is considered to be one way of challenging epistemic injustice wherein lies it relevance for considerations of human rights. However, deeper reflection raises several questions about this approach. These range from fundamental questions concerning who and what justice is for, to other more practical questions concerning who is heard and why, and who is not heard and why in such processes. Ultimately, the question is begged as to whether these processes themselves can distort the experiences drawn upon with the resultant effect that policy can effectively be in the interests of parties other than victim-survivors: a point made by Smart (1989). The question also remains: what is meant by 'lived experience'? This phrase has been used in at least two different ways in the study of violence(s) against women. The first as a way of valuing women's lives as they were lived as in the memorialisation work often associated with femicide advocacy. The second is to use women's experiences of violence(s) and service delivery as data for change. It is the second usage of this term which informs what follows.

Mcintosh and Wright (2019) in reviewing the policy turn to lived experience make the simple but profound point that experience is nothing if it is not lived. This is a simple observation, but it is also a profound and provocative one. For example, whilst Doyle et al. (2021) argue that 'good' policy should be informed by those who are directly affected by it, how this is done and what assumptions it makes about whose knowledge counts are not easily dealt with. As Mcintosh and Wright (2019) point out, the value placed on understanding experience has a long history in social science and that history differently points to the problem of how another person's experience might be known. For the purposes of the discussion here, this returns us neatly to the perennial question for victimologists as to how one might know another's suffering qua Wilkinson (2005). Thus, how might another's experience be seen and heard?

Mcintosh and Wright (2019) push this further by suggesting that an uncritical embrace of 'lived experience' makes assumptions about authenticity which are not necessarily justified. Such a stance can assume that when a person speaks of their experience it is truthful, authentic and real, and moreover, especially in the domain of advocacy, can count for all experiences. Nonetheless, experience carries weight, and this is difficult to deny. As Eriksson et al (2022, p. 8) aver,

> Lived experience research has, for example, illustrated how men's coercive and controlling behaviour entraps women in abusive relationships through violence, subjugation and surveillance, thereby limiting their freedom and reducing their 'space for action', namely their perceived ability to make decisions and be in control of their own lives.

At the same time, experience cannot be *known* by others. Rather like suffering, experiences can be shared but only up to a point. Thus, this poses deep methodological questions about using lived experience as either a basis or a litmus test for policy. It is the case, of course, that incorporating policy users in the policy process has a longer history that the recent favour found with lived experience and there has been considerable work done under the umbrella of participatory action research and/or work designated as co-produced. All of which would fit well within the lived experience lexicon. However, what is newer about the current approach is its interconnection with the rising presence of victim-survivor voices in offering commentary, invited or otherwise, on criminal justice policy. Moreover, on occasion, those victim voices have also been harnessed in the interests of more punitive strategies for responding to offenders (Barker 2007; Ginsberg 2014) raising different but equally important questions about the relationship between victim stories and human rights. Moreover, individual victim stories are not necessarily the same as human rights stories and therein lies a perennial problem for developing victim rights as human rights.

Thus, listening to victim stories can have different emphases and can set the parameters of how to take account of lived experience in relation to policy, including human rights policies, in different ways. In an interesting analysis of three public inquiries/royal commissions in Australia, all concerned with different aspects of violence against women and claiming to include lived experience, Ailwood et al. (2022) reveal that the capacity for these inquiries to listen to these experiences varied from refusing to listen, to failing to listen, to engaging in selective listening. Indeed, there are not only problems with how listening may or may not take shape, there are also difficulties with the concept of voice. As Thill (2015) points out, voices can be powerful, but they can also be one-sided.

Nevertheless, despite all the difficulties associated with the ways in which the policy process has pivoted to this narrative turn (including the tendency to incline towards the white, heterosexual, middle class woman), such experiences (as stories, narratives, biographies and/or in-depth interviews) carry significant collateral (see inter alia, Hegarty et al. 2022). As Ailwood et al. (2022, p. 2) suggest:

> Through giving voice to experiences of gender inequality, violence, and the inadequacy of legal responses to it, as 'stories', 'narratives' and 'testimony', women have challenged the law's claims to neutrality and objectivity. Moreover, they have highlighted the law's partiality and perspectives as those of the powerful, calling for recognition of women's experiences as valid and robust evidence bases for law reform.

At the same time, despite the recognition of partiality noted by Ailwood et al. above, the commitment to seek change through law reform has been and is one of the consistent and persistent presences in all the different feminist-informed endeavours in the field of violence(s) against women. Indeed, there is evidence to suggest that victim-survivors themselves share their stories in the hope for systemic change (Dichter et al. 2022). Moreover, the recourse to the law has also marked the field of human rights endeavours since the Second World War with arguably similar limited outcomes in terms of efficacy, implementation and change as with all the endeavours concerned with violence(s) against women. Thus, whilst in the twenty-first century victim stories (and in the example used here these are victim-survivor stories) might well still constitute human rights stories, questions remain as to how to ensure such stories act in everyone's interests.

Concluding Thoughts: Victim Stories as Human Rights Stories

Some of the concerns outlined in the discussion above led Meyers (2016) to develop a framework of good practice for researchers and activists wanting to engage with victim storytelling, especially when their focus of concern is to utilise these stories in the interest of human rights. Given the relevance of the work of Meyers for the concerns of this chapter, it is worth considering her recommendations in some detail.

Situating her agenda squarely within concerns about ethics and politics, Meyers (2016) is particularly focused on how to avoid becoming what she refers to as 'spiritual bellhops': sensationalising stories to meet a purpose and/or victim-blaming as a defence strategy. As she says: 'voyeuristically objectifying victims and dabbl[ing] in the unseemly pleasures of observing pain while out of danger' (ibid., p. 181). Ultimately for her, the key question is how to respect victims whilst simultaneously using their stories instrumentally. She suggests four virtues for researchers engaged in this way: informed consent that ensures non-re-traumatisation; project transparency on purpose and methods; reflective interviewing that dispenses with typecasting; and respecting the integrity and complexity of the stories told. To these virtues, I would add a more explicit conceptual embrace of human agency. People can and do change over time. Many do not remain forever victimised though some do. Who does and who does not embrace the victim label remain a victimological lacuna (Rock 2002). It might also be useful to render more explicit, as Fassin and Rechtman (2009) do, the structural conditions which inform such stories. In offering an analysis of the impact of the tsunami in Aceh, they stated: 'Both before and after the tsunami survivors in Aceh were already victims of political domination, military repression, and economic marginalisation' (ibid., p. 281). It needs more than the ethically informed use of stories to change such conditions. It needs global political commitment.

Thus, whilst the human desire to avoid ethical loneliness (Stauffer 2015) is immensely powerful and increasingly rendered a prescient feature of public and policy discourse especially through the use of social media and other platforms, the contemporary expression of victim stories as human rights stories needs to be embraced with caution. Some of these stories will be those, as Valier (2004) observed, which reveal conditions unacceptable by anyone in any terms. However not all of them are. To date, this author is unaware of any jurisdiction that has successfully negotiated the challenges of rendering victim rights as human rights. Thus, he challenges for a victimology of human rights remain.

References

Ailwood, Sarah, Rachel Loney-Howes, Nan Seuffert, et al. 2022. Beyond Women's Voices: Towards a Victim-Survivor-Centred Theory of Listening in Law Reform on Violence Against Women. *Feminist Legal Studies*. https://doi.org/10.1007/s10691-022-09499-1.

Barker, Vanessa. 2007. The Politics of Pain: A Political Institutionalist Analysis of Crime Victims' Moral Protests. *Law & Society Review* 41 (3): 619–663.

Brison, Susan. 2002. *Aftermath: Violence and the Remaking of the Self*. Princeton, NJ: Princeton University Press.

Cook, Elizabeth, and Sandra Walklate. 2019. Excavating Victim Stories: Making Sense of Agency, Suffering and Redemption. In *The Emerald Handbook of Narrative Criminology*, ed. J. Fleetwood, L. Presser, S. Sandberg, and T. Ugelvik, 239–257. Bingley: Emerald Publishing Limited.

Cox, Pam, and Sandra Walklate, eds. 2022. *Victims Access to Justice: Historical and Comparative Perspectives*. London: Routledge.

Dichter, Melissa, Alicia Chatterjee, and Bernie S. Newman. 2022. "I'd Go from a Mountain Top and Tell My Story": Perspectives of Survivors of Intimate Partner Violence on Storytelling for Social Change. *Violence against Women* 28 (6–7): 1708–1720. https://doi.org/10.1177/10778012211024267.

Doyle, Caroline, Karenr Gardner, and Karen Wells. 2021. The Importance of Incorporating Lived Experience in Efforts to Reduce Australian Reincarceration Rates. *International Journal for Crime, Justice and Social Democracy* 10 (2): 83–98. https://doi.org/10.5204/ijcjsd.1942.

Eriksson, Loraine, Paul Mazerolle, and Sandra McPhedran. 2022. Giving Voice to the Silenced Victims: A Qualitative Study of Intimate Partner Femicide. Trends and Issues in Crime and Criminal Justice No 645, March. aic.gov.au.

European Commission. 2020. Questions and Answers—Victims' Rights: New Strategy to Empower Victims. https://ec.europa.eu/commission/presscorner/detail/en/qanda_20_1169.

Fassin, Didier. 2012. *Humanitarian Reason: A Moral History of the Present*. Los Angeles: University of California Press.

Fassin, Didier, and Richard Rechtman. 2009. *The Empire of Trauma: An Inquiry into the Condition of Victimhood*. Princeton, NJ: Princeton University Press.

Friedberg, Edna. 2016. Elie Wiesel and the agony of bearing witness: Why should any of us expect people who have suffered profound trauma to relive it for our benefit? *The Atlantic*, July 9.

Furedi, Frank. 2002. *Culture of Fear: Risk Taking and the Morality of Low Expectation.* London: Cassell.

Goodey, Jo. 2005. *Victims and Victimology*. London: Longmans.

Ginsberg, Raphael. 2014. Mighty Crime Victims: Victims' Rights and Neoliberalism in the American Conjuncture. *Cultural Studies* 28 (5–6): 911–946.

Hegarty, Kevin, M. McKenzie, E. McLindon, M. Addison, J. Valpied, M. Hameed, M. Kyei-Onanjiri, S. Baloch, K. Diemer, and L. Tarzia. 2022. "I Just Felt Like I Was Running Around in a Circle": Listening to the Voices of Victims and Perpetrators to Transform Responses to Intimate Partner Violence (Research Report, 22/2022). ANROWS.

Lasch, Christopher. 1979. *The Culture of Narcissism: American Life in an Age of Diminishing Expectations.* New York: Warner Books.

Mawby, Rob, and Sandra Walklate. 1994. *Critical Victimology*. London: Sage.

McGarry, Ross, and Sandra Walklate. 2015. *Victims: Trauma, Testimony, Justice.* London: Routledge.

McIntosh, Ian, and Sharon Wright. 2019. Exploring What the Notion of 'Lived Experience' Offers for Social Policy Analysis. *Journal of Social Policy* 48 (3): 449–467. https://doi.org/10.1017/S0047an279418000570.

Meyers, Diana. 2016. *Victims' Stories and the Advancement of Human Rights.* New York: Oxford University Press.

Miers, David. 1978. *Responses to Victimisation.* Abingdon: Professional Books.

Miers, David. 1989. Positivist Victimology: A Critique. *International Review of Victimology* 1 (1): 3–22.

Morrison, Wayne. 2015. War and Normative Visibility: Interactions in the Nomos. In *Invisible Crimes and Social Harms*, ed. Francis Peter, Tanya Wyatt, and Davies Pam, 178–198. London: Palgrave Macmillan.

Morrison, Wayne. 2021. On 'Visualising the Truth of Genocide' Reflections on Whakapapa and Finding Southern Epistemology, Occasioned by a Tattered

Album from the Nomos of the Holocaust. In *Genocide and Victimology*, ed. Eski Yari, 102–137. London: Routledge.
Pemberton, Antony, Pauline G.M. Aarten, and Eva Mulder. 2018a. Stories as Property: Narrative Ownership as a Key Concept in Victims' Experiences with Criminal Justice. *Criminology and Criminal Justice*, 1–17.
Pemberton, Antony, Pauline G.M. Aarten, and Eva Mulder. 2018b. Stories of Injustice: Towards a Narrative Victimology. *European Journal of Criminology* 16 (4): 391–412.
Rock, Paul. 1998. *After Homicide*. Oxford: Clarendon.
Rock, Paul. 2002. On Becoming a Victim. In *New Visions of Crime Victims*, ed. Hoyle Carolyn and Young Richard, 1–22. Oxford: Hart.
Stauffer, Jill. 2015. *Ethical Loneliness: The Injustices of Not Being Heard*. New York: Columbia University Press.
Smart, Carol. 1989. *Feminism and the Power of Law*. London: Routledge.
Thill, Cate. 2015. Listening for Policy Change: How the Voices of Disabled People Shaped Australia's National Disability Insurance Scheme. *Disability & Society* 30 (1): 15–22.
Valier, Clare. 2004. The Sense of Atrocity and the Passion for Justice. *Critical Review of International Social and Political Philosophy* 7 (2): 145–159.
Walklate, Sandra. 2016. The Metamorphosis of the Victim of Crime: From Crime to Culture and the Implications for Justice. *International Journal for Crime, Justice and Social Democracy* 5 (4): 4–16.
Walklate, Sandra. 2021. Victimology and Genocide; Neglected Stories? In *Genocide and Victimology*, ed. Yarin Eski, 23–37. London: Routledge.
Walklate, Sandra. 2023. *An Advanced Introduction to Victimology*. Cheltenham: Edward Elgar.
Waller, I. 2010. *Rights for Victims of Crime: Rebalancing Justice*. Lanham: Rowman and Littlefield.
Wheildon, Lisa, et al. 2021. The Batty Effect: Victim-Survivors and Domestic and Family Violence Policy Change. *Violence against Women*. https://doi.org/10.1177/10778012211024266.
Wilkinson, Iain. 2005. *Suffering: A Sociological Introduction*. Cambridge: Polity.

13

Gendered Violence: A Human Rights Agenda for Criminology

Nancy Wonders and Sydney Shevat

Criminologists, particularly feminist and critical criminologists, have produced a substantial body of research detailing the etiology, forms, and impacts of gendered harm. Gendered or gender-based violence is harm against persons because of their sex and/or socially constructed gender identity, roles, and relations (True 2021, p. 8). Despite extensive research that documents the physical, economic, and social costs associated with gendered violence and the development of human rights initiatives that call upon states to address gendered violence, gender-based harm continues to be a pervasive and profound justice challenge around the world.

N. Wonders (✉)
Criminology and Criminal Justice, Northern Arizona University, Flagstaff, AZ, USA
e-mail: Nancy.Wonders@nau.edu

S. Shevat
Department of Sociology, University of Tennessee, Knoxville, TN, USA
e-mail: sshevat@vols.utk.edu

L. Weber and M. Marmo (eds.), *A Research Agenda for a Human Rights Centred Criminology*, Palgrave Critical Studies in Human Rights and Criminology,
https://doi.org/10.1007/978-3-031-46289-4_13

This chapter highlights human rights initiatives related to gendered violence, as well as the relatively small body of criminological research that has utilized a human rights frame to examine gendered violence. We call for a future criminological research agenda that targets the dynamics that are producing and exacerbating gendered violence and vulnerability, including: (1) the role of nation-states in producing the 'slow violence' associated with gender inequalities; (2) the gendered impacts of conflicts and climate change, and gendered barriers to mobility; (3) the rise of nationalist and right-wing politics that promote gender-based hierarchies and oppose international institutions; and (4) challenges related to representation and power from above and below. We argue that a human rights-centered criminology requires that gendered violence be viewed as a reflection of structured social inequalities and injustices that are produced by people—and that can be changed by people—if we are to ensure justice for all.

Criminological Research on Gendered Violence

Feminist criminological analysis has drawn attention to the complex role that the social construction of gender plays in the etiology and consequences associated with gendered violence, particularly the way that gender is linked to power and control, resources inequalities, and the production of vulnerability to harm. Gender is not a natural fact but is instead a social construct that must be produced. Feminist scholars have documented the historic forces that have contributed to the construction of a gender binary and gender hierarchies that privilege masculinity/male over femininity/female and heterosexuality over other sexualities (Belknap 2015; Federici 2004; Wonders 2018a). Historically and in the contemporary period, the gender hierarchy has been maintained and enforced through soft social control mechanisms, particularly socialization, and through hard social control mechanisms, including sexual terrorism and violence. According to the World Health Organization '[v]iolence against women remains devastatingly pervasive ....1 in 3 women, around 736 million, are subjected to physical or sexual violence by an intimate partner or sexual violence from a non-partner – a number that has remained largely unchanged over the past decade' (WHO 2021); thus, although gender is not 'real', it is real its consequences. It is essential to emphasize that the harms associated with gender stratification are deeply bound to other forms of structured social inequality, including race, sexuality, and social class (Ritchie 2017).

While gendered violence is often characterized as an individual level harm, many feminist scholars have emphasized that nation-states have been complicit in the maintenance of gender hierarchies by permitting gender discrimination, failing to develop laws and policies that prohibit the use of violence against some groups, and through the use violence by agents of the state, including in the justice system (Caulfield and Wonders 1993). State-facilitated gender hierarchies perpetuate masculine power and privilege and ensure that some people are made more vulnerable to harm than others, producing what some have called the 'feminization of vulnerability' (Detraz 2017; Wonders 2018b).

Although some research has explored how gender constructions shape the violence engaged in and experienced by men, a much larger body of criminological research has focused on men's violence against women and girls. This research has examined many types of gendered violence, including rape, intimate partner violence, dowry death, bride burning, forced marriage, and femicide (for summaries of this scholarship, see Barberet 2014; Carrington 2014; True 2012). Some criminologists have also utilized a gender lens to understand gendered violence directed toward LBGTQ+ identified people (Buist and Lenning 2022), a development which has been important for revealing and unsettling socially constructed gender hierarchies.

A few key observations crosscut the criminological scholarship on gendered violence. Research has established that violence by men against women is pervasive globally; as True (2021, p. 33) contends, it is 'the most prevalent yet least recognized human rights violation'. At the same time, gendered violence is significantly undercounted; what 'counts' as gendered violence is often ambiguous and contested, in part because much harm occurs within the context of intimate relationships and in the privacy of the home (Fitz-Gibbon and Walklate 2021). Indeed, research indicates that intimate partner violence is the most common kind of gendered violence worldwide (True 2021). However, the human rights architecture was largely developed with a masculine bias that prioritized harm experienced by men in the public sphere. Attention to gender-based violence and violence in the private sphere is a much more recent development.

Human Rights Instruments and Initiatives Related to Gendered Violence

A variety of human rights instruments and initiatives pertain to gendered violence. For summary purposes, these can be considered in four broad categories. The first category includes initiatives that focus on equality, non-discrimination, and empowerment of women. These include the Universal Declaration of Human Rights (UDHR); the Commission on the Status of Women (CSW); and the Global Campaign for Women's Human Rights. According to the UN, the CSW is the 'principal global intergovernmental body exclusively dedicated to the promotion of gender equality and the empowerment of women' (UN Global Issues: Gender Equality). Many social, economic, and political rights that bear on gendered violence, including those pertaining to education, marriage, and reproduction, are further elaborated in the International Covenant on Civil and Political Rights; the International Covenant on Economic, Social and Cultural Rights; and the Platform for Action for Equality, Development and Peace. Perhaps the most important instrument pertaining to gendered violence is the Convention on Elimination of All Forms of Discrimination Against Women (CEDAW) which explicitly defines women's rights as human rights. CEDAW's formal recommendations obligate signatory states to protect women from violence and hold states responsible for preventing private acts of violence (Brysk 2016). Feminist criminologists have relied upon these documents when engaging in research on women's rights in the public, social, political, cultural, and economic fields, with the most important document being CEDAW (Barberet and Rodriguez-Spahia 2016; Wonders and Danner 2001, 2015). As True (2012, p. 32) notes, 'the UN's CEDAW (1979), signed and ratified by 189 states, considers that violence against women is a form of gender discrimination that negatively impacts women globally'.

A second category of human rights initiatives addresses gendered violence that occurs in specific contexts. Gendered violence related to conflict and war is discussed in the Declaration of Elimination of Violence Against Women, the UN Convention on the Prevention and Punishment of Genocide, and UN Committee Against Torture. Some criminologists have used these documents to frame gender-based violence during and after conflict as a human rights violation, in part to argue for international intervention and aid (Barberet 2014; Barberet and Carrington 2018). Concern with gendered violence related to imprisonment is contained in the Bangkok Rules which deals with women's rights in prison. Gendered violence related to trafficking of women and children is targeted in the Protocol to Prevent, Suppress and Punish Trafficking in Persons (UN Convention Against Transnational Organized Crime). Because this document relies heavily on a criminal justice response to trafficking, some criminologists have argued that it heightens vulnerability to violence for migrants (Milivojevic et al. 2017).

A third category of human rights initiatives tackles gendered violence by focusing on development. The most expansive to the human right agenda has been the UN Sustainable Development Goals (SDGs). Adopted by the UN General Assembly in 2015, the 2030 SDGs agenda focuses on a range of environmental and human rights issues. Criminologists who study gendered violence have focused on SDG 5, which seeks to 'eliminate all forms of violence against all women and girls in the public and private spheres, including trafficking and sexual and other types of exploitation', as well as 'eliminate all harmful practices, such as child, early and forced marriage and female genital mutilation' (Blaustein et al. 2018, p. 777).

The fourth category of human rights initiatives related to gendered violence addresses sexual orientation and gender identity. The Protection Against Violence and Discrimination Based on Sexual Orientation and Gender Identity considers violence related to sexuality or gender identity. Given that 'as of 2020, more than 70 countries in the world still criminalize same-sex relations or diverse gender identities, 11 of which maintain the penalty of death' (Madrigal-Borloz 2021, p. 173), this instrument is crucial for expanding human rights protections.

Human rights initiatives regarding gendered violence have met with several challenges. Some nations have simply refused to address gendered violence that harms women. As Blaustein et al. (2018, p. 323) note, 'a 2017 Report of the World Bank indicates that 49 countries still have no domestic violence legislation, 45 countries have no legislation addressing sexual harassment and 37 countries do not consider rape a criminal offence if the perpetrator is married to or subsequently marries the victim'. Further, there remains a tragic record of governmental inaction and unwillingness to confront the systemic inequalities that underlie much gendered violence. Much of the legislation that has been passed within nation-states in response to human rights initiatives addresses the impact of gendered violence but fails to address root causes. Typical approaches include criminalizing offenders and providing victim services. Unfortunately, the focus on punitive legislation has often undermined efforts to improve gender justice by criminalizing already marginalized groups (Gruber 2023), while victim services occur *after* the violence has occurred. Another challenge with many human rights initiatives is their tendency to naturalize the gender/sex binary by treating females as a separate category of humanity. Many key human rights documents focus specifically on 'women'. Some criminologists argue that this focus is essential for drawing attention to unique characteristics of gendered violence (Barberet 2014). However, others argue that such an approach challenges the universality of human rights and marginalizes gendered violence, suggesting that a more effective approach might be to reconceptualize gendered harms like intimate partner violence as a 'crime against humanity' or 'state crime' as a strategy to center state responsibility for the structural inequalities that contribute to gendered violence (Collins 2018; Rose 2015). Human rights frames place primary responsibility for 'fixing' the gendered harm on nation-states, but it is important to keep in mind that state action—or inaction—often *is* the problem. As Collins (2018, p. 179) notes, 'the state is overrepresented as a perpetrator of violence' around the world'.

Despite these challenges, framing gendered violence as a violation of human rights has been important for heightening international attention to gender-based harm and for applying pressure on nation-states to enact domestic legislation. As evidence of the positive impact of human rights initiatives and norms, Brysk (2016, p. 146) notes that 'Over 120 countries have now adopted some form of legislation on violence against women'. While legislation does not guarantee reductions in violence, law creation is an important strategy for heightening the accountability of nation-states for gendered violence. Framing gendered violence as a human rights violation has also served as an important tactic for mobilizing action. As Brysk (2018, pp. 9–10) emphasizes, 'human rights is *movement*, not doctrine – a movement of mobilization, a movement of political process toward accountability and empowerment, and a movement towards norms of freedom, dignity and equality'. It is with this understanding of human rights in mind that we consider a future research agenda for criminologists committed to preventing gendered violence.

Future Priorities for a Human Rights Agenda for Criminology

Given the nation-centric bias of criminology, there has been a shortage of criminological research that utilizes a human rights frame to examine gendered violence. Yet, there *is* a significant body of criminological research that has identified many of key drivers of gendered violence. It is our view that future criminological research should utilize—and help expand—the existing human rights architecture to target these key drivers.

In this section, we identify four key dynamics that can be viewed as root causes of gendered violence since they work to *produce* gender inequality, vulnerabilities to violence, and harm. Framing these dynamics as human rights challenges has the potential to scale up discourse about gendered violence to the international level as a strategy to apply normative pressure to nation-states to heighten their accountability for gendered violence via legal and policy change, and to scale it downward to the local level as a vehicle for mobilizing local action and community engagement to address gendered violence.

The Slow Gendered Violence of Structural Inequality

Slow violence is defined as violence that is not sudden, but rather builds incrementally and produces inequalities and impacts that may not be felt for years or centuries (Nixon 2011; Wonders 2018b). Future criminological research must take seriously the accumulated research that evidences that the slow violence of gender inequality is foundational to gendered violence in virtually all forms. As Walklate et al. (2020, p. 9) emphasize:

> The drivers of gender violence, and intimate partner violence, as the most common type of such violence, are consistently linked to gender inequality. This inequality is manifest in many subtle, obvious, and diverse ways across the globe: from the wages gap, the absence of limited presence of women in leadership positions in politics and in public space, the exclusion of women from education, to the refusal to ensure women's educational achievements translate into careers that match those of their less educated male counterparts, to mention but a few examples.

A focus on the drivers of gender inequality suggests the need for a broad research portfolio for criminology that remains focused on the various forms of gendered violence but prioritizes research on the conditions that create vulnerabilities to violence in the first place. In addition to the list of inequalities identified by Walklate et al. (2020) above, we would also encourage greater criminological focus on inequalities and harm linked to gender socialization, reproductive labor and care work, and those linked to class, race, ethnicity, sexuality, and other socially constructed differences that contribute to gendered injustice (Henne and Torshynski 2019). As True (2021, p. 180) explains, a focus on economic empowerment is particularly important since '[s]tructural interventions linking economic strengthening to gender transformation are increasingly being recognized as critical to tackling the intersections of women's risks of and vulnerability to violence'.

An understanding of structural inequalities that affect gendered violence must also include inequalities between nation-states and those produced by global and transnational dynamics. Gendered violence is not evenly distributed worldwide; 'violence disproportionately affects women living in low and lower-middle income countries' (WHO 2021). Recent criminological research about and from the Global South provides a valuable foundation for considering gendered violence with the context of global inequalities (Carrington et al. 2016). It is especially important to focus research on the 'political economy of gendered violence' and the extreme harm and inequality generated by neoliberal economic policies and neo-colonialism (Ciocchini and Greener 2021). One research strategy for more deeply engaging international inequalities between nations and elevating the priorities of the Global South is for criminologists to focus research on the potential for the International Covenant on Economic, Social and Cultural Rights to be used to address gender inequality given its attention to economic and cultural rights. Another is to continue to build on the nascent and promising research on the UN Sustainable Development goals as a way to directly target structural global inequalities (Blaustein et al. 2018).

Criminological research can help to unpack the ways that nation-states are complicit in creating the conditions that make gendered violence so common. We particularly value the work of feminist and critical criminologists who have focused attention on gendered violence that is state facilitated (Barak 2021; Collins 2018). For example, some recent scholarship has utilized a human right frame to highlight how femicide is often state facilitated, with the goal of heightening state accountability, tracking, and violence reduction (Walklate et al. 2020; Walkate et al. 2019). As Collins (2018, p. 186) notes 'Gender-based violence…is not simply a feature of micro-level interactions between individual actors, but is deeply and historically embedded in communities, institutions, and most importantly the state itself'.

State sovereignty is deeply embedded within the human rights regime, but the changing character of the state under globalization, particularly its pivotal role in advancing neoliberal capitalism globally, requires that approaches to human rights shift and change as well. Human rights instruments provide a useful set of normative tools for criminologists who wish to assess state compliance with international standards for promoting gender justice within, between, and beyond nation-states in a globalized world.

Gendered Impacts of Conflict and Climate Change—And Gendered Barriers to Mobility

Criminological research has documented the gendered character of the mobility and displacement caused by contemporary conflicts and climate change, as well as gendered barriers to mobility (Pickering 2011; Pickering and Cochrane 2013; Wonders 2018b). These dynamics are expected to increase dramatically in the very near future given the anticipated increase in conflict and displacement associated with global warming (Wonders and Danner 2015).

While neoliberal globalization ensures that capital and the wealthy are able to cross borders with ease, nation-states have developed sophisticated strategies for regulating the mobility of less advantaged border crossers (Milivojevic et al. 2017; Weber 2015; Wonders and Jones 2021). Bordering has become an increasingly powerful strategy for constructing difference and allocating privilege (Pickering and Weber 2011; Wonders and Jones 2021). The global mobility regime reflects and produces inequalities, including gendered vulnerabilities that are being further exacerbated by conflict and climate change.

National restrictions on mobility are increasingly justified by framing migration as a crisis. However, research has evidenced that existing inequalities, including gender hierarchies, are amplified by the use of crisis frames (Shevat 2023; Wonders 2018b; Wonders and Jones 2021). Dominant framings of violence, risk, and security tend to increase women's insecurity and vulnerability to violence. Criminologists can play a valuable role in reframing women's displacement and insecurity as human rights concerns; doing so breaks the link between the rhetoric of 'crisis', securitization, and the legitimation of gendered violence.

Migration is one of the primary adaptation strategies for many people facing the effects of conflict and climate change. However, there is a gendered 'adaptation deficit' given that women are more likely to have resource deficits, care responsibilities that constrain their mobility, and limited voice in decision-making regarding adaptation strategies. These dynamics contribute to higher mortality rates for women during environmental disasters (True 2012). Research has also found that gender-based violence increases in post-disaster contexts (Quan 2015). Female climate refugees are more vulnerable to violence and victimization when compared to their male counterparts because of the profound inequalities they experience across social and political life; as Quan (2015, p. 114) explains 'the common violations of women's rights that make them more vulnerable to climate change effects include discrimination as regards education, gender role stereotyping, and public participation'.

Currently, international law fails to provide effective protection to those displaced by environmental danger and national border regimes relegate many climate refugees to stateless subjects without the rights of citizenship and state protection, producing the structural conditions driving the high rates of gendered violence experienced by migrants and refugees (Pickering 2011). Human rights discourse and instruments are strategic tools that criminologists can utilize to document the gendered harm experienced by those who are displaced and to frame global challenges like conflict and climate change as unjust; they also serve an essential vehicle for displaced people to claim rights beyond the boundaries of citizenship.

Right-Wing and Religious Extremism and the Resurgence of Nationalism

Another contemporary challenge that warrants focused criminological attention is the resurgence of nationalism and the rise of right-wing and religious extremism in many countries around the world. Right-wing and religious extremists fuel patriarchal, misogynistic, and racist attitudes that contribute to gendered violence. They have also fostered hostile discourses toward international bodies that seek to hold nation-states accountable for violence that occurs domestically and, in doing so, pose a threat to an already fragile international human rights regime.

Recent events in the United States provide a disturbing illustration of these dynamics which are giving new durability to gender inequalities.

The ascendance of Donald Trump to the US Presidency provided a global platform for the airing of misogynistic views and public attacks on gender and sexual difference, as well as advocacy for reduced rights and social exclusion of minoritized groups, a dynamic that can be observed in other countries as well (Henne and Troshynski 2019; Koulish and van der Woude 2020). The Trump administration was successful in transforming the US Supreme Court and federal courts by appointing extremely conservative judges (Wonders and Danner 2020), a tactic that is key for understanding the historic reversal of the *Roe v. Wade* landmark decision regarding abortion. Given the lengthy terms of federal judges, this transformation of the judiciary portends significant future attacks on reproductive rights, as well as further rollbacks on rights linked to gender and sexual expression. The growing influence of the extreme right over legislatures and the judiciary in the US has led to public policies that restrict and virtually eliminate abortion rights in some states and impose serious restrictions on the expression of alternative sexual identities. As Celorio (2022, p. 84) emphasizes, 'it is important to underscore that sexual and reproductive rights are an integral part of the human rights of women'. The Trump administration also began a process of regulatory rollbacks that sought to dismantle many important social protections, with disproportionate impacts on women and LGBTQ+ people (Wonders and Danner 2020). The political capture of the courts by the extreme right and religious fundamentalists has become part of a global game plan that is well underway in many countries, yet an independent judiciary is fundamental to the protection of rights.

While rights for minoritized genders and sexualities are being rolled back in some of the democracies of the West, in many other countries, such as Afghanistan and Iran, women's access to basic political and civil rights remain sharply curtailed and state violence is being used to silence and demobilize those who advocate for basic rights and gender justice.

It is essential to focus criminological attention on the efforts of the extreme right, religious fundamentalist, and nationalist groups to enforce—and restore—traditional gender hierarchies, reduce reproductive rights, and reinforce masculine power and privilege given the threat these efforts pose to gender justice and to democratic processes that are the foundation of contemporary human rights regime.

Power from Above and Below

Around the world, women and minoritized sexualities are underrepresented in governmental and justice system decision-making, including in key institutions responsible for promoting human rights (Runyan 2019). It matters that it is primarily wealthy white men who dominate decision-making about the character of justice. Gendered barriers to power ensure the continuation of patriarchy. In a globalized world, power is exercised at multiple scales—international, national, and local—and it is crucial for more diverse voices to gain power and representation at each level. While some international bodies and nation-states have implemented gender quotas, given that gender and sexual identities are increasingly unstable signifiers and cross-cutting with other kinds of difference, new interdisciplinary research is needed to gauge whether and how power from above can best be achieved. Research is also needed to explore how challenges to gender and sexual binaries, particularly by LGBTQ+ communities, can further expand the boundaries of representation, human rights discourse, and the pursuit of gender justice. Yet, it is crucial to acknowledge that political rights and representation are not sufficient for creating change; they must be accompanied by broader social and cultural change. As Weber et al. (2014, p. 63) note, 'Patriarchy is an example of systemic discrimination against women that is supported widely by social, cultural and religious beliefs, and so deeply entrenched in everyday practices that it often goes unnoticed'. Research plays an important role in making these dynamics visible.

Given the intransigence of nation-states with respect to gender inequality and gendered violence, criminologists must consider the localization of human rights as one strategy for creating change. Some criminologists have drawn attention to women-only police stations and transit systems in countries of the Global South as examples of local responses to gendered violence (Barberet and Carrington 2018). Other criminologists have examined city-level strategies that protect the human rights of border crossers (Wonders and Bessa-Fernández 2021). This research reveals that many subnational levels of governance have the capacity to offer the substantive human rights protections nation-states are refusing to provide.

Future criminological research can contribute to theoretical and practical understanding of how to facilitate utilization of human rights discourse and instruments to leverage change from below. For example, some criminologists have been successful in creating high-profile institutes that focus on gendered violence and facilitate direct collaboration between researchers and those most affected by violence, as well as organizations and policymakers who are best positioned to implement effective solutions. Taking human rights discourse to the local level grounds commitments to a particular place where the diverse needs of local and indigenous cultures can be taken into account.

Another strand of criminological research reveals that migrants are playing a fundamentally important role in 'transforming borders from below' by unsettling conceptions of gender, race, citizenship, and demanding rights protections and global justice; by framing irregular migration as a social movement, criminological theorizing and research can help to elevate demands for human rights protection and change (Segrave and Wonders 2019; Wonders and Jones 2021). Similarly, those most affected by gender injustices are increasingly mobilizing through NGOs and women's rights organizations to demand that solutions be considered from their vantage point and perspectives. The pursuit of international gender justice requires that criminologists prioritize attention to the voices of those most affected by gender injustices and gendered violence if we are to effectively understand and address the complex dynamics that produce inequalities and harm in the first place.

A human rights-centered criminological agenda for the future will wisely help to identify how the dynamics that drive gendered violence can be changed from above, at all levels of governance and decision-making about human rights and gender justice, and from below, in the many places where people have power in everyday life—and where the personal is always political.

References

Barak, Maya Pagni. 2021. Family Separation as State-Corporate Crime. *Journal of White Collar and Corporate Crime* 2 (2): 109–121.

Barberet, Rosemary. 2014. *Women, Crime and Criminal Justice: A Global Enquiry*. London: Routledge.

Barberet, Rosemary, and Kerry Carrington. 2018. Globalizing Feminist Criminology: Gendered Violence During Peace and War. In *The Palgrave Handbook of Criminology and the Global South*, ed. R. Hogg, R.J. Scott, and M. Sozzo, 821–845. New York: Palgrave.

Barberet, Rosemary, and Diana Rodriguez-Spahia. 2016. Feminist Criminology and Human Rights. In *The Routledge International Handbook of Criminology and Human Rights*, ed. L. Weber, E. Fishwick, and M. Marmo, 1st ed. London: Routledge. https://doi.org/10.4324/9781315679891.

Belknap, Joanne. 2015. *The Invisible Woman: Gender, Crime and Justice*. Stamford, CT: Cengage.

Blaustein, Jarett, Nathan W. Pino, Kate Fitz-Gibbon, and Rob White. 2018. Criminology and the UN Sustainable Development Goals: The Need for Support and Critique. *The British Journal of Criminology* 58 (4): 767–786.

Brysk, Alison. 2016. Violence Against Women: Law and Its Limits. *Deusto Journal of Human Rights* 1: 145–173.

Brysk, Alison. 2018. Expanding Rights: New Frames for Violence Against Women. In *Expanding Human Rights: 21st Century Norms and Governance*, ed. A. Brysk, 77–93.

Buist, Carrie L., and Emily Lenning. 2022. *Queer Criminology*. New York: Routledge.

Carrington, Kerry. 2014. *Feminism and Global Justice*. New York: Routledge.

Carrington, Kerry, Russell Hogg, and Maximo Sozzo. 2016. Southern Criminology. *British Journal of Criminology* 56: 1–20.

Caulfield, Susan. L., and Nancy A. Wonders. 1993. Personal AND Political: Violence Against Women and the Role of the State. In *Political Crime in Contemporary America: A Critical Approach*, ed. K.D. Tunnel. New York: Garland Press.

Celorio, Rosa. 2022. Sexual and Reproductive Rights: A Gender Equality and International Law Approach. In *Women and International Human Rights in Modern Times: A Contemporary Casebook*, 184–216.

Ciocchini, Pablo, and Joe Greener. 2021. Mapping the Pains of Neoliberalism. *The British Journal of Criminology* 61: 1612–1629.

Collins Victoria E. 2018. Feminist Perspectives on State Crimes Against Women. In *The Routledge International Handbook of Violence Studies*, ed. W.S. DeKeseredy, C.M. Rennison, and A.K. Hall-Sanchez, 179–189.

Detraz, Nicole. 2017. Gender and Environmental (In)security: From Climate Conflict to Ecosystem Instability. In *Routledge International Handbook on Gender and Environment*, ed. S. Macgregor. New York: Routledge.

Federici, Sylvia. 2004. *Caliban and the Witch: Women, the Body, and Primitive Accumulation*. New York: Autonomedia.

Fitz-Gibbon, Kate, and Sandra Walklate. 2021. Eliminating All Forms of Violence Against All Women and Girls: Some Criminological Reflections on the Challenges of Measuring Success and Gauging Progress. In *Emerald Handbook of Crime, Justice and Sustainable Development*, ed. J. Blaustein, K. Fitz-Gibbon, N.W. Fine, and R. White, 315–332. Emerald Publishing.

Gruber, Aya. 2023. The Critique of Carceral Feminism. *Yale Journal of Law and Feminism* 34 (2): 55–62.

Henne, Kathryn, and Emily L. Torshynski. 2019. Intersectional Criminologies for the Contemporary Moment: Crucial Questions of Power, Praxis and Technologies. *Critical Criminology* 27: 55–71.

Koulish, Robert, and Maartje van der Woude. 2020. *Crimmigrant Nations: Resurgent Nationalism and the Closing of Borders*. New York: Fordham University Press.

Madrigal-Borloz, Victor. 2021. The Price That Is Paid: Violence and Discrimination Based on Sexual Orientation and Gender Identity and Poverty. In *Research Handbook on Human Rights and Poverty*, ed. M. F. Davis, M. Kjaerum, and A. Lyons. Elgar.

Milivojevic, Sanja, Marie Segrave, and Sharon Pickering. 2017. The Limits of Migration-Related Human Rights: Connecting Exploitation to Immobility. In *The Routledge Handbook of Criminology and Human Rights*, ed. L. Weber, E. Fishwick, and M. Marmo, 291–300. New York: Routledge.

Nixon, Rob. 2011. *Slow Violence and the Environmentalism of the Poor*. Cambridge: Harvard University Press.

Pickering, Sharon. 2011. *Women, borders and violence: Current issues in asylum, forced migration, and trafficking*. New York: Springer.

Pickering, Sharon, and Brandy Cochrane. 2013. Irregular Border Crossing Deaths and Gender: Where, How and Why Women Die Crossing Borders. *Theoretical Criminology* 17 (1): 27–48.

Pickering, Sharon, and Leanne Weber. 2011. *Globalization and Borders: Death at the Global Frontier*. New York: Palgrave Macmillan.

Quan, Ryan J.D. 2015. Securing Women's Rights Amid the Changing Climate. *Atteneo Law Journal*, 60: 98–125.
Ritchie, Andrea. 2017. Enduring Legacies. *Invisible No More: Police Violence Against Black Women and Women of Color*. Boston: Beacon Press.
Rose, Evelyn. 2015. A Feminist Reconceptualization of Intimate Partner Violence Against Women: A Crime Against Humanity and a State Crime. *Women's Studies International Forum* 53: 31–42.
Runyan, Anne Sisson. 2019. *Global Gender Politics*. New York: Routledge.
Segrave, Marie and Nancy A. Wonders. 2019. Special Issue, "Introduction: Transforming Borders from Below: Theory and Research from Across the Globe," *Theoretical Criminology* 23 (2): 133–135.
Shevat, Sydney. 2023. Framing Climate Change Induced Displacement: Causes, Consequences, and Solutions. Unpublished Master's Thesis. Northern Arizona University.
True, Jacqui. 2012. *The Political Economy of Violence Against Women*. New York: Oxford University Press.
True, Jacqui. 2021. *Violence Against Women: What Everyone Needs to Know*. New York: Oxford University Press.
Walkate, Sandra, Jude McCulloch, and Kate Fitz-Gibbon. 2019. Criminology, Gender and Security in the Australian Context: Making Women's Lives Matter. *Theoretical Criminology* 23 (1): 60–77.
Walklate, Sandra, Kate Fitz-Gibbon, Jude McCulloch, and JaneMaree Maher. 2020. *Towards a Global Femicide Index: Counting the Costs*. Routledge.
Weber, Leanne. 2015. *Rethinking Border Control for a Globalising World: A Preferred Future*. New York: Routledge.
Weber, Leanne, Elaine Fishwick, and Marinella Marmo. 2014. *Crime, Justice and Human Rights*. Basingstoke: Palgrave Macmillan.
Wonders, Nancy A. 2018a. Gender, Crime, and Justice. In *Investigating Difference: Human and Cultural Relations in Criminal Justice*, 3rd ed., ed. S. Prior and L. Jones, 69–90. New York: Pearson.
Wonders, Nancy A. 2018b. Climate Change, the Production of Gendered Insecurity, and Slow Intimate Partner Violence. In *Intimate Partner Violence, Risk and Security: Securing Women's Lives in a Global World*, ed. K. Fitz-Gibbon, S. Walklate, J. McCullloch, and J. Maher, 34–51. New York: Routledge.
Wonders, Nancy A., and Cristina Bessa-Fernández. 2021. Border Struggles, Political Unity, and the Transformative Power of the Local: U.S. Sanctuary Cities and Spain's Cities of Refuge. *International Journal for Crime, Justice and Social Democracy* 10 (3): 1–15.

Wonders, Nancy A., and Mona Danner. 2001. Globalization, State-Corporate Crime, and Women: The Strategic Role of Women's NGOs in the New World Order. In *Controversies in White Collar Crime*, ed. G.W. Potter. New York: Routledge.

Wonders, Nancy A., and Mona J.E. Danner. 2015. Gendering Climate Change: A Feminist Criminological Perspective. *Critical Criminology* 23 (4): 401–416.

Wonders, Nancy A., and Mona J.E. Danner. 2020. Regulatory Rollbacks and Deepening Social Inequality. *Journal of White Collar and Corporate Crime* 1 (2): 103–112.

Wonders, Nancy A., and Lynn C. Jones. 2021. Challenging the Borders of Difference and Inequality: Power in Migration as a Social Movement for Global Justice. In *Handbook of Migration and Global Justice*, ed. L. Weber and C. Tazreiter. Elgar.

World Health Organization. 2021. Devastatingly Pervasive: 1 in 3 Women Globally Experience Violence. https://www.who.int/news/item/09-03-2021-devastatingly-pervasive-1-in-3-women-globally-experience-violence. Accessed 22 May 2023.

14

Toward a Human Rights Criminology of Public Health

Raymond Michalowski and Rebecca Annorbah

Parable 1: Two Deaths

Imagine two young people, Amy and Jack are walking in a small park in the Streeterville section of Chicago, United States. They spot a white man, about 60 years old, strolling ahead of them. His clothes and his watch mark him as good pickings. Amy attracts his attention by asking for the time. While the man is looking down at his Rolex, Jack steps behind him and fires a .22 caliber bullet into the back of his head, execution style, killing him instantly. They grab the victim's wallet and watch, and make their get-away.

Few would doubt that this was murder. This killing, however, was more than an instant in time. As a white resident of Streeterville, their

R. Michalowski (✉) · R. Annorbah
Northern Arizona University, Flagstaff, AZ, USA
e-mail: Raymond.Michalowski@nau.edu

R. Annorbah
e-mail: ra854@nau.edu

L. Weber and M. Marmo (eds.), *A Research Agenda for a Human Rights Centred Criminology*, Palgrave Critical Studies in Human Rights and Criminology,
https://doi.org/10.1007/978-3-031-46289-4_14

victim had a good chance of living to 90 years of age—the average life expectancy for people in that neighborhood (Habitat Chicago 2020). In addition to his watch and wallet, they likely stole as much as 30 years of his life. If they faced a wrongful death lawsuit, those 30 years would be critical in determining the damages awarded the victim's heirs (ZD Law 2022).

Imagine now, that just as they were committing this murder, a 60-year-old African-American man in Chicago's Englewood neighborhood died from a stroke due to untreated high blood pressure. Since he had reached the average life expectancy for male Englewood residents, there was little surprise. In his neighborhood, he was, in Ehrenreich's (2018) words, 'old enough to die.' A wrongful death lawsuit would be unlikely because there is no obvious guilty party. And even if there was, the value of any award would be minimal because the victim's life expectancy was all but exhausted.

Core Questions

Our parable is played out in real life every day, around the United States and across the globe. Put simply, the affluent live longer, healthier lives than those from lower income strata (Glei et al. 2022). Research has increasingly confirmed a positive relationship between higher income and longer life expectancy (Chetty et al. 2016; Deaton 2013; Marmot 2015; Waldron 2013). One 2017 study of Seattle and its surrounding county, for example, found an 18-year difference in the life expectancy of men living in census tracts with the highest life expectancy compared to those from tracts with the lowest (Dwyer-Lindgren et al. 2017). Similarly, other studies have shown a gap in life expectancy based on race, class, and gender (Harper et al. 2007; Riddell et al. 2018). One study, tracing Black-White disparities in Washington DC from 2000 to 2016 showed that African Americans, on average, died 17 years younger than Whites in that city (Roberts et al. 2020). These class and race dynamics are not limited to the United States, but have been found in other developed countries as well. After assessing the relationship between income and mortality in developed countries, Wilkinson

(1992, p. 167) concluded that 'there is clear evidence of the relationship between society's income distribution and the average life expectancy of its population.'

The demonstrable interconnection among economic status, racial identity, and exposure to beneficial or harmful social determinants of health raises three meta-theoretical questions that animate this chapter:

Are the average shorter lives and worse health of poorer and/or minority populations *within* the United States, or in other nations a violations of human rights?
Are the differences in life expectancy and average health *between* those living in less developed as compared to more affluent nations a violation of human rights?
Does the gap in life and health between the affluent and the poor, both within and between nations have anything to do with a human rights criminology?

It is our contention that the lost years of our imaginary Englewood stroke victim, like those of so many actual people, are not stolen by people acting with criminal intent, but by agents of social systems who, *deliberately, casually, and without feeling guilt*, allocate positive social determinates of health to some, while promoting institutional arrangements, policies, and practices that withhold them from others. Insofar as these outcomes are predictable and avoidable they are, to use Agnew's (2011, p. 194) term 'morally blameworthy social harms.' As such, they are appropriate objects of criminological inquiry.

Some mainstream criminologists might object to the idea that criminology can appropriately incorporate acts that have not been designated as crimes by law into the subject matter of criminology. However, failing to do so renders the field a hermetically sealed, tautological enterprise. There is nothing new or radical in this observation. Nearly 150 years ago, the nineteenth-century Italian criminologist Rafael Garafolo (1885/1914, p. 59) observed that 'the attempt to show us what the law views as crime ends in our being told that crime, in the eyes of the law, is the doing of that which the law itself forbade.' In a similar rejection of criminology as a subset of law, in the first edition of his foundational textbook,

Criminology, Edwin Sutherland (1924, p. 20) proposed that 'the legal definition of crime is purely formal and inadequate.' From our perspective, harm takes many forms, but only some of them are singled out for legal control. Some harms are over-selected for criminalization, while others are under-selected (Weis 2017). One of the central tasks of criminology *should be* to identify what explains those differences, although it is a task that is often ignored.

How perfectly legal acts can allocate poor health and early death to some, and comparatively healthy lives to others was made particularly clear during the Trump administration in multiple ways. One was Trump's promotion of resistance to public health measures during the COVID-19 pandemic such as mask wearing, aimed at slowing community spread of the disease. Others included the promotion of bogus treatments and the tacit (and sometimes explicit) ways Trump and his political operatives helped mobilize a social movement against intervention strategies (Hotez, 2023; Coles 2020).

In addition to malign COVID-19 policies, the Trump administration undertook a broad assault on regulatory policies, practices, and institutions designed to protect public health. This assault was both ordinary and extraordinary. It was ordinary insofar as neo-liberal economic theory, since the 1980s, has served as a warrant for Conservative efforts to limit government regulation of markets, including rolling back regulations created to protect life and health (Claybrook 1984; Eilperin 2017; Patterson 1967; Lloyd and Davenport 2013). In this way, Trump's regulatory rollbacks were ordinary pro-business efforts to protect the private accumulation of capital.

Trump's rollbacks, however, were extraordinary for (1) the breadth of regulations targeted, (2) their attempt to undermine the operational structure of the regulatory system, (3) the replacement of science with ideology as the basis for regulatory rule-making, and (4) promoting workplace strategies to demoralize those employed by regulatory agencies (Lewis 2018). Together, these signaled an anti-regulation lurch to the right that remains proactive at this writing, threatening the life, health, and development of humans and other animals, as well as long-term environmental risks whose effects remain in the mists of the future

(Michalowski and Brown 2019). This increasingly malignant intersection of corporate profit-seeking and anti-regulatory government policies is one example of what Aulette and Michalowski (1993) identified as *state facilitated corporate crimes* that should be incorporated into human rights criminology of public health as explored below.

The Human Right to Health

The Universal Declaration of Human Rights (UDHR), the socio-legal foundation for the contemporary understanding of human rights, recognizes that health and the pre-conditions for it are human rights, *to wit*:

> Article 25
> Everyone has the right to a standard of living adequate for the health and well-being of himself and of his family, including food, clothing, housing and medical care and necessary social services, and the right to security in the event of unemployment, sickness, disability, widowhood, old age or other lack of livelihood in circumstances beyond his control. (United Nations 1948)

The UDHR, however, was an aspirational document. Fulfilling those aspirations required additional legal frameworks and organizational structures. Two important steps in this direction were the creation of the World Health Organization (WHO) in 1948 and the adoption of International Covenant on Economic, Social and Cultural Rights (ICESCR) in 1966.

The WHO (1948) charter defines *health* as 'the complete physical, mental, and social well-being of the whole person, not merely the absence of disease or infirmity,' and holds that 'the enjoyment of the highest attainable standard of health is one of *the fundamental rights of every human being* without distinction of race, religion, political belief, economic or social condition'[1] (Authors' emphasis). In 1966, ICESCR set forth a set of steps countries should follow to achieve the 'highest attainable standard of health.' Specifically:

> The steps to be taken by the States parties to the present Covenant to achieve the full realization of this right shall include those necessary for: (a) The provision for the reduction of the stillbirth-rate and of infant mortality and for the healthy development of the child; (b) The improvement of all aspects of environmental and industrial hygiene; (c) The prevention, treatment and control of epidemic, endemic, occupational and other diseases; (d) The creation of conditions which would assure to all medical service and medical attention in the event of sickness.

The language of the World Health Organization, the UNDHR, the ICESCR as well as many regional documents like the European Social Charter recognizes that the right to health includes a fundamental right to positive *social determinants of health*. According to the WHO, social determinants of health are the conditions in which people are born, grow, live, work, and age and the wider set of forces and systems shaping the conditions of daily life (Commission on Social Determinants of Health 2008; WHO 2013). These determinants shape individuals' opportunities to lead healthy lives and can have a profound impact on their health outcomes.

The practical and organizational pathways to achieving equitable distribution of positive social determinants of health require affirmative actions at national and local levels (Wallace 2007). It is at these levels that governments, acting on their own, or in concert with economic institutions, often work to preserve or extend status-quo, unequal distribution of positive social determinants of health in contravention of the formally recognized human rights to health.

Providing equitable access to positive social determinants of health would require major structural and cultural changes in political-economic practices (Fox 2013; Sharma et al. 2018). The core change needed would require moving away from a global political economy structured in accordance with the profit-seeking imperatives of multinational and transnational corporations, and toward one structured more closely around the needs of natural persons rather than corporate ones (Biehl and Petryna 2013; Wist 2010).

Despite the substantial structural barrier to creating equitable distribution of positive social determinants of health, the conditions that make it possible are well established as fundamental human rights under in international law, as well as the national laws of the 160 countries have ratified the ICESCR. With more than 80 percent of countries recognizing the ICESCR, it is now international customary law and can be considered applicable to all countries, even those few like the United States, that have not ratified the treaty (International Committee of the Red Cross 2023). Thus, we argue that actions by individuals, corporate entities, and political states, acting individually or together, that create avoidable threats to health (acts of commission), or fail to take available steps to avoid or mitigate these threats (acts of omission), are no less guilty of crimes than those who engage in or facilitate other violations of human rights. We term these acts *public health crimes*.

Public Health and Criminology

In the 1980s, the concept of *population health* became an increasingly important component of public health research and policy-making. Population health extends beyond the cumulative health of individuals. It involves identifying how health is distributed across different, identifiable social groupings (Dutton, 2008; Starfield 2001). By focusing on the divergent health outcomes for identifiable population groups based on characteristics such as gender, race/ethnicity, location, or social class, population health studies spurred a growing recognition of the importance of understanding and addressing *group-based health disparities.* This served as the foundation for the contemporary movement for *health equity* (Kolars and Conger 2023).

It is worth noting that the attention to group-based disparities in health that emerged in the last decades of the twentieth century parallels similar trends in criminological research, particularly those strands falling under the broad umbrella of critical criminology. Feminist criminology targeted the victimization of women, not just through crimes of sexual assault, but for a broad variety of social harms that weigh particularly heavy on women, such as poverty, war, and global climate change (Belknap 2020; Van Wormer 2008; Wonders 2017). The prison abolition movement focused attention on the racial and ethnic disparity in incarceration and other forms of carceral control (Gilmore 2007; Miller 2014; Piché and Larsen 2010). Similarly, queer criminology analyzed the many ways both civil law and criminal justice systems brutalize and disadvantage those who do not conform to the dominant heterosexual mandate (Kosenko and Nelson 2018; Russell 2017). However, although public health and the various forms of critical criminology were on parallel tracks, they only rarely intersected explicitly, even though each was increasingly concerned with the way subaltern and socially disadvantaged groups were disproportionately subject to harms against their physical, psychological, economic, and emotional well-being.

The subject matter of both mainstream and critical criminology is crimes and social harms that, in many cases, are either direct or indirect threats to public health. Consider the following state-corporate crime of omission. In 1979, the Centers for Disease Control in the United States identified one of the central topics of mainstream criminology—direct, person-to-person violence—as a public health problem. In 1992, it established the National Center for Injury Prevention and Control (NCIPC) to study the causes of violence and propose ways to reduce its presence (Romano et al. 2021). The NCIPC initiative focused primarily on the psychological and social-psychological causes of violence. Less attention was given to the structural forces that increase levels of violence. Nevertheless, it might have been an initial step in forging a link between the study of crime and the study of public health. This fledgling effort, however, died an early death in 1996 at the hands of the 'Dickey Amendment,' passed at the behest of the America's powerful gun-industry lobby. This amendment to that year's spending bill barred the CDC from funding research that might lead to gun control legislation. Insofar as firearms were (and are) by far the most common cause of violent deaths in the United States, this accommodation to the profit-making interests of gun manufacturers undercut what would have been twenty years of federally funded research into controlling gun violence in the United States. The result was an increased availability of the high-power, high-capacity weapons that make contemporary mass shootings more likely and more lethal than they were when the Dickey Amendment was passed (Busse 2021). We nominate this as a clear state-corporate crime against the human right to life and bodily integrity. The gun lobby/government nexus did not pull any triggers. But they made sure there would be many more triggers for fingers to pull. The death of federal public health research into gun violence also curtailed what could have been significant cross-cutting linkages between criminology and public health.

One area where criminology and public health have intersected is research and programs focused on physical and behavioral health problems among prison and jail populations (Massoglia and Pridemore 2015; Wallace and Wang 2020). These approaches focus primarily on end-point relations between street crime and health of offenders, particularly when in custody. Largely absent are considerations of the relationship between macro-social forces shaping unequal distributions of positive determinants of social health and the likelihood of becoming enmeshed in the criminal justice system.

More promising linkages between a human rights criminology and public health are found in studies of environmental crime, in recent analyses sparked by the COVID-19 pandemic, Southern criminology, and queer criminology. Of particular note are contributions from environmental or 'green criminology,' as it is sometimes called. These take two forms. One focuses on the relationship between environmental conditions and retail crimes, that is, those where individuals directly harm others. Stretesky and Lynch's (2004) work showing the linkage between concentrations of air-borne lead and violent crime across counties in the United States is one example of this kind of inquiry. Another is Caruso's (2017) inquiry into the intersection of public health and criminal behavior. The other focuses on inquiries that examine choices made by corporations and states to pursue policies and practices that contribute to environmental degradation and biospheric harms that threaten health in violation of existing standards of human rights.

Even though preventable harms to health frequently results from *choices* made in corporate boardrooms and governmental agencies, analyses of corporate and state crimes manifest a curious lacuna when it comes to public health. While these analyses frequently focus on the harmful public health consequence of state and corporate behavior, they rarely identify the harm specifically as a public health problem, or incorporate public health data, methods, and theory into the analyses. Rather, their focus tends to more often be on identifying the criminal actors, whether natural or corporate persons, who are guilty of the wrongdoing.

As a corrective, we offer three propositions. First, a vibrant linkage between the disciplines of criminology and public health can contribute to a better understanding of the societal and organizational bases of what we term *public health crimes*, including both illegal acts and legal but wrongful harms to human well-being (Freudenberg 2014). As we elaborate below, the concept of public health crimes, by virtue of the definition of public health, is inherently located within the frame of human rights violations.

Second, criminologists concerned with corporate crime, state crime, state-corporate crime, and other crimes of power are particularly well positioned to develop what we call an *upstream criminology of public health*.

Finally, if done well, a public health criminology can be more than an academic exercise. It can be an opportunity for criminologists to engage with public health advocates who are working to right the wrongs of health disparity.

Parable 2: Looking Upstream for Public Health Crimes

Public health writers and speakers often use the 'parable of the stream' to call attention to how macro-social forces generate poor health outcomes. The parable typically goes like this: Two women, Madison and Ginny, settle down to picnic next to a swift-flowing river. Soon, however, they hear the shouts of a woman being swept past them in the current. Madison, dives in and rescues the woman. Not long after, a young man appears struggling in the current. Ginny grabs his hand and brings him to the shore. But it didn't stop. People kept coming down the river, and Madison and Ginny were exhausting themselves trying to save them from the current. Madison decided to find out why so many people were at risk of drowning. She ran upstream and soon came upon….and here the parable varies. Sometimes it is because there is a hole in the bridge crossing the stream. Sometimes it is because people struggling with one another along the banks of the river, pushing each other into the current.

At this point in the usual public health narrative, the story ends with some corrective that solves the problem—repairing the hole, putting up a warning sign, or convincing the people to stop fighting. The parable ends with the admonition that we have to look *upstream* for the source of the health problems faced by populations and healthcare systems. As far as it goes, this parable is useful for conceptualizing how macro-social forces generate individual and population health outcomes. We suggest, however, that it ends too soon. So let's add a political-economic component.

When Madison asked why people were trying to push others into the water, they said there was not enough land for everyone to live on. When asked why there wasn't enough land, they said most of it was owned by a few people, and the rest had to try to survive on what little remained.

Parables are not reality. They are stories invented to make a point. The parable of the stream underscores that contemporary and proximate harms do not arise from nowhere. The present is always shaped by the decisions and choices made by people operating within specific social conditions in the past as well as the present (Marx, 1852). Understanding transgressions against human rights to health requires examination of historical and contemporary, macro-social conditions that generate wrongful, downstream harms to public health.

A human rights criminology can make an important contribution to understanding threats to public health by interrogating the way upstream factors are often the source of public health crimes. We further suggest that the theories of *structural violence* (Galtung 1968) and *slow violence* (Nixon 2011) are useful starting points for identifying corrosive economic and political processes that lead to violations of the human right to health, even though they often occur at social locations well removed from actual manifestations of harm. Theories such as these ask us to pull the lens back so that we can observe wider forces that are so often left outside the frame of highly-focused analyses (Biehl and Petryna 2013). This is particularly critical when considering violations of human rights. Many human rights violations appear both immediate and as the consequence of individual malfeasance, such as discriminatory treatment or violence against individuals because of their racial, gender, sexual, religious, or national identities. However, these violations nearly always occur within systemic frameworks that promote, facilitate, or passively permit these violations in pursuit of political, economic, or organizational interests. The same is true of violations of the human right to health. When communities of color, for instance, find themselves differentially exposed to the health threats of hazardous waste or unsafe drinking water, it is often relatively easy to identify the specific decisions that led to these conditions. Unveiling the *context* that made those decisions possible, however, requires a wider sociological lens. It is this lens toward which we turn now.

Conclusion: An Agenda for Public Health Criminology

To further the development of a public health criminology, we offer the following chart as a preliminary framework.

This chart is meant to be illustrative rather than an all-inclusive framework for the way macro-social forces produce violations of the human right to health. In keeping with public health discourse, the column on the far left identifies three levels of causation: downstream, midstream, and upstream. These correspond with what social analysts often term the individual, organizational, and macro-social levels of social action. For heuristic reasons, we show these as discrete levels. In actuality, the line from individual to societal is a continuum insofar as individuals are always enmeshed in organizations and institutions that reflect macro-social frameworks. The middle column represents illustrative characteristics of each level, while the third column identifies public health harms resulting from the forces in column two.

We are not arguing that all of the malign health consequences in column three *are* crimes under law (though some are, and some others should be), but rather that these harms are analogous to injuries recognized as crime under law (Michalowski 1985). This similarity of outcomes raises a fundamental human rights question as to why some violations of human rights are sanctioned by and others are not. Finally, because many of these harms result from the actions of corporations and governments, we suggest that the theoretical and methodological tools of critical criminological studies of corporate, state, and state-corporate crimes are a useful starting point to build an intersection between public health, criminology, and the study of violations of the right to health.

In addition to offering a general framework for a public health criminology, Chart 14.1 is suggestive of potential research agendas and strategies. Each cell in column three identifies potential violations of the human right to health. Each of these violations, in turn, is related vertically and horizontally to structural conditions, organizational actions, and behavioral choices. As an exercise, pick a particular public health harm and then begin drawing lines to other factors and forces on the chart to which it is likely related. The result will be a multi-level, conceptual path model, an expanded sociological framework for inquiry into the specific problem chosen.

As noted above, we present the framework Chart 14.1 only as a preliminary and partial model for conceptualizing public health crimes.

Criminology of Public Health Framework

UPSTREAM ➡	**Macrosocial Forces** ✦ Wide economic disparity ✦ Poverty ✦ Racism ✦ Sexism	**Unhealthy Structural Conditions** ✦ Unsafe housing and water ✦ Food deserts and inadequate diet ✦ Differential health care access ✦ Elevated stress levels
MIDSTREAM ➡	**Organizational Deviance** ✦ State laws facilitating malign macro-social arrangements ✦ Corrupt state-corporate relations ✦ Production, sale, promotion of harmful or fraudulent goods and services	**Threats to Population Health** ✦ Differential access to SDoH by class, race, gender ✦ Failure to effectively regulate health-harming corporate actions, e.g. pollution, ✦ Promotion of known harms (e.g., Opioids). ✦ Medical frauds (e.g., Theranos, med equipment)
DOWNSTREAM ➡	**Behavioral Practices** ✦ Unhealthy diets ✦ Dangerous legal consumption ✦ Criminalized addiction ✦ Health risking behavior	**Health Consequences** ✦ Diabetes, hypertension, heart disease ✦ Overuse of alcohol and prescribed drugs ✦ Physical/ mental health problems worsen ✦ Smoking, inactivity, health care avoidance due to cost

Chart 14.1 Criminology of public health framework

However, we hope that it points to how the concepts and methods of critical studies of crimes of power can provide a deeper contextual understanding of violations of the human right to health.

Note

1. Animal rights theorists, researchers, and activists would argue that a similar right to life and well-being extends to non-human as well as human animals (Singer 1990; Beirne 2009). We do not reject this argument, but set it aside here for reasons of complexity and length.

References

Agnew, Robert. 2011. *Toward a Unified Criminology: Integrating Assumptions About Crime, People, and Society*, vol. 1. New York: NYU Press.

Aulette, Judy, and Raymond Michalowski. 1993. Fire in Hamlet: A Case Study of a State-Corporate Crime. In *Political Crime in Contemporary America*, ed. K. Tunnell, 171–206. New York: Routledge.

Beirne, Piers. 2009. *Confronting Animal Abuse: Law, Criminology, and Human-Animal Relationships*. Lanham, Maryland: Rowman and Littlefield.

Belknap, Joanne. 2020. *The Invisible Woman: Gender, Crime, and Justice*. Sage.

Biehl, João, and Adriana Petryna, eds. 2013. *When People Come First: Critical Studies in Global Health*. Princeton University Press.

Busse, Ryan. 2021. *Gunfight: My Battle Against the Industry That Radicalized America*. Washington, D.C.: Public Affairs.

Caruso, Gregg. 2017. *Public Health and Safety: The Social Determinants of Health and Criminal Behavior*. UK: Researchers Links Books.

Chetty, Raj, Michael Stepner, Sarah Abraham, Shelby Lin, Benjamin Scuderi, Nicholas Turner, Augustin Bergeron, and David Cutler. 2016. The Association Between Income and Life Expectancy in the United States, 2001–2014. *JAMA* 315 (16): 1750–1766.

Claybrook, Joan. 1984. *Retreat from Safety. Reagan's Attack on America's Health.* New York: Pantheon Books.

Coles, T.J. 2020. *Capitalism and Coronavirus.* London: Ursa Major.

Commission on Social Determinants of Health. 2008. Closing the Gap in a Generation: Health Equity Through Action on the Social Determinants of Health: Final Report of the Commission on Social Determinants of Health. World Health Organization.

Deaton, Angus. 2013. *The Great Escape: Health, Wealth and the Origins of Inequality.* Princeton, NJ: Princeton University Press.

Dwyer-Lindgren, Laura, Rebecca W. Stubbs, Amelia Bertozzi-Villa, Chloe Morozoff, Charlton Callender, Samuel B. Finegold, Shreya Shirude, et al. 2017. Variation in Life Expectancy and Mortality by Cause among Neighborhoods in King County, WA, USA, 1990–2014: A Census Tract-Level Analysis for the Global Burden of Disease Study 2015. *The Lancet Public Health* 2 (9): e400–e410.

Ehrenreich, Barbara. 2018. *Natural Causes: An Epidemic of Wellness, the Certainty of Dying, and Killing Ourselves to Live Longer.* Hachette, UK.

Eilperin, Juliet. 2017. Trump Administration Works Toward Renewed Drilling in Arctic National Wildlife Refuge. *The Washington Post*, September 17. https://www.washingtonpost.com/politics/trump-administration-working-toward-renewed-drilling-in-arctic-national-wildlife-refuge/2017/09/15/bfa5765e-97ea-11e7-87fc-c3f7ee4035c9_story.html.

Dutton, Paul. 2008. *Differential Diagnoses: A Comparative History of Health Care Problems and Solutions in the United States and France.* Ithaca, NY: Cornell University Press.

Fox, Daniel M. 2013. Health Inequality and Governance in Scotland Since 2007. *Public Health* 127 (6): 503–513.

Freudenberg, Nicholas. 2014. *Lethal But Legal: Corporations, Consumption, and Protecting Public Health.* Oxford University Press.

Garafalo, Rafael (1885). *Criminologia: Studio sul Delitte, Sulle sue Cause e sui Mezzi di Repressione.* Torino, IT: Fratelli Bocca.

Galtung, Johan. 1968. A Structural Theory of Integration. *Journal of Peace Research* 54: 375–395.

Gilmore, Ruth. 2007. *Golden Gulag: Prisons, Surplus, Crisis, and Opposition in Globalizing California.* Berkeley: University of California Press.

Glei, Dana A., Chioun Lee, and Maxine Weinstein. 2022. Income, Wealth, and Black-White Disparities in Cognition. *Social Science & Medicine* 310: 115298.

Habitat Chicago. 2020. Housing and Health During Covid-19: Community Conditions. https://www.habitatchicago.org/news/housing-and-health-during-covid-19-community-conditions.

Harper, Sam, John Lynch, Scott Burris, and George Davey Smith. 2007. Trends in the Black-White Life Expectancy Gap in the United States, 1983–2003. *JAMA* 297 (11): 1224–1232.

Hotez, Peter. 2023. *The Deadly Rise of Anti-science: A Scientist's Warning*. Baltimore, MD: Johns Hopkins University Press.

International Committee of the Red Cross. 2023. War and Law. https://www.icrc.org/en/war-and-law/treaties-customary-law/customary-law.

Kolars, Joseph, and Amy Conger. 2023. A Global Movement to Advance Equity in Health. https://globalhealthequity.umich.edu/news-events/blog/global-movement-advance-equity-health.

Kosenko, Kami A., and Elizabeth A. Nelson. 2018. Identifying and Ameliorating Lesbian, Gay, Bisexual, and Transgender Health Disparities in the Criminal Justice System. *American Journal of Public Health* 108 (8): 970.

Lewis, Michael. 2018. *The Fifth Risk*. New York: W.W. Norton.

Lloyd, Gordon, and David Davenport. 2013. *The New Deal & Modern American Conservatism: A Defining Rivalry*. Hoover Press.

Marmot, Michael. 2015. The Health Gap: The Challenge of an Unequal World. *The Lancet* 386 (10011): 2442–2444.

Marx, Karl. 1852. *The Eighteenth Brumaire of Louis Bonaparte*. https://www.gutenberg.org/files/1346/1346-h/1346-h.htm.

Massoglia, Michael, and William Alex Pridemore. 2015. Incarceration and Health. *Annual Review of Sociology* 41: 291–310.

Michalowski, Raymond. 1885. *Order, Law, and Crime*. New York: New York: Random House.

Michalowski, Raymond, and Meredith Brown. 2019. Old Wine, New Bottles: Contextualizing Trump's Regulatory Rollback. In *Explorations in Critical Criminology in Honor of William J. Chambliss*, 90–115. Brill.

Romano, Sebastian D., Anna J. Blackstock, Ethel V. Taylor, Suad El Burai, Stacey Adjei Felix, Christa-Marie. Singleton, Jennifer Fuld, Beau B. Bruce, and Tegan K. Boehmer. 2021. Trends in Racial and Ethnic Disparities in COVID-19 Hospitalizations, by Region—United States, March–December 2020. *Morbidity and Mortality Weekly Report* 70 (15): 560.

Miller, Reuben Jonathan. 2014. Devolving the Carceral State: Race, Prisoner Reentry, and the Micro-Politics of Urban Poverty Management. *Punishment & Society* 16 (3): 305–335.

Nixon, Rob. 2011. *Slow Violence and the Environmentalism of the Poor*. Harvard University Press.

Patterson, James. 1967. *Congressional Conservatism and the New Deal*. Frankfort, KY: University of Kentucky Press.

Piché, Justin, and Mike Larsen. 2010. The Moving Targets of Penal Abolitionism: ICOPA, Past, Present and Future. *Contemporary Justice Review* 13 (4): 391–410.

Riddell, Corinne A., Kathryn T. Morrison, Jay S. Kaufman, and Sam Harper. 2018. Trends in the Contribution of Major Causes of Death to the Black-White Life Expectancy Gap by US State. *Health & Place* 52: 85–100.

Roberts, Max, Eric N. Reither, and Sojung Lim. 2020. Contributors to the Black-White Life Expectancy Gap in Washington DC. *Scientific Reports* 10 (1): 1–12.

Russell, Emma K. 2017. Queer Penalties: The Criminal Justice Paradigm in Lesbian and Gay Anti-Violence Politics. *Critical Criminology* 25: 21–35.

Singer, Peter. 1990. *Animal Liberation*. New York, New York: New York Review Books.

Sharma, Malika, Andrew D. Pinto, and Arno K. Kumagai. 2018. Teaching the Social Determinants of Health: A Path to Equity or a Road to Nowhere? *Academic Medicine* 93 (1): 25–30.

Starfield, Barbara. 2001. Basic Concepts in Population Health and Health Care. *Journal of Epidemiology & Community Health* 55 (7): 452–454.

Stretesky, Paul, and Michael Lynch. 2004. The Relationship Between Lead and Crime. *Journal of Health and Social Behavior* 45 (2): 214–229. https://doi.org/10.1177/002214650404500207.

Sutherland, Edwin H. 1924. *Criminology*. Philadelphia, PA: JB Lippincott Company.

United Nations. 1948. *Universal Declaration of Human Rights*. https://www.un.org/en/about-us/universal-declaration-of-human-rights.

Van Wormer, Katherine. 2008. Anti-Feminist Backlash and Violence against Women Worldwide. *Social Work & Society* 6 (2): 324–337.

Waldron, Hilary. 2013. Mortality Differentials by Lifetime Earnings Decile: Implications for Evaluations of Proposed Social Security Law Changes. *Social Security Bulletin* 73: 1.

Wallace, Barbara C. (editor). 2007. *Toward Equity in Health: A New Global Approach to Health Disparities*. New York, New York: Springer.

Wallace, Danielle, and Xia Wang. 2020. Does In-Prison Physical and Mental Health Impact Recidivism? *SSM-Population Health* 11: 100569.

Weis, Valeria Vegh. 2017. *Marxism and Criminology*. Leiden, Netherlands: Brill.

Wilkinson, Richard G. 1992. Income Distribution and Life Expectancy. *British Medical Journal* 304 (6820): 165.
Wist, William. 2010. *The Bottom Line or Public Health: Tactics Corporations Use to Influence Health and Health Policy, and What We Can Do to Counter Them.* New York: Oxford.
Wonders, Nancy. 2017. Gender, Crime, and Justice. In *Investigating Difference: Human and Cultural Relations in Criminal Justice*, 18–21. New York: Pearson.
World Health Organization. 2013. Social Determinants of Health, Key Concepts. World Health Organization. https://www.who.int/news-room/questions-and-answers/item/social-determinants-of-health-key-concepts.
World Health Organization. 1948. *Charter*. https://www.who.int/about/accountability/governance/constitution.
ZD Law. 2022. How Is Life Expectancy Calculated in Wrongful Death Claims? https://www.zdfirm.com/wrongful-death/calculate-life-expectancy-claim/.

15

Aged Care and the Convention Against Torture: 'It Was Like Guantanamo Bay'

Claire Loughnan and Steven Caruana

Introduction

On 24 May 2023, Claire Nowland, a 95-year-old woman living with dementia in a Residential Aged Care Facility (RACF) in Australia, died several days after facility staff requested police intervention: she was in possession of a kitchen knife and said to be behaving erratically. Nowland

'It Was Like Guantanamo Bay': This quote is taken from a statement by a family member of someone in the Oaken Aged Care Facility regarding evidence of abuse (Bachelard and Tomazin 2017).

C. Loughnan (✉)
School of Social and Political Sciences, University of Melbourne, Parkville, VIC, Australia
e-mail: clairebl@unimelb.edu.au

S. Caruana
University of Melbourne, Melbourne, VIC, Australia

Australia OPCAT Network, Sydney, Australia

L. Weber and M. Marmo (eds.), *A Research Agenda for a Human Rights Centred Criminology*, Palgrave Critical Studies in Human Rights and Criminology,
https://doi.org/10.1007/978-3-031-46289-4_15

suffered fatal injuries after being hit by a police Taser. This news was met with public horror and disbelief at the force of the intervention, despite persistent police claims that this was a necessary response to risk: that is, that '[t]he threat was so grave, police decided, that they needed to deploy the most serious use of force option available to them, bar drawing their firearm' (Knaus and Beazley 2023). Yet Nowland was walking at a slow pace, with a walking frame, and weighed only 45 kilograms (Green and Achenza 2023). The incident attracted widespread criticism of excessive police force (Ryan 2023), of a poor understanding of dementia, and lack of sensitivity to the care that Nowland needed and deserved (McFarlane 2023): human rights seem routinely breached in such circumstances (Steele et al. 2020). A similar report subsequently aired of an instance in which another resident was held down forcibly in a RACF. Police were called to handcuff her simply to remove a staff lanyard from her grip when she took it from a staff member (Delaney 2023).

What was additionally disturbing was the decision initially taken by RACF management in calling police to the 'home,' reacting to what was framed as an emergency (Green and Achenza 2023). There was a clear inability to work in a respectful way with people with dementia, and/or a lack of desire to do so. There are alternatives: police force is not one of them. Poor staff conduct, lack of training, over-stimulation and pain, can all result in people becoming agitated and aggressive (McFarlane 2023). As a manager in an RACF motivated by an ethic of care and hospitality remarked several years ago, such distress emerges when a person's needs are not being met (Loughnan 2020). There is a bigger story to tell about the treatment of people in such closed institutions.

Six years earlier, an article in the Melbourne newspaper *The Age* in September 2017 was headlined with a statement by Margaret Daly, the wife of a former resident of Oakden residential aged care 'home' in Adelaide, that her husband's experience of living there was 'so dehumanising, it was like something you would witness at Guantanamo Bay' (Bachelard and Tomazin 2017).

S. Caruana
e-mail: steven_caruana1@hotmail.com

The documentation in 2017 of widespread neglect and violence in other aged care sites by Australian television programme *Four Corners* led to the prompt announcement of an Australian Royal Commission into Aged Care Quality and Safety (hereafter referred to as Royal Commission).

This chapter calls upon criminologists to engage more attentively with sites of care and the human rights breaches they often generate. Typically, criminology has focused on experiences of 'incarceration in prisons [which have] deflected attention away from other changes in the custodial landscape' (O'Donnell and O'Sullivan 2020, p. 2). And yet criminologists bring unique perspectives to the characteristics of these sites that are often under-appreciated. We start by exploring the significance of sites of care as deserving of criminological inquiry, including from a human rights perspective. We then turn to potential avenues for change, through the application of the Optional Protocol to the Convention Against Torture, and other Cruel, Inhuman or Degrading Treatment or Punishment (OPCAT) to RACFs. We conclude by cautioning, however, against an uncritical turn to human rights as a remedy to systemic abuse and violence in sites of care marked by confinement, restrictive practices and constructed vulnerabilities (Dehm et al. 2021).

Why Criminologists should Care About Aged Care[1]

Prisons, and youth and immigration detention sit at the extreme end of a continuum of sites of confinement and control, given that they are purposed (whether in law or not) as a form of deterrence and punishment. At the other end of this continuum lie aged and disability care sites and institutions such as orphanages which function, ostensibly, as places of care and protection, while exhibiting many parallels with prisons and detention centres. People in aged care often live there against their will, have little or no chance of 'release,' and are sometimes subject to chemical and physical restraints that diminish their agency and their personal liberty. There is a relative absence of criminological engagement with aged care, both as sites of confinement and control, and as places where human rights are regularly breached. The significance of this is profound. Monitoring human rights in places where people are deprived of agency in multiple ways is not straightforward. Being held within such sites diminishes a person's ability to ensure that their rights are protected: who will claim them on behalf of those who cannot claim rights themselves? Families concerned to do so on behalf of their older relatives are typically wary of intimidation and reprisals against those whose very rights are already tenuous (Loughnan 2020).

Although some aged and disability care sites are marked by a clear commitment to ethical conduct, RACFs are nonetheless appreciable then, as 'quasi-carceral' spaces (Repo 2019). They are characterised by diverse modes of surveillance and control, often functioning as sites of risk and vulnerability for those living there. Harms can range from clear breaches of international human rights treaties to more subtle and pervasive forms of control which are nonetheless intrusive, and which undermine human dignity. The use of restrictive practices, whether chemical or physical (Maker and McSherry 2019), has resulted in calls for greater monitoring of aged care sites. This includes through advocacy for RACFs to fall within the remit of a National Preventive Mechanism (NPM) within the framework provided by the OPCAT.

The literature on aged care and human rights breaches therein has focused largely on sexual abuse or restrictive practices in aged and disability care (see, for example, Fileborn and Barrett 2019; Maker and McSherry 2019). This research has typically been published in disciplines other than criminology, with some exceptions (Fileborn and Barrett 2019; Greener 2020). Contrastingly, there is extensive literature examining human rights breaches in disability settings that nonetheless intersect with concerns in aged care (e.g. Ben-Moshe et al. 2014; Gooding 2021)—including by criminologists (Spivakovsky 2014, 2017). There remains an apparent reluctance to address the reality of abuse in aged care settings. Indeed 'the very terminology of 'care' in the naming of institutions tends to limit our appreciation of how coercive control and neglect emerge in these settings' (Loughnan 2022, p. 3). However, in her study of a Finnish nursing home, Virve Repo (2019, pp. 235, 237) remarked that '"careless" control' too easily transmutes into 'quasi-carceral experiences.' This is fostered both by austerity measures and by differential power relationships between staff and typically vulnerable aged care residents (Greener 2020). Although aged care does not sit within the criminal justice system (O'Donnell and O'Sullivan 2020), it is thus distinctly pertinent to criminological analyses of organisational harms and breaches of human rights: the potential for harm is higher where those confined are held in closed or 'total institutions' (Goffman 1962).

While acknowledging the distinctions between places of punishment or 'protection,' a criminological analysis delivers insights into experiences of vulnerability, restrictive practices, isolation, violence and institutional/corporate harms that also align with those characterising prisons and detention centres. This extends to systematic human rights breaches, often with limited or no avenues for redress. These are sites of institutional harm that are also productively comprehended within the work of prominent criminological analyses of state and corporate crime (Cohen 1993; Scraton 1999) as well as within studies of those who are victims, whether structurally or individually (Holder 2017, p. 421; McDonald 2023).

Human rights are a criminological concern simply because 'crime and justice are inherently political' (McCulloch 2017, p. 326, citing Cohen). Indeed, human rights are 'central to defining and understanding state crime' (McCulloch 2017; Green and Ward 2004). Criminological literature addressing human rights tends, broadly speaking, to focus on individuals subjected to either punishment, such as prisons, policing and detention on the one hand, or state and organisational crime on the other (Cohen 1993; Stanley 2017). This sees attention either on individuals subjected to police violence or imprisonment, or on structural violence resulting in breaches of human rights by the state or by corporations (Scraton 1999). There is little criminological engagement with structural harms in sites of 'care' let alone with the everyday, systemic breaches of human rights in some RACFs.

Arguably, a human rights-informed criminology (Weber et al. 2016; 2014) is of greatest value in addressing structural causes of harm and violence: without this, there remains a tendency to focus centrally on individual experiences of human rights breaches, while leaving the system that led to such harms, intact (Boochani and Loughnan 2023, forthcoming). Often legal remedies are also 'piecemeal,' failing to address structural harm (Stanley 2017, p. 507). The relevance of a criminological focus on human rights breaches in aged care is therefore most productively indicated by a critical analysis of organisational and structural harms (Scraton 1999; Green and Ward 2004). This is especially as residents in aged care are often effectively squeezed out of the official mechanisms intended to protect them (Stanley 2017, p. 507). Even when subjected to police power, as we saw in the case of Claire Nowland, those policed are not effectively regarded as rights-bearing subjects (McClanahan and Brisman 2017, p. 335) whether vulnerable or not (Chelberg 2023). As observed by Claire Spivakovsky (2017, p. 207), 'involuntary detention and compulsory treatment cannot take place without limiting people's rights to freedom, liberty, security, autonomy … in each of these cases, risk-based logics and public protection arguments have succeeded.' Although our focus here is on RACFs, such observations also extend to disability 'care' and the mental healthcare system. As mental healthcare survivor, Indigo Daya has remarked, for those categorised as 'risk' in the mental health care system (or indeed of people with dementia):

> [t]he suspension of ordinary rights and legal protections disappear … reflecting the biopolitical division between bodies that matter, and bodies that don't. At the same time, the very notion that legal rights can be suspended in these sites is 'normalised' and accepted' and 'lawful violence' – such as chemical and physical restraints, and police intervention in aged care facilities – becomes permissible. (Daya 2022)

The extension of OPCAT to RACFs is one potentially important, preventative mechanism against institutional violence.

The Optional Protocol to the Convention Against Torture and Other Cruel, Inhuman or Degrading Treatment or Punishment

Evidence of mistreatment and institutional violence in RACFs presented to the Royal Commission comprised an unequivocal breach of the Convention Against Torture and Other Cruel, Inhuman or Degrading Treatment of Punishment (hereafter referred to as 'the Convention'), amounting to cruel, inhuman or degrading treatment. The imperative for a preventive approach to human rights breaches in RACFs is potentially enabled through the monitoring processes under the OPCAT.

Article 16 of the Convention (United Nations General Assembly 1984) states that:

> Each State Party shall undertake to prevent in any territory under its jurisdiction other acts of cruel, inhuman or degrading treatment or punishment which do not amount to torture as defined in article I, when such acts are committed by or at the instigation of or with the consent or acquiescence of a public official or other person acting in an official capacity.

In short, actions that don't comply with the strict definition of torture in Article 1 of the Convention nonetheless fall within the ambit of the Convention.

The Convention is notable since it enshrines the right to freedom from such treatment as a 'non-derogable right.' That is, it cannot be diminished or made conditional upon any other circumstances or claims by, notably, the state and state authorities. And yet the state can draw on significant resources—legal, discursive, social and political—which dilute its compliance with this significant human rights treaty. In the case of our elders, many of the restraints (physical and chemical) used to control movement and agency are ostensibly defended as necessary for the safety of the individuals concerned, as well as for the safety of others (Maker and McSherry 2019).

Importantly, the monitoring of rights in prisons and detention centres is necessitated by the closed nature of these sites. The concept of a universal monitoring system comprising visits to such places where people are deprived of their liberty was deliberated upon during the drafting of the Convention in the 1980s (Association for the Prevention of Torture 2007). This would establish a mechanism for monitoring and inspections of sites that might involve breaches of the Convention. An Optional Protocol to the Convention placed an important emphasis on *prevention*, with regular visits to sites where deprivation of liberty is evident, seen as a critical preventive measure. However, it was not until late 2002 that the OPCAT was adopted by the UN General Assembly, and not until 2006 when it formally entered into force. Despite delays from concept to practise, the OPCAT has been described as arguably 'the most powerful mandate for torture prevention that has yet been devised by the global community' (Evans 2016). The Special Rapporteur on Torture has noted that OPCAT visits are 'one of the most important shields we have against the abhorrent practice of torture and other ill-treatment' (Edwards 2023).

The OPCAT treaty establishes a two-tiered system of international and national visits to places where people are deprived of their liberty. State parties to the OPCAT are obliged to establish one or several independent NPMs with the power to undertake regular unannounced visits to all places of detention, conduct private interviews with all detainees and make recommendations to relevant authorities with the aim of preventing torture and improving detention conditions. OPCAT also enables periodic visits from the Subcommittee of Prevention of Torture (SPT). The SPT is comprised of 25 independent experts elected by State parties to the OPCAT. The SPT also assists and advises State parties on the establishment of their NPM.

Australia ratified OPCAT on 21 December 2017 to fulfil a voluntary pledge in its campaign for membership on the UN Human Rights Council (Bishop 2017) and as a direct response to gross mistreatment and abuse uncovered at the Don Dale Youth Detention Centre by the Royal Commission into the Detention and Protection of Children in the Northern Territory (SBS News 2017). However, at the time of ratification, Australia invoked Article 24 of OPCAT to postpone its obligations to establish an NPM until January 2022. The Australian Government elected to adopt a multiple-body monitoring system with the Commonwealth, States and Territories asked to designate their own NPM(s) within their relevant jurisdictions. The Office of the Commonwealth Ombudsman was nominated as the NPM Coordinator, responsible for visiting places of detention under federal jurisdiction. At the time of writing, thirteen NPM bodies make up the Australian NPM with representation across Western Australia, South Australia, the Northern Territory, the Australian Capital Territory and Tasmania. New South Wales, Queensland and Victoria have yet to designate their NPMs. For this reason, and due to the COVID-19 pandemic, the Australian Government formally requested that the deadline for meeting its obligations be postponed, which was granted by the UN Committee Against Torture, with 20 January 2023 was set as the revised date for compliance (United Nations Committee Against Torture 2023).

Article 4 (2) of the OPCAT defines 'deprivation of liberty' to mean 'any form of detention or imprisonment or the placement of a person in a public or private custodial setting which that person is not permitted to leave at will by order of any judicial, administrative or other authority' (UN General Assembly 2003). Article 4 (1) provides a qualifying element in that the deprivation of liberty must occur within State parties' 'jurisdiction and control… either by virtue of an order given by a public authority or at its instigation or with its consent or acquiescence' (UN General Assembly 2003). The SPT has elaborated that 'as extensive an interpretation as possible should be made in order to maximize the preventive impact of the work of the national preventive mechanism' (United Nations Subcommittee on Prevention of Torture 2016), while recognising that some preventive mechanisms have encountered obstacles in 'conducting visits to places of places of deprivation of liberty' (United Nations Subcommittee on Prevention of Torture 2016).

The Australian Government's position on 'deprivation of liberty' runs counter to the spirit and intent of the OPCAT treaty (United Nations Committee Against Torture 2022; Grenfell and Caruana 2022). It has consistently argued that Australia's NPM will prioritise activities in those it deems 'primary places of detention,' as opposed to *all* places where people may be deprived of their liberty. 'Primary places of detention' is defined to include: adult prisons; juvenile detention facilities; police lock-up or police station cells (where people are held for equal to, or greater than, 24hrs); closed facilities or units where people may be involuntarily detained by law for mental health assessment or treatment (where people are held for equal to, or greater than, 24hrs); closed forensic disability facilities or units where people may be involuntarily detained by law for care (where people are held for equal to, or greater than, 24hrs); immigration detention centres; and military detention facilities (Commonwealth Ombudsman 2019).

Notably, it has failed to consider the extension of the OPCAT to places typically regarded as sites of care, despite its nearest neighbour, New Zealand, opting to do so. Yet social care settings are as important as obvious places of detention (Chesterman and Naylor 2023) and so proactive OPCAT monitoring provides the best guarantee that residents will be treated with humanity and dignity (Grenfell et al. 2021). For example, the Special Rapporteur on the rights of persons with disabilities acknowledged that 'persons with disabilities extensively experience unique, disability specific forms of deprivation of liberty' and are 'exposed to additional human rights violations, such as forced treatment, seclusion and restraints' (United Nations Human Rights Council 2019). Likewise, the Independent Expert on the Enjoyment of all Human Rights by Older Persons reported that 'older persons are exposed to heightened risks of violence, abuse and neglect when they are forcibly placed and deprived of their liberty' (United Nations Human Rights Council 2022).

In its 2020 submission to the SPT, the Australia OPCAT Network recommended the incorporation of human rights plans in any national monitoring network, extending to a *preventative* approach to breaches of the convention and not merely a monitoring and inspectorate role (Australia OPCAT Network 2020, p. 17). The report also recommended an *expansive* definition of places of detention, to include aged and disability care (Australia OPCAT Network 2020, p. 19). The Australia OPCAT Network argued that locked and segregated units in RACFs operate as places of detention and so must be subject to the terms of the Convention: residents of these units are at a high risk of torture or cruel, inhuman or degrading treatment. As it noted: '[m]any aged care residents are detained in locked units in RACFs: most are subject to government-sanctioned orders or schemes which require or permit this detention' (Australia OPCAT Network 2020, p. 127). Additionally, the limited mobility of many residents in RACFs combined with the high usage of restrictive practices means that many residents are effectively detained in what might be appropriately described as 'civil detention' (Australia OPCAT Network 2020)—irrespective of whether they are in a locked unit—and at high risk of torture or cruel, inhuman or degrading treatment. Where this is in breach of law, such detention is arbitrary, meaning that some aged care sites are effectively places of detention.

A report by the SPT noted that 'the Optional Protocol was intended to extend to all places where persons may be deprived of their liberty by instigation, consent or acquiescence, and not just places where persons are deprived of liberty through a formal order' and that the definition of places of detention should, therefore, be sufficiently broad to encompass all circumstances where people might be subjected to forms of control and loss of freedom beyond their consent. Accordingly, despite ratifying OPCAT in 2017, Australia's progression towards fulfilling its treaty obligations has been considerably listless, prompting the Australian Human Rights Commissioner to describe it as 'simply not good enough.'

These concerns were compounded by the suspension and subsequent termination of the SPT visit in 2022–23 (United Nations Office of the High Commissioner for Human Rights 2022, 2023). Australia is one of only two State parties to have had a visit terminated, now facing the imminent risks of being placed on the SPT's Article 17 list for substantial non-compliance (Sadler 2023). The Australian Human Rights Commissioner, Lorraine Finlay (2023), has remarked that 'it is profoundly disappointing that six years after ratifying OPCAT we have still not delivered on our promises and have failed to meet our already extended OPCAT implementation deadline.'

Conclusion

Criminologists have a responsibility to act with and on behalf of those communities who are subjected to state and institutional violence in ways that routinely breach their human rights (Canning et al. 2023) and to draw attention to such breaches. In the light of this, advocacy by criminologists for the implementation of OPCAT is significant: it has the potential to provide a *preventive* approach to human rights protections, should it be extended to Australian RACFs. In contrast, inquiries and commissions, although important, only offer a retrospective 'witnessing' of such harms (Cohen 1993; Scraton 1999). Yet the promise of human rights as a source of protection must be 'continually articulated, enacted, remembered and fought over' (Stanley 2017, p. 503). Along with the power to deliver human rights protections, the state also possesses enormous power to deny them (Cohen 1993). We therefore caution against an unambiguous attachment to human rights: human rights often fail to deliver on their promise. This is borne out by persistent abuse, neglect and violence endured by those living in *all* sites of confinement, from aged care to prisons. Although advocating for the extension of OPCAT to RACFs is preferable to these sites lying outside its remit, we are mindful that this doesn't deliver an ironclad guarantee of rights protections in sites that in actuality *produce* vulnerability to mistreatment, neglect and abuse (Dehm et al. 2021). Ongoing institutional abuse, despite numerous inquiries and investigations, suggests a disturbing reality that laws are potentially unable to fix. There also remains a risk that such laws will effectively perpetuate violent systems as an effect of reformist strategies. Accordingly, any research agenda within criminology must engage robustly with those who are directly impacted by living in closed sites, including aged and disability care, as well as with the limits of law and of human rights, and with how such limits manifest within carceral and confined sites. This includes an acknowledgement of how vulnerability is produced as an effect of confinement. It is with this in mind that we extend an 'invitation to explore what a society based on political inclusion and the building of more just communities might look like' (Dehm et al. 2021, p. 102). Any monitoring of human rights is meaningless without a culture of respect and ethical relationality which typically exceed the legal imperatives and boundaries of human rights.

Note

1. This wording is drawn from an important article by Leanne Weber. 2001. The Detention of Asylum Seekers: 20 Reasons Why Criminologists Should Care. *Current Issues in Criminal Justice* 14 (1): 9–30.

References

Association for the Prevention of Torture. 2007. Letting in the Light: 30 Years of Torture Prevention, 6–7. https://www.apt.ch/sites/default/files/publications/apt30years.pdf.

Australia OPCAT Network. 2020. The Implementation of OPCAT in Australia. https://reliefweb.int/attachments/fdb6f676-0b22-3a02-b0e0-c1ab4f90ea81/Implementation_of_OPCAT_in_Australia.pdf.

Bachelard, Michael, and Farrah Tomazin. 2017. Nursing Home Accused of Being Like Guantanamo Bay. *Sydney Morning Herald*, 24 September.

Ben-Moshe, Liat, Chris Chapman, and Alison Carey, eds. 2014. *Disability Incarcerated: Imprisonment and Disability in US and Canada*. New York: Palgrave Macmillan Press.

Bishop, Julie. 2017. Ratification of OPCAT Caps Year of Significant Human Rights Achievements for Turnbull Government, 15 December. https://www.foreignminister.gov.au/minister/julie-bishop/media-release/ratification-opcat-caps-year-significant-human-rights-achievements-turnbull-government.

Boochani, Behrouz, and Claire Loughnan. 2023. Human Rights and the White Saviour Pattern in Australia's Immigration Detention Industry. *Australian Journal of Human Rights* (forthcoming).

Canning, Victoria, Greg Martin and Steve Tombs. 2023. *Emerald International Handbook of Activist Criminology*. Emerald Publishers.

Chelberg, Kristina. 2023. *'Vulnerable Monsters': Constructions of Dementia in the Australian Royal Commission into Aged Care*. International Journal for the Semiotics of Law.

Chesterman, John, and Bronwyn Naylor. 2023. Complying with OPCAT in Social Care Settings. Acumen, 11 May. https://www.rmit.edu.au/news/acumen/complying_with_OPCAT.

Cohen, Stanley. 1993. Human Rights and the Crimes of the State: The Culture of Denial. *Australia and New Zealand Journal of Criminology*. 26 (2): 97–115.

Commonwealth Ombudsman. 2019. Implementation of the Optional Protocol to the Convention Against Torture and Other Cruel, Inhuman or Degrading Treatment or Punishment (OPCAT), September, p. 8. https://www.ombudsman.gov.au/__data/assets/pdf_file/0025/106657/Ombudsman-Report-Implementation-of-OPCAT.pdf.

Daya, Indigo. 2022. Russian Dolls and Epistemic Crypts: A Lived Experience Reflection on Epistemic Injustice and Psychiatric Confinement. *Incarceration: An International Journal on Imprisonment, Detention and Coercive Control* 3 (2).

Dehm, Sarah, Claire Loughnan, and Linda Steele. 2021. COVID-19 and Sites of Confinement: Public Health, Disposable Lives and Legal Accountability in Immigration Detention and Aged Care. *UNSW Law Journal* 44 (1): 60–103.

Delaney, Ailish. 2023. Confronting Video Shows Dementia Patient Handcuffed by Police at Sydney Nursing Home, 22 May. https://7news.com.au/news/nsw/confronting-video-shows-dementia-patient-handcuffed-by-police-at-sydney-nursing-home-c-10724629.

Edwards, Alice. 2023. Keynote Presentation to the United Kingdom's National Preventive Mechanism Annual Conference, 13 April. https://view.officeapps.live.com/op/view.aspx?src=https%3A%2F%2Fwww.ohchr.org%2Fsites%2Fdefault%2Ffiles%2Fdocuments%2Fissues%2Ftorture%2Factivities%2FKeynote-UKNPM-Annual-Conference-SRT.docx&wdOrigin=BROWSELINK.

Evans, Malcolm. 2016. Statement by Sir Malcolm Evans, Chairperson of the Subcommittee on Prevention of Torture and Other Cruel, Inhuman or Degrading Treatment or Punishment at the 71st Session of the General Assembly, 18 October. https://www.ohchr.org/en/statements/2016/10/statement-sir-malcolm-evans-chairperson-subcommittee-prevention-torture-and. Accessed 16 April 2023.

Fileborn, Bianca, and Catherine Barrett. 2019. Sexual Violence Against Older Women: Documenting the Practices of Aged Care Service Providers. In *Violence Against Older Women*, vol. II, ed. H. Bows. Palgrave Studies in Victims and Victimology, 101–122. Cham: Palgrave Macmillan.

Finlay, Lorraine. 2023. Australia Needs to Deliver on Our Treaty Promises, 20 January. https://humanrights.gov.au/about/news/opinions/australia-needs-deliver-our-treaty-promises.

Goffman, Irving. 1962. *Asylums: Essays on the Social Situation of Mental Patients and Other Inmates*. Chicago: Aldine.

Gooding, Piers. 2021. Can Laws "Commit" Governments to Provide Mental Health Services? A Role for Human Rights in Securing Resources. In *Innovations in Global Mental Health*, ed. Okpaku Samuel, 1st ed., 1439–1461. Springer International Publishing.

Green, Eli, and Madeline Achenza. 2023. Police Reveal What Happened in Moments Before 95-Year-Old Clare Nowland Was Tasered by Police. https://www.news.com.au/national/nsw-act/crime/investigation-launched-after-elderly-woman-tasered-at-aged-care-homby-police/news-story/617055bdd08b9aedfdaf2d326c022694.

Green, Penny, and Tony Ward, eds. 2004. *State Crime: Governments*. Violence and Corruption: Pluto Press.

Greener, Joseph. 2020. Performative Compliance and the State-Corporate Structuring of Neglect in a Residential Care Home for Older People. *Critical Criminology* 28 (4): 651–668.

Grenfell, Laura, and Steven Caruana. 2022. Are We OPCAT Ready? So Far, Bare Bones. *Alternative Law Journal* 47 (1): 54–59.

Grenfell, Laura, Anita Mackay and Julie Debeljak. 2021. Human Rights Accountability for Systems of Ill-treatment in Residential Aged Care. *Monash University Law Review* 47 (3).

Holder, Robyn. 2017. Seeing the State: Human Rights Violations of Victims of Crime and Abuse of Power. In *The Routledge International Handbook of Criminology and Human Rights*, ed. Leanne Weber, Elaine Fishwick, and Marinella Marmo, 419–428. Routledge.

Knaus, Christopher, and Jordyn Beazley. 2023. Clare Nowland: NSW Police's Decision to Taser 95-Year-Old Woman Leaves Community 'Gobsmacked'. https://www.theguardian.com/australia-news/2023/may/20/clare-nowland-nsw-polices-decision-to-taser-95-year-old-woman-leaves-community-gobsmacked.

Loughnan, Claire. 2020. *Towards a Restorative Model in Aged Care in Human Rights for People Living with Dementia: An Australian Anthology*, ed. Linda

Steele, Kate Swaffer, Lyn Phillipson and Richard Fleming, 38–39. Sydney: University of Technology Sydney.

Loughnan, Claire. 2022. The Scene and the Unseen: Neglect and Death in Immigration Detention and Aged Care. *Incarceration: An International Journal of Imprisonment, Detention and Coercive Confinement* 3 (2).

Maker, Yvette, and Bernadette McSherry. 2019. Regulating restraint use in mental health and aged care settings: Lessons from the Oakden Scandal. *Alternative Law Journal* 44 (1): 29–36.

McClanahan, Bill, and Avi Brisman. 2017. Police Violence and the Failed Promise of Human Rights in The Routledge International Handbook of Criminology and Human Rights, ed. Leanne Weber, Elaine Fishwick, and Marinella Marmo, 333–341. Routledge.

McCulloch, Jude. 2017. Police and Human Rights. In *The Routledge International Handbook of Criminology and Human Rights*, ed. Leanne Weber, Elaine Fishwick, and Marinella Marmo, 323–332. Routledge.

McDonald, David. 2023. The Work of Acknowledgment: 'Loud Fence' as Community-Level Response to Institutional Child Sexual Abuse Testimony. *Social and Legal Studies*.

McFarlane, Steve. 2023. When Someone Living with Dementia is Distressed or Violent, De-escalation Is Vital, May 18. https://theconversation.com/when-someone-living-with-dementia-is-distressed-or-violent-de-escalation-is-vital-205988.

O'Donnell, Ian, and Eoin O'Sullivan. 2020. Coercive Confinement: An Idea Whose Time Has Come? *Incarceration: An International Journal of Imprisonment, Detention and Coercive Confinement* 1 (1).

Repo, Virve. 2019. Spatial Control and Care in Finnish Nursing Homes. *Area* 51 (2): 233–240.

Ryan, Emma. 2023. Why Doesn't Australia Have Greater Transparency Around Taser Use by Police? The Conversation, 24 May. https://theconversation.com/why-doesnt-australia-have-greater-transparency-around-taser-use-by-police-206085.

Sadler, Denham. 2023. Exclusive: UN Set to Sanction Australia Over Human Rights Abuses. *Saturday Paper*, May 20–26, No. 450. https://www.thesaturdaypaper.com.au/news/law-crime/2023/05/20/exclusive-un-set-sanction-australia-over-human-rights-abuses#hrd.

SBS News. 2017. Oversight May Have Prevented Don Dale: AG, 9 February. https://www.sbs.com.au/news/article/oversight-may-have-prevented-don-dale-ag/wvwjesdc0.

Scraton, Phil. 1999. Policing with Contempt: The Degrading of Truth and Denial of Justice in the Aftermath of the Hillsborough Disaster. *Journal of Law and Society* 26 (3): 273–297.

Spivakovsky, Claire. 2014. From Punishment to Protection: Containing and Controlling the Lives of People with Disabilities in Human Rights. *Punishment & Society* 16 (5): 560–577.

Spivakovsky, Claire. 2017. Human Rights and the Governance of Cognitive Impairment and Mental Illness. In *Routledge Handbook of Criminology and Human Rights*, ed. Leanne Weber, Elaine Fishwick and Marinella Marmo, 200–209. Routledge.

Stanley, Elizabeth. 2017. Human Rights as a Protective Force. In *The Routledge International Handbook of Criminology and Human Rights*, ed. Leanne Weber, Elaine Fishwick and Marinella Marmo, 503–512. Routledge.

Steele, Linda, Ray Carr, Kate Swaffer, Lyn Phllipson, and Richard Fleming. 2020. Human Rights and the Confinement of People with Dementia in Care Homes. *Health and Human Rights Journal* 22 (1): 7–19.

UN General Assembly. 1984. Convention Against Torture and Other Cruel, Inhuman or Degrading Treatment or Punishment, United Nations, Treaty Series, 10 December, vol. 1465. https://www.refworld.org/docid/3ae6b3a94.html.

UN General Assembly. 2003. Optional Protocol to the Convention Against Torture and other Cruel, Inhuman and Degrading Treatment or Punishment, A/RES/57/199, 9 January. https://www.refworld.org/docid/3de6490b9.html.

United Nations Committee Against Torture. 2022. Concluding Observations on the Sixth Periodic Report of Australia [41], 5 December. https://docstore.ohchr.org/SelfServices/FilesHandler.ashx?enc=6QkG1d%2FPPRiCAqhKb7yhsoQ6oVJgGLf6YX4ROs1VbzEru4wycL%2FqQoIrzLep%2BJZyT2kIvroOhuMbJG1ioCx4Z3eXyrZ%2FkEdUDMwgHAnBoh0v9T4FjuSgv4v9weZd7XDc.

United Nations Committee Against Torture. 2023. Decision Adopted by the Committee on the Request Submitted by Australia Under Article 24 (2) of the Optional Protocol to the Convention (CAT/C/73/3), 3 June.

United Nations Human Rights Council. 2019. Rights of Persons with Disabilities: Report of the Special Rapporteur on the Rights of Persons with Disabilities [14], 11 January. https://documents-dds-ny.un.org/doc/UNDOC/GEN/G19/005/03/PDF/G1900503.pdf?OpenElement.

United Nations Human Rights Council. 2022. Older Persons Deprived of Liberty Report of the Independent Expert on the Enjoyment of All Human Rights by Older Persons, Claudia Mahler [56], 9 August. https://documents-dds-ny.un.org/doc/UNDOC/GEN/G22/447/00/PDF/G2244700.pdf?OpenElement.

United Nations Office of the High Commissioner for Human Rights. 2022. UN Torture Prevention Body Suspends Visit to Australia Citing Lack of Co-operation, 23 October. https://www.ohchr.org/en/press-releases/2022/10/un-torture-prevention-body-suspends-visit-australia-citing-lack-co-operation.

United Nations Office of the High Commissioner for Human Rights. 2023. UN Torture Prevention Body Terminates Visit to Australia, Confirms Missions to South Africa, Kazakhstan, Madagascar, Croatia, Georgia, Guatemala, Palestine, and the Philippines, 20 February. https://www.ohchr.org/en/press-releases/2023/02/un-torture-prevention-body-terminates-visit-australia-confirms-missions.

United Nations Subcommittee on Prevention of Torture. 2016. Ninth Annual Report of the Subcommittee on Prevention of Torture and Other Cruel, Inhuman or Degrading Treatment or Punishment, Annex Compilation of Advice Provided by the Subcommittee in Response to Requests from National Preventive Mechanisms, CAT/C/57/4 [1–3], 22 March. https://documents-dds-ny.un.org/doc/UNDOC/GEN/G16/059/73/PDF/G1605973.pdf?OpenElement.

United Nations Subcommittee on Prevention of Torture. 2016. Draft General Comment No. 1 on Places of Deprivation of Liberty (Article 4) [5]. https://www.ohchr.org/sites/default/files/documents/hrbodies/spt-opcat/call-inputs/draft-GC1-on-art1-for-public-consultation-en.pdf.

Weber, Leanne, Elaine Fishwick and Marinella Marmo. 2014. *Crime Justice and Human Rights*.

Weber, Leanne, Elaine Fishwick and Marinella Marmo. 2016. *The Routledge International Handbook of Criminology and Human Rights*.

Index

L. Weber and M. Marmo (eds.), *A Research Agenda for a Human Rights Centred Criminology*, Palgrave Critical Studies in Human Rights and Criminology, https://doi.org/10.1007/978-3-031-46289-4

SPRINGER NATURE

GPSR Compliance

The European Union's (EU) General Product Safety Regulation (GPSR) is a set of rules that requires consumer products to be safe and our obligations to ensure this.

If you have any concerns about our products, you can contact us on ProductSafety@springernature.com

In case Publisher is established outside the EU, the EU authorized representative is:

Springer Nature Customer Service Center GmbH
Europaplatz 3
69115 Heidelberg, Germany

The manufacturer's authorised representative in the EU is Springer Nature Customer Service Centre GmbH, Europaplatz 3, 69115 Heidelberg, Germany. If you have any concerns regarding our products, please contact ProductSafety@springernature.com

Printed and bound by CPI Group (UK) Ltd, Croydon, CR0 4YY

30/09/2026

02225311-0008